Real-Time Systems and Software

ALAN C. SHAW
University of Washington

JOHN WILEY & SONS, INC.
New York / Chichester / Weinheim / Brisbane / Singapore / Toronto

Acquisitions Editor   *Paul Crockett*
Marketing Manager   *Katherine Hepburn*
Senior Production Editor   *Sandra Russell*
Senior Designer   *Harold Nolan*
Production Management Services   *Suzanne Ingrao*

This book was set in New Caledonia by Pine Tree Composition and printed and bound by R. R. Donnelley & Sons/Crawfordsville. The cover was printed by Lehigh Press, Inc.

This book is printed on acid-free paper. ∞

Library of Congress Cataloging in Publication Data:
Shaw, Alan C., 1937–
    Real-time systems and software / Alan C. Shaw.--1st ed.
      p. cm.
    Includes bibliographical references.
    ISBN 0-471-35490-2 (pbk. : alk. paper)
      1. Real-time data processing.   2. Computer software.   I. Title.

QA76.54.S298 2001
004'.33--dc21

                                    00-043924

Printed in the United States of America

10 9 8 7 6 5 4 3 2 1

Preface

Since the late 1980s, the focus of my research has been real-time systems and software. At the same time, I have been developing and teaching courses on this subject, primarily to university students but also to working engineers. This text is the result of those efforts. The prerequisite background assumed is the equivalent of single-term courses in programming, data structures, computer organization, and operating systems.

The university version is a one-term course for computer science and engineering majors at the senior and graduate student levels. It has been a regular course offering at the University of Washington, and has also been taught at the University of Paris VI, the University of California at Santa Cruz, and Ecole Nationale Superieure Des Telecommunications (Paris). Short, intensive industrial classes, without homework and projects, have also been given at NTU by satellite television, at the Summer Institute in Computer Science at the University of California at Santa Cruz, and on-site.

A course that uses the text would fit naturally into a school's offerings in computer systems and software engineering. It could also be a component of a more general systems engineering curriculum, or it could be part of a specialized program, for example, in control systems or embedded systems.

The text emphasizes concepts and principles. Another approach to presenting a systems topic, especially a relatively new one such as real-time software, is through case studies. A case-study approach was rejected because it is inherently less efficient, requiring the learning of many unnecessary details; also, an emphasis on concepts forces the student and teacher to understand the underlying principles that apply to many situations. On the other hand, many examples of commercial and research systems are used throughout the book to explain and justify concepts. I have also tried to avoid the other extreme, which might be a text devoted to the theory of real-time systems.

To achieve a reasonable balance between concepts and practice, it is also recommended that some sort of laboratory experience accompany any course based on the text. The appendix describes a project on air traffic monitoring and control that provides this kind of experience. I have used variations of this project in one-term classes in both software engineering and real-time systems.

The book's ten chapters can be divided into four general areas. The first two chapters give some general definitions and architectural frameworks for designing and building real-time software. Chapters 3, 4, and 5 cover formal and informal methods for specifying requirements and designs, with some emphasis on state-based schemes and assertional notations. The next three chapters focus on different aspects of time—deterministic scheduling, prediction of program execution times, and keeping time on computers. Chapters 9 and 10 discuss software implementation mechanisms; there are separate chapters on real-time programming languages and operating systems. A large number of exercises are specified. These appear at the end of the sections.

The material is technically diverse, for example, including state machines, logic, concurrent programming, and scheduling algorithms. One unifying theme is *time*. Every chapter is concerned with some aspect of time—specifying, analyzing, implementing, or monitoring timing behaviors (or doing these things with time itself).

The text contains a large number of citations to the major publications of the field. The home page of the IEEE Computer Society Technical Committee on Real-Time Systems, *http://cs-www.bu.edu/pub/ieee-rts*, is a fairly comprehensive source for many aspects of real-time systems. It has links to most of the relevant journals, books, conferences, and workshops; to research groups at universities and elsewhere; and to commercial tools and systems.

▶ EXAMPLES

The text contains a variety of real and toy real-time examples. For easy reference, the major ones are listed below, along with the section(s) where they appear most prominently. The examples are defined in the italicized sections. The exercises and other parts of the book also use these examples, but to a lesser extent, and also present some other examples.

Example	Section(s)
Air Traffic Control	1.1.2, 2.5, 3.2, *Appendix*
Alarm Clock	*4.1.3*
Bounded Buffer	2.5, 3.4, *4.1.1*, 4.1.2, 9.2.1, 9.5
Digital Watch	*4.2.1*
Highway Entry Control	3.3
Mouse Button Click Recognizer	*4.1.3*, 5.3, 9.6
Nuclear Power Plant Monitor	2.3, 4.3.1
Railway Crossing Gate	3.3, 3.4, 5.1, 5.2.1, 5.3, 9.6
Software Clock	7.3.2, *8.3*
Traffic Light Control	*5.1*, 5.3

Acknowledgments

I am grateful to Insup Lee, Nancy Leveson, Chang-Yun Park, and Sean Sandys for their constructive comments on earlier versions of the manuscript.

Alan Shaw

Contents

CHAPTER 1

Introduction: The World of Real-Time Systems

▶ 1.1 WHAT ARE REAL-TIME SYSTEMS?

Real-time systems are computer systems that monitor, respond to, or control an external environment. This environment is connected to the computer system through sensors, actuators, and other input-output interfaces. It may consist of physical or biological objects of any form and structure. Often, humans are part of the connected external world, but a wide range of other natural and artificial objects, as well as animals, are also possible.

The computer system must meet various timing and other constraints that are imposed on it by the real-time behavior of the external world to which it is interfaced. Hence comes the name *real time*. Another name for many of these systems is *reactive systems*, because their primary purpose is to respond to or react to signals from their environment. A real-time computer system may be a component of a larger system in which it is embedded; reasonably, such a computer component is called an *embedded system*.

Applications and examples of real-time systems are ubiquitous and proliferating, appearing as part of our commercial, government, military, medical, educational, and cultural infrastructures. Included are:

- vehicle systems for automobiles, subways, aircraft, railways, and ships
- traffic control for highways, airspace, railway tracks, and shipping lanes
- process control for power plants, chemical plants, and consumer products such as soft drinks and beer
- medical systems for radiation therapy, patient monitoring, and defibrillation
- military uses such as firing weapons, tracking, and command and control
- manufacturing systems with robots

- telephone, radio, and satellite communications
- computer games
- multimedia systems that provide text, graphic, audio, and video interfaces
- household systems for monitoring and controlling appliances
- building managers that control such entities as heat, lights, doors, and elevators

A simple example of a reactive system is a digital watch that responds to button presses for displaying and setting various times, stopwatches, and alarms. This is also obviously a real-time system because it must respond to clock signals predictably and rapidly enough to display the time accurately. An automobile cruise control system is a good example of an embedded system. It regulates car speed by sensing the drive axle rotations, speedometer, cruise control switch, and throttle to control the brake and throttle; it clearly has timing and other constraints related to performance and safety.

1.1.1 Real-Time versus Conventional Software

Computer hardware for real-time applications typically consists of a number of fairly standard components such as processors, memory units, buses, and peripherals, connected to some real-time input and output devices such as sensors and actuators. Our concern is mainly with the software or programs running on this hardware. Real-time software differs significantly from conventional software in a number of ways.

First is the dominant role of *timing constraints*. A program must not only produce the correct answer or output, but it must also compute the answer "on time." In other words, a program must be both logically and *temporally* correct. More generally, real-time software must also satisfy timing assertions that involve relations over relative and absolute times. The most common and simplest such assertion is a *deadline*—a limit on the absolute or relative time when a computation must complete. In a robot control system, for example, there may be a deadline or limit between the time that a moving robot senses an obstruction in its path and the time that an actuator, such as a wheel controller, is activated to move the robot in a safer direction.

A qualitative distinction can be made between *hard* and *soft* real-time systems. Hard real-time systems are those that, without exception, must meet their timing constaints—if a constraint is violated, the system fails. At the other extreme are soft real-time systems which can still be considered successful, that is, perform their mission, despite missing some constraints. There is a continuum between the extremes of "hardness" and "softness," and most systems fit somewhere in between.

For example, a very hard system might be one that controls the vertical motion of an elevator; missing a particular timing constraint could mean that the elevator stops between two floors, requiring emergency procedures to rescue the occupants. A very soft subsystem might be one that counts the number of vehicles per unit of time entering a highway, and does this when the system has nothing else to do; by definition, it can fail to complete a count. A communication system that occasionally loses messages (but informs the sender) fits in the middle of the hard/soft spectrum. Another example of a softer application is a telephone system that sometimes fails to make a connection; the sender just dials again.

Most timing constraints are *deterministic*, that is, nonstatistical, in nature. Deadlines and other assertions involving time are expressed in terms of exact or fixed values, rather than aggregate measures such as averages. The reason, of course, is that failures to meet deterministic guarantees often mean mission failures, especially for harder real-time systems. For example, a railway crossing gate on a road must always be closed by the time a train reaches the crossing, not closed "most of the time" or on the average. These kinds of deterministic constraints can be contrasted with standard software performance and other timing measures which are usually treated as governed by some stochastic process.

A second distinguishing feature of real-time systems is *concurrency*. Computer systems use concurrency to improve performance, for example, by employing several processors running in parallel. Many systems also use concurrency as a model to represent logically parallel activities, even though they may be implemented by interleaving the activities on a single processor. In addition to these reasons, real-time systems must also deal with the inherent physical concurrency that is part of the external world to which they are connected. Signals from the environment can arrive simultaneously; physically disjoint and parallel activities may be monitored and controlled by a single computer system; it is often necessary to know the real time at which signals are received; and output signals may need to be emitted at approximately the same time due to timing constraints.

Systems design becomes especially difficult when one combines the problems of concurrency with those related to time. In an illuminating article on real-time programming, [Wirth77] defined an informal hierarchy of program complexity: The first or lowest level of software complexity—the least complex—are sequential programs; next in complexity are multiprograms which create an illusion of parallelism by factoring out time (eliminating interrupts at the higher level), implementing logical parallelism typically via coroutines, and providing for synchronization and resource management; the highest and most complex level are real-time programs which include the parallel features of multiprograms but are also execution-time dependent.

A third major characteristic of real-time systems is the emphasis on and significance of *reliability* and *fault tolerance*. Reliability is a measure of how often a system will fail. Alternatively, to paraphrase [Leveson95, p.172], it is the probability that a system will perform correctly over a given period of time. However, virtually no system is perfectly reliable and failures must be expected. Fault tolerance is concerned with the recognition and handling of failures. Errors and failures can be very costly, causing, for example, money losses, property damage, mission failures, or loss of human life. Consequently, it is very important to avoid failures if possible, through techniques for reliability, and to respond appropriately, gracefully, and with as little cost as possible to failures that do occur (fault tolerance).

Systems or parts of systems can be classified according to their *criticality*, which is a measure of the failure cost—the higher the cost of failure, the more critical the system. A very critical system with high failure cost might control an aircraft or a nuclear power plant. Note that criticality is a different dimension than hardness/softness, even though hardness and criticality often go together, as in the last examples. A computer game might still be a hard system, even though it is not a critical one; if a constraint is not met, the game might fail but the failure may be benign to the participant(s).

Most conventional computer systems are general purpose. They run several applications at the same time, and the applications are often unknown to the system designers. Real-time systems, on the other hand, are often *application-specific* and *stand-alone*. That is, all of the software, including the operating system, is tailor-made or adapted for the particular application.

While there are examples of completely automatic real-time systems, the more common configurations and applications have one or more humans who interactively control and monitor the system behavior. The *human–machine interfaces* need to be designed especially carefully in order to prevent human errors and confusion.

A final difference between real-time and conventional programs relates to *testing* and *certification*. Because of the high costs associated with failures, it is usually not feasible to test and debug systems with their actual complete environments. Instead, one must rely upon simulations, testing of subsystems, careful specifications, comprehensive analysis of designs, and extensive run-time procedures for fault detection and handling.

1.1.2   A Comprehensive Example: Air Traffic Control

Air traffic control systems (ATC)[1] provide particularly good examples for a number of reasons. First, they are certainly an important, widely known, and difficult application [Perry97], and there are many of them throughout the world. They also contain instances of all of the distinguishing features of real-time systems presented in the previous section. Finally, parts of them can be abstracted to illustrate various technical ideas.

We consider the ATC network that monitors aircraft flying in the United States airspace. Figure 1.1 shows the basic control points in the U.S. air traffic control environment. The airspace is divided into volumes called *sectors*. If a plane is flying in a controlled airspace, there is an air traffic controller, a person, responsible for that aircraft. As aircraft pass from one sector to another, control of that aircraft passes from one controller to another. The sectors near airports are called *Terminal Radar Approach Control* (TRACON) sectors; here, the air traffic controller directs traffic to the tower for landing, and away from the tower to *En Route* sectors after takeoff.

The main goals of these systems are safety, efficiency, and performance. We want to prevent collisions and the occurrence of other hazards. For this purpose, air traffic controllers need to assure that adequate aircraft separation distances are maintained; and that weather hazards, natural obstacles, and restricted airspaces are avoided. Efficiency and performance goals include maximizing airspace capacity and airport throughput, minimizing aircraft delays, and minimizing fuel consumption.

At each individual center, there may be a variety of computer workstations and servers. There are also many forms of communications among components and between centers. Proposed changes in ATC include the ability for controllers to send flight plans directly from ground ATC to flight management systems on-board an aircraft. Radar will be augmented by aircraft that can report their position—determined through communication with global positioning systems (GPS)—directly to ground control.

---

[1]We use the abbreviation ATC to mean air traffic control, air traffic control system, and air traffic control systems, relying on the context to distinguish among the three possibilities.

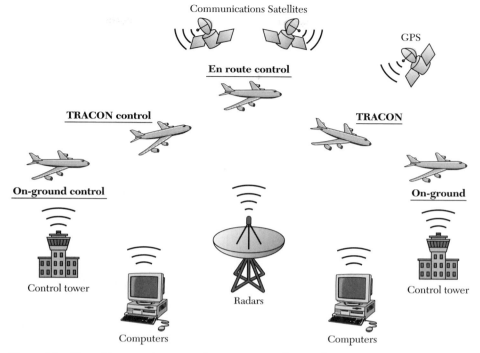

Figure 1.1 Air traffic control systems: Components and control points.

A Simplified ATC

Consider the following simplified version of an ATC [Scallon&Nast87] as a more detailed example. The purpose of the system is to keep track of all aircraft in a given three-dimensional airspace and to ensure that the aircraft maintain a minimum separation distance at all times. Figure 1.2 shows the computer system and its external environment.

A radar tracks the position of each aircraft in the space. When an aircraft enters the space, its presence is announced through a digital communications subsystem; on leaving the space, the computer system broadcasts a notice of its departure to neighboring sites. The communications subsystem can also be used to communicate directly with an aircraft. A console with keyboard and graphics display interfaces to a human operator; it displays the track of each aircraft and responds to operator commands. Operator commands include ones to interrogate the status and descriptive data for an aircraft and to transmit messages to aircraft, for example, to change direction in order to avoid a collision.

The radar can scan any portion of the airspace, given space coordinates. If the radar detects an object at the commanded position, it returns a "hit." An aircraft is considered lost if the radar fails to produce a hit; in this case, the operator must be notified and corrective action taken. The radar is also used to scan the space for unknown objects and lost aircraft.

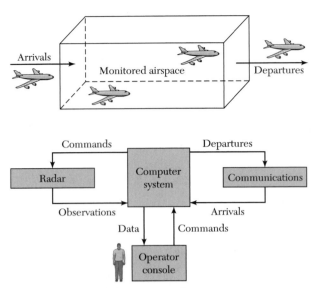

Figure 1.2 Simplified ATC example.

Some reasonable timing constraints for handling the various devices and the environment are:

1. The radar should track each plane in the space at a rate of at least one observation every 10 seconds per plane.
2. The current position and track of each plane should be updated and displayed at least once every three seconds.
3. A response must be provided to an operator command within two seconds.

Where do these constraints come from? The objectives are to give the operators sufficient time to understand the state of the airspace, to control the position of aircraft by sending messages to them, and to respond quickly to unusual or emergency situations, involving, for example, potential collisions or overloads. The informally defined global objectives are translated into the above more detailed and precise constraints.

Note also the inherent parallelism in the environment monitored by the computer. Radar observations, new arrivals, and operator commands can arrive independently and simultaneously. Similarly, the output signals, radar, display, and departures, are logically concurrent.

▶ EXERCISES 1.1

1. Which of the following computer systems are real-time systems? Justify your answer in terms of the characteristics described in the text.

• An automatic teller machine that dispenses cash to credit card and bank customers.
• An elevator system that responds to patron requests inside and outside an elevator, controlling the elevator and door operations.

- A payroll system that produces employee paychecks every two weeks.
- A sports system that registers, maintains, and displays scores during sporting events, such as baseball games or track and field.
- A gate controller at the intersection of railway tracks and a road that controls the opening and closing of a gate, to ensure that the road is blocked whenever a train is in the intersection area.
- A system that monitors and controls the environment (heat, lighting, air quality, security, etc.) of a large building.
- A disc controller for a computer system.
- The floating point unit for a computer.

- A medical record-keeping system that maintains medical histories of patients in a clinic.

2. The degree of hardness and criticality of an application can be represented by a point in a criticality/hardness graph, where the y-axis denotes criticality and x-axis gives hardness:

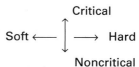

Name and place at least two applications in each of the four quadrants of the graph.

► 1.2 SOME HISTORY

Before modern developments in digital computers, most of the functions of real-time systems were performed by analog circuitry, electromechanical switching systems, and much human decision making and interaction. Human operators were especially involved in integrating the results from various subsystems during their execution— that is, in monitoring their behavior, reacting to external events, and controlling their operation.

The first uses of computers in this area were as direct replacements for analog components and electromechanical switching logic. Commercially, applications comprised small independent subsystems for performing such tasks as data acquisition, conversion from analog to digital signals, control of single devices, and monitoring signals from simple processes. More elaborate applications were developed in the course of research and development in the experimental sciences. This work occurred in universities, and in government, and industrial laboratories; for example, in physics, aerospace, and biomedicine, complex instruments were used to capture, control, and study the behavior of physical and biological phenomena.

Typically, system design was done by the scientist or engineer most directly involved with the application. Alternatively, computer hardware engineers, usually electrical engineers, were responsible for designing and building the real-time components. Hardware design was emphasized, with little thought given to software. It is fair to state that the software was ad hoc.

Some large commercial and government systems were constructed during the 1950s and1960s, particularly in the United States. Examples included air defense systems, telephone switching systems, airline reservation systems, and systems for the manned space program. The design of software for these and similar systems was discussed in an early text on real-time systems [Martin65]. Some of the first real-time operating systems, as distinguished from general purpose ones, were also produced during this period. These systems were concerned mainly with low-level issues in interrupt handling, input-output device control, timing, and scheduling—issues that remain with us today. [Laplante_et_al95] contains a detailed review of many of the early U.S. systems.

Despite many successes, the earlier real-time systems suffered from many problems and errors, mainly because the relevant software techniques and methodologies did not exist. Software engineering technology for requirements, design, implementation, testing and debugging, and maintenance was poorly understood in the real-time area. This was especially the case as systems became larger and required more systematic design, modelling, analysis, and organization. In all kinds of systems, but particularly in real-time ones, software complexity can be overwhelming without some underlying methodological help.

Techniques for assuring reliability and for preventing, detecting, and recovering from faults were not available, and not easily discovered or invented. For example, the standard hardware technique for improving reliability and recovery from faults is to replicate components; this idea just doesn't work for software. For many of these older systems, requirements and designs were not specified prior to coding. Concurrency and timing errors appeared frequently, were often not reproducible, and were extremely hard to find and correct. An extreme example of software engineering problems and a related disastrous timing error is the Therac accidents studied by [Leveson&Turner93]: A real-time computer system controlling a radiation therapy machine was the cause of several accidents, resulting in patient deaths.

The situation changed, starting from the late 1970s. For the first time, the computer science and engineering community devoted substantial attention and resources to solving some of the unique problems of real-time computing. What caused this change? There are several catalysts.

One of these catalysts was a U.S. government initiative. In the late 1970s, the U.S. Department of Defense (DoD) sponsored a contest for the design of a new programming language, named Ada, for command and control applications. Ada was to be adopted by DoD and all of its contractors as its standard programming language. The winning language was, arguably, the first widely used real-time language. The challenge of designing, using, compiling, and providing run-time support for Ada, as well as the requirement that it be used, stimulated both researchers and practitioners. A second cause was the growing and more urgent need to find solutions to the software engineering problems mentioned above. It was during these years that the number and importance of real-time applications grew dramatically and was recognized. Lastly, the availability of inexpensive microprocessors made it feasible to monitor and control both simple and complex systems much more efficiently, precisely, and reliably.

More recently, there has also been a dramatic increase in the number and variety of softer real-time applications. Here, we include game and entertainment systems, and consumer embedded systems such as hand-held cell phones and navigation devices. The infamous year 2000 problem, the *Y2K Problem*, has made everyone aware of the difficulties and pitfalls in dealing with time and dates in computer systems, and especially of the enormous costs incurred when systems aren't designed correctly in the first place.

All of this attention has resulted in some substantial advances. Ideas from operating systems and programming languages have been adapted and extended to real-time software. Computer science modelling and analysis methods, employing techniques in discrete mathematics, were developed for real-time problems. Formal notations for specifying requirements and designs were invented or modified. Our knowledge and toolbag have grown impressively, but many challenging problems and issues remain.

► 1.3 COMPUTER HARDWARE FOR MONITORING AND CONTROL

Real-time computer hardware has different requirements than general purpose computer systems. Its run-time behavior must be *predictable*, so that software designers can, in turn, predict applications behavior. Hardware must be *reliable* and *fault tolerant*, so that costly errors are prevented, when possible, and handled predictably, otherwise. For the same reasons, computer resources, such as memories, caches, processors, controllers, input-output devices, and communications elements, need to be program accessible and controllable. Lastly, because of tight timing constraints, it is often necessary that components and systems operate at *high speeds*.

This section offers a very brief overview of real-time hardware and how these requirements are approximated. It should be observed that there are substantial differences between software, hardware, and the environment, with respect to predictability. Whatever uncertainties exist in the connecting environment, such as when data arrive and what the values might be, are a given; they are normally beyond the designers' control and must be handled as is. At the other extreme, the software designer can exercise a great deal of control over the construction of her artifacts and, in principle, deduce its behaviors. Hardware is in the middle. It is often off-the-shelf, general purpose, and predetermined and must be adapted to real-time use; and yet it can be controlled usually to yield predictable results.

From a logical point of view, a generic real-time hardware configuration doesn't appear too different from a conventional one, consisting of several nodes connected through a communications network, as illustrated in Figure 1.3. There is a larger variety of sensors, actuators, and displays; and a number of more precise clocks and timers may be present. One could also view a single node in the figure as a network itself, with one or more buses as the communications network. At the other extreme, a node may consist of a single processor system alone.

In order to satisfy real-time requirements, some care must be taken in implementing and using this architecture. Virtual memories, if they are used at all, should be controllable to some extent by the applications programmer. In particular, parts of virtual memory need to be locked or permanently resident in physical main memory, so that unpredictable page or segment faults and associated, but also unpredictable, fault handling times are not incurred. Similarly, instruction and data caches, if they are used, should be preloaded.[2] At a lower level, other common performance-enhancing features, such as instruction and data pipelining and branch prediction, make timing prediction difficult.

Input-output (IO) subsystems can range from quite simple controller-driven devices to complicated IO channel connections. It is important, but normal, that the system provide both polling and priority interrupts, for real-time sensors and actuators as

---

[2]How to obtain the performance benefits of caches and, at the same time, obtain predictable and reproducible execution times is a subject of much recent and current research.

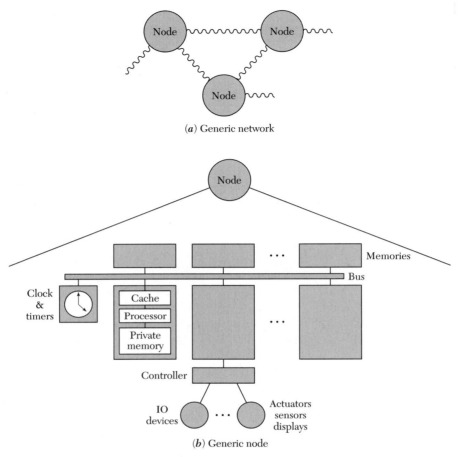

(a) Generic network

(b) Generic node

Figure 1.3 Generic computer configuration.

well as for the usual IO devices. IO and processors may access the same memory simultaneously and sometimes share the same bus lines. This resource sharing and competition can cause unpredictable performance. Hardware and programming solutions exist for avoiding or mitigating these problems. For example, separate IO bus lines may be used; and programs can be organized so that processors and IO devices are not accessing the same memory elements at the same time.

It is more difficult to guarantee deterministic timing over a network, depending on its structure and communications method. If there exist several paths from one node to another, or more than one transmission medium, or if the network is shared, then message transmission times can be unpredictable. A standard hardware solution and constraint are to have a single path, dedicated lines, and pre-allocation of lines or time slots within a line. Hardware reliability, within a node and between nodes, is obtained through redundancy. Safety-critical systems will typically have multiple processors, memories, devices, and interconnection hardware that either vote on results or are enabled sequentially when faults occur.

▶ EXERCISE 1.3

Discuss the timing predictability of each hardware component of a contemporary workstation or high-end personal computer.

▶ 1.4 SOFTWARE ENGINEERING ISSUES

The field of software engineering is concerned with the techniques, methodologies, and processes for constructing software. Like other engineering disciplines, it is an applied science. In this case, the science is computer science. The "applied" part normally means that the software is constructed in a cost-effective manner and that the software must meet certain societal goals. In this section, we briefly outline some general ideas in software engineering and discuss some issues that are particularly relevant to the real-time domain.

The software "life cycle" defines the stages in the life of a software system as it develops from its initial specification through its final deployment and use. It has been classified into five sequential phases or tasks, as diagrammed in Figure 1.4.[3]

The first phase is *requirements*: what the software must do. Next comes *design*: how the software meets its requirements. The third task is *implementation*: this involves the actual construction, that is, programming, of the application. *Testing* is next: here, an attempt is made to assure the correctness of the software experimentally by debugging. The last phase is *maintenance*: inevitable changes—deletions, additions, and modifications due to changing conditions—have to be made. While these tasks occur logically in sequence, in reality, feedback loops connecting each of the phases exist. For example, design and requirements problems may be discovered during implementation, causing revisions of the work of these earlier phases; and maintenance, by definition, requires attention to the other tasks. The dotted lines in the figure trace all possible feedback paths.

It is useful to view requirements in terms of a client–contractor relationship. The contractor is responsible for providing the software for a client. Requirements describe an agreement or contract between the two parties, specifying what the software must do to pass an acceptance test. The user view of the system is emphasized; in the extreme, many of the requirements can be described or inferred by preparing a user manual. Typically, this would also include a description of the environment and hardware interfaces of the system, and the details of the computer and software support components, if known or mandatory. Software needs are specified in terms of the required response to various events and conditions, timing constraints, and how to handle external

---

[3]This organization, sometimes called the waterfall model, is somewhat controversial as a realistic depiction of the software development process, but it is certainly useful for discussing the various required tasks. Other models, for example, evolutionary, incremental, spiral, and transformational ones, have also been proposed or used [Ghezzi_et_al91]. In practice, hybrid approaches that combine aspects of all models are commonly employed.

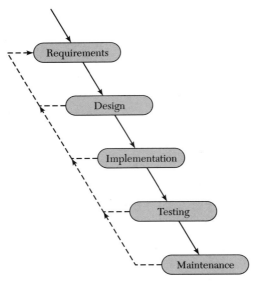

Figure 1.4 Software life cycle.

faults. [Heninger80] contains a detailed discussion of many of the elements that should appear in a requirements document.

The importance of this first phase has been confirmed in many projects (e.g., [Brooks87]). In fact, it is generally acknowledged that most systems' errors and costs can be traced back to incomplete, unclear, or incorrect requirements. As a consequence, a precise, formal, and unambiguous method for specifying requirements is recommended. With such a method, it becomes possible to describe, analyze, simulate, verify, and monitor many of the required behaviors and properties of a system.

Many systems have required *safety* properties. These are often stated in the negative in the form: The system should never be in certain (undesirable) states. Colloquially speaking, "the system should not do bad things." A fundamental safety property in an ATC, for example, is that airplanes should never come closer than a given minimum separation distance. Another example is a railway crossing system that controls a gate at the intersection of a railway and a road; the gate should never be open when a train is in the intersection area.

However, it is often the case that a "dead" system, one that doesn't do anything useful, will satisfy required safety properties. For example, one could just keep the railway crossing gate closed permanently, or never allow any planes to enter the airspace, thus assuring safety in both cases. *Progress* or *liveness* properties are meant to handle these situations. These properties describe the required "live" and desirable behaviors of a system; colloquially, they state that "the system should do some good things." Two examples are: The gate should be open whenever there are no trains in the area; and planes requesting entry to the airspace are allowed to enter eventually and make progress through the space.

The design phase is concerned with both "in-the-small" or low-level design and "in-the-large" or architectural design. Low-level issues include the definitions of algorithms and data structures, and the detailed design of individual parts such as procedures, modules, and files. (The name "low level" clearly does *not* mean that this phase is unimportant.) The higher architectural level emphasizes the definition, organization, and relationships of the software objects or modules that could be employed to meet the requirements. This phase also focusses on the interfaces of the architectural components.

Some analysis is typically done to assure that requirements or designs are consistent, and that they satisfy certain desirable properties that may not be immediately obvious from the specifications. A safety property may be incompatible with another safety property or with a progress property; for example, in an ATC, it may be impossible to maintain minimum aircraft separation distance and, at the same time, guarantee that airplanes will traverse the space within a given time interval. Formal proofs of such properties may also be generated, where possible, either manually or with some machine help. More often, analysis is performed through computer testing of various executable forms of parts of the requirements or designs. Executable specifications, prototypes, and simulations are particularly useful in real-time systems for debugging specifications. They can illuminate problems at an early enough stage for easy and inexpensive correction; they also provide some idea of the run-time behavior of the system, giving a basis for a user to refine or change specifications.

By the implementation stage, programming language and operating system decisions have been made. The software is now actually coded. The main intellectual task is to construct the program modules and their detailed interfaces. Some care must be taken to ensure that the design is followed. Individual objects or elements are debugged using traditional in-the-small techniques. Such unit testing may be of the "white box" kind that examines the actual code in detail, or of the "black box" type that does not look inside a component but determines only whether the behaviors of the interfaces satisfy specifications.

What is the relationship among these first three phases? Informally, we can say that the implementation must satisfy the design and the design must satisfy the requirements. More formally, let R represent the set of valid sequences of timed input-output *events* specified by the requirements, where each sequence consists of a single execution history over time of the system. Each sequence, for example, must satisfy simultaneously all of the safety and progress specifications. These event sequences represent the interface or input-output behavior between the environment and computer system. Analogously to R, let D and I denote the set of timed event sequences described by the design and implementation, respectively, where the events are restricted to the same interface classes as in R. The required relationship among these three is: $I \subseteq D \subseteq R$.

This relationship means that, with respect to those events that control and sample the environment, the implementation and design must obey the requirements. Also, there may be timed execution histories in the requirements or design that don't appear in the actual implemented system. For example, the requirements might be stated using continuous or dense time and real-valued environmental variables, whereas implementations are restricted to discrete values. Computer clocks, for example, measure time in terms of discrete ticks; and the (x, y, z) position coordinates of an airplane could be represented as integers representing feet or meters. This kind of formal framework relating R, D, and I is developed and employed in detail in [Heitmeyer&Lynch94].

The testing part of the software engineering process is the in-the-large form, known as integration testing. Components are combined incrementally, checking that each resulting subsystem satisfies the required global properties during run time. Typically, this composition is done in both a top-down and bottom-up manner.

Many phases of the software life cycle have to be repeated in part during maintenance after the software is in use. Improvements in hardware technology, new theoretical developments, the availability of better support software, the discovery of errors, and changes in client needs can all result in a continuing demand for changes in a system. A recommended approach is to explicitly document both potential changes and parts of the system that will not change, and to do this during the requirements phase. This information can be used during the next phase so that changes are anticipated in the design.

▶ EXERCISE 1.4

The text argues for the relations $I \subseteq D \subseteq R$. But why shouldn't these relations be reversed, that is, $I \supseteq D \supseteq R$?

For example, it is desirable that a design *at least* meet the requirements, but it would presumably be even better if a design exceeded the requirements.

CHAPTER 2

Software Architectures

An architectural description of a system specifies the structure and style of the elements comprising the system. Software architectures for real-time systems also include the possible kinds of software components, how these components may be organized, how they interact with each other, and the underlying abstractions and models.

▶ 2.1 PROCESS AND STATE-BASED SYSTEMS MODEL

In our highest level global view, a real-time system is considered a closed world containing two components, an environment and a computer system, that interact through messages, signals, or events at their interface. Typically, both the environment and computer system are further subdivided into smaller component parts.

At any time, a system may be in one of a (possibly infinite) number of *states*. Generally, each state denotes a particular set of values of variables or set of relations among variables that represent the environment and computer. The system changes state due to *events* that change the values of, or relations among, these state variables; such a state change is called a state *transition*. The transition-causing events may be *interface* events that are transmitted between the environment and computer system, or they could be *internal* events that are generated and consumed solely within the system. For organizational and design reasons, it is often convenient to group subsets of states into named objects. These groupings are termed *modes* or *superstates*, and may be nested.

▶ Examples of States, Modes, and Transitions

1. An aircraft control system might have three distinct modes or superstates of operation: *takeoff*, *cruising*, and *landing*. The *takeoff* mode itself may consist of two modes: *on_ground* and *airborne*. A transition from a subset of the *on_ground* states to an initial *airborne* state occurs, for example, when an event is sensed indicating that the load on the landing gear has decreased below a given threshold.

2. A communications system might be in either a *send* mode or a *receive* mode.

3. A digital watch could operate in any of three modes: *stopwatch*, *set_time*, or *normal*. One of the superstates within *set_time* could be *hms* (for *hours*, *minutes*, and *seconds*). Pressing one of the watch buttons while in *hms* mode could increment the *hours* variable by one (modulo 24), thereby causing a transition to a new state—the one with the new value for *hours*. ♦

The most common model for real-time software is adapted from the one used in operating systems and concurrent programming: the standard process model (See, for example, [Bic&Shaw88]). The software that implements states, modes, and transitions consists of a set of interacting processes. Processes interact by sending messages to each other, by sharing hardware and software, and by competing for resources. There are a variety of incarnations of the process notion with different names, most notably, threads and tasks, but we shall not distinguish among them at this point.

The process is the active object of a system and is the logical unit of work scheduled by the operating system. It has a "state," normally represented by a data descriptor or process control block (PCB). The descriptor stores such information as the values of the process's variables, its program counter, and the resources that have been allocated to it, for example, main storage or IO devices. A process may be running (executing on a processor), ready (ready to run but waiting for an available processor), or blocked (waiting for the allocation of some resource other than a processor).

2.1.1 Periodic and Sporadic Processes

Real-time systems generally contain two types of processes: *periodic* and *sporadic*. Periodic processes are activated on a regular basis between fixed time intervals. They are used typically for systematically monitoring, polling, or sampling information from sensors over a long time interval. For example, one may employ a periodic process to read a liquid temperature every 50 milliseconds or to scan an airspace every 3 seconds.

In contrast, sporadic processes are event driven; they are activated by an external signal or a change of some relationship. A sporadic process could be used to react to an event indicating a fault of some piece of equipment or a need to change modes, such as a change from the *on_ground* to *airborne* modes (Example 1, Section 2.1). In the simplified ATC application described in Section 1.1.2, it would be natural to design a periodic process to control the display and a sporadic process to handle arrival notifications through the communications subsystem.

A periodic process has a predetermined amount of work to do every cycle or period, and is normally activated or *released* at the beginning of each cycle. The code for a process P can be represented by the fragment

```
P:: loop Wait_for_start_of_next_cycle ; P_code; end loop ;,
```

where *P_code* denotes the program for process P. P is made ready at the start of each period and is blocked after it completes the execution of *P_code*.

In its simplest form, a periodic process P is characterized by a triple (c, p, d), where c gives the computation time, usually a worst case estimate, for *P_code*, p is the period or cycle time, and d is a deadline, with $c \leq d \leq p$. The relationship among these variables

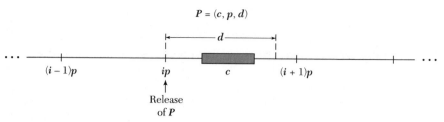

Figure 2.1 The periodic process.

is illustrated in Figure 2.1. The meaning is that the process is activated every p units of time and its computation must be completed before its deadline d expires. More formally, the process is activated every $t_0 + ip$ units of time, where $i = 0, 1, \ldots$, t_0 is the time of the initial release of the process, and the ith activation must complete before

$$t_0 + (i - 1)p + d.$$

The period and deadline are obtained or derived from the system requirements; p and d are often identical. Computation time is found through simulation, measurement, or analysis. This simple characterization of a periodic process is often employed, especially for analysis and early design, because it is formally tractable and gives a reasonable approximation to reality in many cases. More complex versions are also used in practice. For example, the deadline could be greater than the period, the period could be allowed to "slip" or vary depending on the load, or the release time could occur at some time later than the beginning of the period.

A sporadic process P can be represented by the code

```
P:: loop Wait_for_event; P_code; end loop ;.
```

P is blocked until the event occurs and is then made ready. Once the computation of *P_code* is complete, it is blocked again waiting for the next instance of the event.

A sporadic process is also commonly represented by a triple (c, p, d) with $c \leq d \leq p$. Here, c and d have a similar meaning as in the periodic case. On the occurrence of the event, the computation must be completed within the specified deadline; that is, the completion time t must satisfy

$$t \leq t_e + d,$$

where t_e is the event occurrence time. p gives the minimum time between events; that is, successive events are separated by at least p. Note that the requirements for a sporadic process could be met by a periodic process that looks or polls for the event sufficiently often. In Chapter 6 we show how to define such an equivalent periodic process.

Another form of event-driven task permits events to arrive simultaneously ($p = 0$) or within an arbitrarily small time of each other. These are sometimes called *aperiodic* processes. Theoretically, timing constraints can no longer be deterministic in this case since an unbounded burst of events could occur at any time. However, in practice, it is sometimes possible to use the deterministic constraints, provided that they aren't violated too often and that there are robust procedures for reacting to timing faults. Alternatively, the constraints are specified statistically, for example, as average response times that must be satisfied. It is then convenient to describe event arrivals by a probability density function. Aperiodic processes are thus soft real time. Most of our presentation ignores this class.

The above standard definitions for periodic and sporadic processes fail to include the effects of process interactions. If two processes share resources, for example, using critical sections protected by common locks, they may be blocked by each other at various times during their execution. Blocking times, the times that processes wait for required resources or messages, need to be included in a more realistic model.

Yet another important effect that often demands attention is *jitter*. There are various kinds of jitter that can occur in a system, but the term generally means the variation, from cycle to cycle or from event to event, of the time to complete a task or to produce some output to an actuator (e.g., [Locke92]). This variation could be defined as the difference between the worst case and the best case execution times of a process activation, or it could be the difference between the worst and best case completion times where the times are measured starting from the process activation. Process interactions, jitter constraints, and other practical issues, such as the effects of operating system overheads for context-switching, are treated in Chapter 6.

Figure 2.2 shows part of a possible implementation of the ATC example of Section 1.1.2 in terms of periodic and sporadic processes. The major data structure is a *Track File* that is shared by several processes. It stores such information as current position, time-stamped previous positions, velocity, and identification for each aircraft in the space. The arrows in the figure denote data flow or message passing.

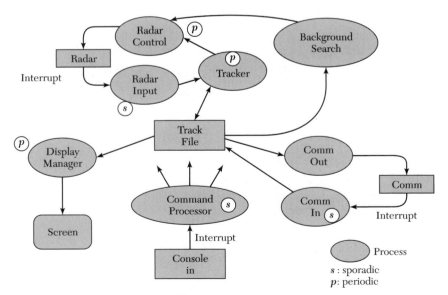

Figure 2.2   ATC software: partial design.

The major functions of each process are

Tracker:	Maintains the *Track File*, controls radar output, and processes radar hits.
Background Search:	Searches airspace for unknown objects.
Command Processor:	Receives and interprets operator input, and directs it to the appropriate internal process.
Display Manager:	Displays airspace contents, the response to operator commands, and any other output of interest to the operator.
Radar Input and *Output*:	Controls and handles IO for the radar subsystem.
Comm In and *Out*:	Controls and handles message IO for the communications subsystem.

▶ **EXERCISE 2.1**

ATC Example: Give some reasonable periods and separation times for the periodic and sporadic processes outlined in Figure 2.2. Use the ATC timing data presented in Chapter 1, Section 1.1.2, as a basis.

▶ **2.2 CYCLIC EXECUTIVES**

Historically, one of the most widely used methods for organizing real-time software is the cyclic executive approach. The method handles only periodic processes. Sporadic processes are either translated into equivalent periodic ones or treated on an ad hoc basis, for example, by assuming that they take negligible processing time and executing them immediately after their triggering events are received. The principal aim is to ensure that tasks meet their deadline constraints, given one or more processors to perform their computations; in this section, a single processor is assumed.

This goal is accomplished by predefining explicitly, and before run time, an interleaving of process executions that produces a feasible execution schedule. A *cyclic executive* (CE) program controls the execution of the processes according to this pre-run-time schedule. Because the controlled tasks are periodic, the CE is also periodic or cyclic. The CE approach has been very popular, especially to early designers, because it is simple, generates an efficient run-time system, and produces highly predictable behavior. On the other hand, it is a very low level and inflexible method, making systems difficult to design, change, and maintain. Our discussion follows the treatment and analysis presented in [Baker&Shaw89].

2.2.1 CE Definitions and Properties

The program code S for a periodic process is broken into a sequence:

$$S = S_1; S_2; \ldots; S_n,$$

where each element S_i is called a *scheduling block*, *slice*, or *action*, and has a (worst case) computation time. Each such block is scheduled as a unit by the CE, and is nonpreemptible. Typically, each S_i could be a procedure call, a sequence of straight-line code, or a one-in/one-out block such as a loop. The computation time for each block is derived from the time of its associated process.

A *major schedule* is an allocation of blocks to the processor such that the deadlines and periods of all processes are met. A major schedule is cyclic so that it can be repeated by the CE. It is made by packing the blocks into a time line. The *major cycle time (MCT)* is the minimum time required to execute through a major schedule. During a major cycle, every process will execute through at least one of its periods. A major schedule is divided into a sequence of *minor cycles or frames*; the frame size or time is called the *minor cycle time (mct)*. Timing is defined and enforced *only* at frame boundaries, through clock tick events. Actions or blocks are allocated to particular frames. These notions are illustrated in Figure 2.3.

In the figure, T and t are the major and minor cycle times, respectively. A sequence of actions A_i is allocated to a frame. However, because a timing event, a clock tick, only occurs at frame boundaries, the exact start and end times for each action are not known; one can just guess, using computation time estimates for the actions. For example, a particular instance of an action time is typically smaller than its estimate, and occasionally larger.

► Example: A Major Schedule and CE

Consider four periodic processes, A, B, C, and D, each defined by (c, p, d) triples:

$$A = (1, 10, 10), B = (3, 10, 10), C = (2, 20, 20), \text{ and } D = (8, 20, 20).$$

Deadlines and periods are equal in all cases. Assume that A, B, and C are handled as single slices and that D is divided into two slices D_1 and D_2, where D_1 has a computation time of 2 and D_2 has a computation time of 6. The MCT is 20, because the entire schedule can be repeated every 20 time units and 20 is the smallest time for which this is true. We select 10 as the *mct*. By packing slices or actions into frames, the major sched-

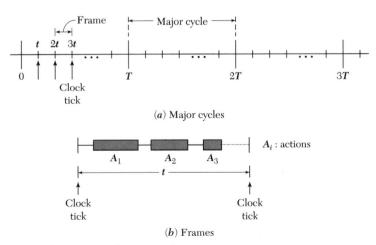

(a) Major cycles

(b) Frames

Figure 2.3   Major and minor cycles.

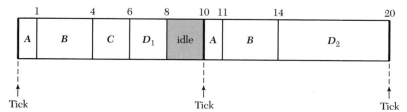

Figure 2.4 A major schedule.

ule can be constructed as shown in Figure 2.4. This form of schedule is also known as a Gantt chart. Note that we could have alternatively inserted the actions in the first frame in another order, such as $B\ D_1\ A\ C$.

A cyclic executive controlling this set of four processes is described as follows in an Ada-like language.[1] *Clock* is a function that returns current time; *delay_until x* will cause a task to block (delay) until real or calendar time has reached at least x.

```
CE :: . . .
    mct: constant := 10 ; -- minor cycle time
    next_time: time := Clock + mct ; -- next tick time
    Frame_Number: integer := 1 ;
    loop delay_until next_time ;
        Frame_Number := (Frame_Number+1) mod 2 ;
        case Frame_Number is
            when 0 => A ; B ; C ; D1 ;
            when 1 => A ; B ; D2 ;
        end case ;
        next_time := next_time + mct ;
        if Clock > next_time
        then Handle_Frame_Overrun ; end if ;
    end loop ;
    . . .◆
```

The CE detects and handles one form of fault that can easily happen. If a frame takes too long to compute, for example, because of incorrect computation time estimates, then the *Handle_Frame_Overrun* procedure is invoked. We discuss appropriate overrun responses later in the section.

Some basic properties of major and minor cycles are now presented. Let a system contain a set of n periodic processes $\{(c_i, p_i, d_i) : i = 1 \ .\ .\ n\}$. Also, assume that all processes are started at the same time, that is, they are all started *in phase* with the same initial release time. The major cycle time *MCT* must be the lowest common multiple (*lcm*) of the periods:

$$MCT = \mathrm{lcm}(p_1, \ldots, p_n).$$

For example, if $n = 2$, $p_1 = 2$, and $p_2 = 3$, the *MCT* is $2 \times 3 = 6$. The *lcm* is the correct and only possibility because it is the shortest repeatable time within which all processes can execute at least once.

---

[1]In the Ada-like code, many important practical issues such as resource sharing, task priorities, and interrupts are ignored. It is also assumed that the CE runs on a dedicated machine.

The *mct* clearly must divide the *MCT*, and be greater than or equal to the computation time of the largest block. Less obviously, it is required that $mct \leq d_i$ for all $i = 1..n$. If this were not the case, it would not be possible to place an action in a frame and determine at run time whether the associated process meets its deadline—time is known only at frame boundaries where clock ticks occur. For example, consider block A_2 in Figure 2.3. If this were the last action for a cycle of the process (c, p, d) and if the minor cycle time t were greater than d, then the deadline d could expire somewhere inside the frame and it could not be ascertained whether A_2 finished before or after the d expired.

An even stronger result for the *mct* that subsumes the above one is derived from a worst case scenario. This occurs when the period of a process starts just after the beginning of a frame and, consequently, the process can not be activated until the next frame. The relation is

$$mct + (mct - \text{gcd}(mct, p_i)) \leq d_i \; (^*)$$

where *gcd* is the greatest common divisor function (see exercises). This result assumes that all times can be represented discretely as integers. Recall that the greatest common divisor of two positive integers is the largest integer that divides evenly into both of them; thus $\text{gcd}(8, 20) = 4$, $\text{gcd}(20, 10) = 10$, and $\text{gcd}(21, 32) = 1$.

▶ Example: Derivation of *MCT* and *mct*

Suppose there are three processes, specified by the triples $(1, 14, 14)$, $(2, 20, 20)$, and $(3, 22, 22)$. Then

$$MCT = \text{lcm}(14, 20, 22) = 1540.$$

$mct \leq 14$ since we require that $mct \leq d_i$. Let the blocks be identical to the processes. Then $mct \geq 3$, yielding the candidates 3 through 14. The values 4, 5, 7, 10, 11, and 14 remain after those that do not divide 1540 are eliminated. Accepting only those that satisfy the relationship $(^*)$ above, we obtain the final set of possible values for the *mct* as $\{4, 5, 7\}$. For example, trying $mct = 10$, we get $10 + (10 - \text{gcd}(10,14)) = 10 + (10 - 2) = 18 > 14$; therefore, 10 is rejected. ◆

2.2.2 Discussion

The cyclic executive approach has many attractive features. It is simple and efficient. A CE controlling program is much less complex than a more general operating system and performs its functions with low overhead. Context switches between scheduling blocks are fast and require less saving of program state such as register contents, because the blocks are known beforehand and are normally selected as logical objects. Prescheduling also means that the run-time system behavior is more timing predictable, compared to an alternative policy that dynamically schedules blocks during execution and has unplanned preemptions.

Despite the above, deadlines are occasionally missed, because computation times exceed their estimates or because of system overloads. Note that these faults may be deliberate; the cost of avoiding them may be too high and it may be the case that they can be detected and resolved with little damage. For example, an action may have a "normal" execution time that is much less than the worst case estimate; if the worst case occurs very rarely and an isolated missed deadline can be tolerated, then a reasonable policy may be to use the "normal" time for the action when constructing a schedule.

Missed deadlines can often be easily detected at frame boundaries. In the CE program example given in the previous subsection, a deadline will be missed if *Clock* > *next_time* after executing frame 1. Given a frame overrun, any of several responses may be possible depending on the application. A simple and common procedure is to terminate the execution of the overrunning frame and begin the next frame. Alternatively, it may be possible to just suspend the offending frame and complete it later. Yet another possible solution is to complete the frame, and start the next minor cycle late in the hope that it will not overrun its cycle. In any case, a record of frame overrun faults is normally kept; if the number of consecutive faults exceeds some threshold, a more serious fault may be signalled and a more complicated recovery procedure can be initiated.

The CE organization generates some natural places to implement mode changes. When a mode transition is indicated, the system must terminate the old mode cleanly and initialize the new one. The latter normally involves starting or restarting some new processes, and consequently starting a different schedule. A major issue is when to make the transition. Again, depending on the circumstances, the change could be made immediately upon receiving the signalling event, thereby interrupting the slice, at the end of the current action, at the completion of the frame, or when the major cycle finishes.

The scheme also provides a straightforward way to handle many resource allocation problems. For example, a task may require exclusive access to some resource, such as a file, data structure, storage block, or IO device, for a short period during its execution. Because each action in a CE is nonpreemptible, it can be treated as a critical section of code, corresponding to the exclusive allocation of some resource to the process. Similarly, precedence constraints among tasks can be taken into account when blocks are prescheduled. Consequently, both of these problems are solved at zero cost at run time.

There are several serious limitations and disadvantages with the CE methodology, however. One difficult problem is how to divide each process into a sequence of actions or scheduling blocks. This is almost always done manually, using natural units such as critical sections, procedures, or one-in/one-out code blocks as a basis. Some proposals have been made to do this automatically, for example, as a byproduct of a compilation, but this has not proven successful yet. Of course, this particular problem can be avoided entirely if processes do not have to be divided; that is, the entire process activation can be used as the scheduling unit for each process. Such a choice is often possible, for example, when the largest period is a small multiple of all of the smaller periods and the computation times are sufficiently small; an example is the process set

$$\{ (1, 5, 5), (2, 10, 10), (3, 20, 20), (3, 20, 20) \}.(^{**})$$

An associated important issue that is still the topic of much research is timing prediction for the actions. The CE scheme assumes that accurate estimates of execution times for each block are available. These, however, are not easy to ascertain. This problem is a variation of the standard prediction problem—how to find the "c" of (c, p, d). We address the standard problem in detail in Chapter 6.

Given the major and minor cycle times, the periods and deadlines of each process, and the actions with their computation times, a schedule must be made. In order to produce a schedule, a time-consuming bin-packing procedure is necessary in general, covering the *lcm* of the periods. This apparently requires an exponential amount of work in the worst case, because the problem is NP-hard for one processor. Results from deterministic scheduling theory (Chapter 6) can be used as guidelines, that is, heuristics, to choose candidate schedules. The principal reason that these results cannot be applied with complete assurance is that they assume that processes can be preempted at arbitrary points, whereas in the CE schemes predetermined preemptions occur only at the termination of a scheduling block.

The use of the CE method seems to imply that a low-level programming style is necessary. Modern concurrent programming techniques are incompatible with the need to break code into predictable blocks and preschedule these blocks. The method is also inflexible and brittle with respect to changes. Small changes in process parameters or in program requirements often involve much changes in the system—typically, blocks need to be redefined and schedules have to be redone. For example, any increase in the computation time of either process A or B in the example of Section 2.2.1 (Figure 2.4) would cause the schedule to "break," requiring at least a redivision of process D into different size slices, perhaps divisions of the other processes, and potentially, a selection of a smaller minor cycle.

▶ EXERCISES 2.2

1. Prove that the major cycle time (MCT) must be the lcm of the periods of the processes.

2. Show that 10 is the only choice for the *mct* for the four processes, A, B, C, and D, given in the example of Section 2.2.1 (Figure 2.4), assuming the same division into slices.

3. Using the same example as in Question 2, suppose that A's computation time is increased to 2. Show that it is impossible to produce a feasible schedule assuming the same slices for B, C, and D, and no division of A.

4. Prove the result (*) in Section 2.2.1 for the minor cycle time (*mct*). Hint: Show that

$$mct + (mct - \delta_i) \le d_i,$$

where $0 < \delta_i \le mct$ and $\delta_i = k \times p_i - j \times mct$ for some $k > 0$ and $j \ge k$.

5. Suppose that a system has three periodic processes $A = (2, 10, 10)$, $B = (5, 10, 10)$, and $C = (3, 25, 25)$. Let A's com-

putation be divided into 2 sequential slices A_1 and A_2 with worst case execution times of 2 and 1, respectively, and B's into 2 blocks B_1 and B_2 with times 2 and 3, respectively; assume that C is not divided. Construct a major CE schedule for this system, having an MCT of 50 and an *mct* of 5.

6. A system has three periodic processes $A = (2, 9, 9)$, $B = (4, 12, 12)$, and $C = (1, 15, 15)$.
(a) What is the MCT for a cyclic CE schedule for this system?
(b) Assuming that blocks are identical to the complete code for all processes, derive the possible values for the *mct*.
(c) Pick one of your answers for (b) and construct a major schedule for the three processes.
(d) Replace C by $C' = (5, 15, 15)$. Using the *mct* values computed in (b), show that a CE schedule *cannot* be constructed.

7. Assume the process set given by (**) in Section 2.2.2 and that the processes are not divided into smaller slices. Exhibit a suitable MCT and *mct*, with a feasible schedule.

▶ 2.3 FOREGROUND–BACKGROUND ORGANIZATIONS

An approach that is even simpler than the cyclic executive has been used for many years and also leads to predictable implementations is based on the *foreground–background* model. All real-time processes are considered to be periodic. The unadorned version of this organization assumes that a system consists of two sets of processes, a high-priority foreground set *FG* and a low priority background set *BG*. The periodic real-time processes are allocated to *FG*. Processes in *FG* are nonpre-emptible, that is, they cannot be interrupted once started. Those in *BG* are pre-emptible by those in *FG*. The idea is to assign the non-real-time, soft real-time, and noncritical processes to the background.

The system executes its foreground work periodically, according to a pre-determined schedule. When there is free time, processes in *BG* are dispatched. During each cycle, a dispatcher allocates the processor sequentially to each element of *FG* and then, if time, to elements in *BG*. A timer interrupt signalling the start of a new cycle will cause a preemption of the current background process. One can view the foreground organization and control as an extreme instance of a cyclic executive system, where all periods are the same, the major cycle time equals the minor cycle time, and the blocks for each process are identical to the entire process code.

The same foreground–background idea can, of course, be used in more elaborate CE and other organizations where, for example, there may be several different periods associated with the real-time processes. Whenever there is idle time in a frame, batch-like or non-real-time processes from a background set are resumed to fill up the available processor space with useful work. Normally, there will almost always be some idle processor time; because it is extraordinarily diffficult to predict timing behavior with great precision, systems should always be designed so that there is some slack time after real-time tasks are handled.

▶ **Example: Nuclear Power Plant Monitor [Alger&Lala86]**

This example is abstracted from the description of an actual system that monitors the coolant flow in an experimental nuclear reactor. At the computer hardware level, the system operates with quadruple redundancy and voting on results. This permits 100% operation in the presence of a single hardware fault, including detecting a second fault. At initialization, a separate software component establishes instruction and timer syn-chronization among the four machines. The software organization for the application processes is sketched in Figure 2.5(*a*).

There are three foreground processes. A timer process (*T*) has responsibility for maintaining elapsed time for use by a background alarm clock task and for timestamp-ing events. A second task in *FG*—*F* in the figure—detects, isolates, and handles faults by reconfiguring the hardware. The *S* process performs the principal application func-tions of reading and processing coolant flow and related data from sensors. The back-ground tasks (*B*) contain less critical processes for testing and display.

The *Dispatcher* is triggered by a timer interrupt on a 100 millisecond cycle [Figure 2.5(b)]. On each cycle, it successively activates *T*, *F*, and *S*; each runs to completion and then returns to the *Dispatcher*. The processes of *B* are then dispatched in the remain-ing cycle time. The software organization of this safety-critical system has been kept as simple as possible in order to achieve the necessary reliability and predictability. ◆

One straightforward extension to the simple version presented above provides for different priorities in the *BG* set. In fact, this is the case for the monitor example—on each cycle, the dispatcher resumes the highest priority background process first, and

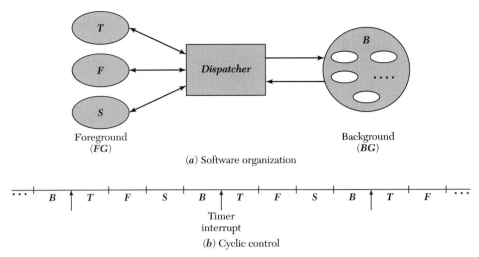

(a) Software organization

(b) Cyclic control

Figure 2.5   A coolant monitor.

continues resuming *BG* processes in priority order until the timer interrupt occurs. In a manner similar to the CE architecture, a foreground–background scheme also relies on very simple and predetermined interactions among the real-time processes. For many applications, this scheme is far too simplistic and more general methods are necessary.

▶ 2.4 STANDARD OS AND CONCURRENCY ARCHITECTURES

The most general organization, and the one that is used in most contemporary systems, follows a conventional operating system (OS) and concurrency control architecture. Figure 2.6 presents a functional hierarchy of this architecture in a real-time setting. The lower level mechanisms are used by the higher level ones in performing their functions.

The kernel level typically implements processes with their illusion of concurrency, process synchronization methods, process scheduling and switching, and basic timer services, as well as handling interrupts. Much of the executive control required by the CE and foreground–background styles consists of simple kernel routines that realize these functions. More complex procedures and data structures are employed here.

The resource management level does storage management, input–output device control, and other resource allocation tasks. These components could be organized as procedures or as OS processes. The periodic and sporadic processes defining the real-time application are at the highest level. (There could also be non-real-time "background" processes, not shown in the figure.)

Timing and other constraints, such as the importance of a process or its criticality, are translated into process *priorities*. These may be explicitly assigned, for example, by directly giving a priority value to a process. Alternatively, the priority may be implicit; for example, the priority could vary inversely with the process activation time, the earlier the activation, the higher the priority, thus corresponding to a first-in/first-out pol-

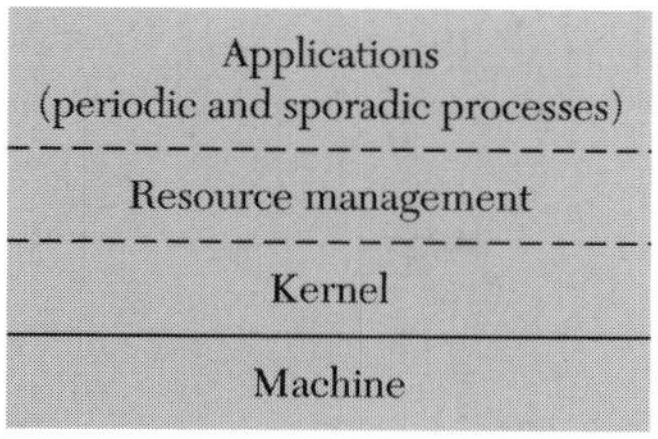

Figure 2.6 Operating system architecture.

icy. The scheduler ensures that the highest priority ready process receives the CPU whenever a scheduling change is possible.

Systems may have fixed or dynamic priorities. In a fixed priority system, the priorities are set before run time or at process initialization, and remain unchanged during execution. Systems with dynamic priorities permit priority changes during execution to reflect changing or unanticipated conditions. Nonpreemptive systems permit a process to run to completion once they are dispatched. In a preemptive system, once a process becomes ready, it will preempt any lower priority running process from the CPU, causing a context switch. Most systems have both preemptive and nonpreemptive components, and combine elements with both fixed and dynamic priorities. Scheduling techniques using priority and preemption notions are discussed in detail in Chapter 6.

There are many advantages to this organization, even for real-time computing. Because of the numerous developments and experiences with the approach and model, there are now standard and tested ways to design, analyze, and build the controlling operating system and ensure its logical correctness. Many of the most difficult problems, especially those related to concurrency control, have been solved and solutions appear in most textbooks, for example, [Bic&Shaw88]. Off-the-shelf software can often be used for some of the more complicated parts.

The major issue and problem is how to achieve predictability while maintaining these advantages. Assigning priorities to reflect timing and other constraints is not an easy problem in general. This is especially the case when process interactions are included and when operating systems processes with their priorities are also competing for the processor and other resources. The effects of a general-purpose operating system are normally not deterministically predictable; OS functions may preempt applications processes at unpredictable times and their execution times are often not known precisely. For these reasons, modifications of the general architecture are made, but often in an ad hoc way. In Chapter 10, we cover this topic in a deeper and more systematic manner.

▶ 2.5 SYSTEMS OBJECTS AND OBJECT-ORIENTED STRUCTURES

Periodic and sporadic processes are the basic *active* objects of real-time systems. They can be realized as independent programs that do not directly share resources, especially data and address spaces, and that communicate through message passing, events, or files; or they can be more closely coupled *threads* that can directly share resources. In either case, something is missing. These other missing parts include the *passive* elements of the system that are used by processes and the objects within which processes are embedded. Examples are data, events, messages, hardware resources, buffers, and modules.

2.5.1 Abstract Data Types

Abstract data types (ADTs) are one kind of object that provide a general mechanism for modelling and implementing these missing passive parts. ADTs encapsulate a data type and its values, and define or export an external interface of procedures for accessing and manipulating the data. Access and changes to the data can only be made through the interface procedures. The addition of a class mechanism allows more convenient specification of these objects. Processes and ADTs are suggested as a suitable architectural framework for real-time systems, for example, in [Shaw89].

▶ ADT Examples

1. The *Track File* in the ATC example of Figure 2.2 (Section 2.1.1) is a natural candidate for an ADT organization. The internal aircraft data stored by the object should be encapsulated so that it is only accessible through a well-defined set of interface procedures and functions. These could include such operations as: *Remove*, *Add*, *Update*, *Retrieve*, and *Extrapolate*, which access and/or update particular aircraft data; and *Retrieve_All* and *Retrieve_Space*, which return all tracks or the tracks in some subspace of the airspace.
2. An ADT of class *Aircraft* could be defined to represent the generic behavior of an airplane; particular ADT instances, say Air_1 and Air_2, may then be declared and identified by name. ◆

▶ A Process/ADT Architecture: Producer–Consumer Model

A higher-level model that explicitly includes process interactions and ADTs is the real-time *producer–consumer* model (PC) introduced in [Jeffay89]. Processes are all sporadic. They are triggered by message events and may send messages to other tasks; message communications occur on nonshared, unidirectional channels. For communications between processes or between processes and IO devices, sending is nonblocking and receiving is blocking. There is a producer–consumer relationship between senders and receivers of messages. Tasks also interact and compete for resources which are represented by abstract data types (ADTs); mutually exclusive access is guaranteed for each ADT.

A process has the generic form or pattern:

```
loop  Wait_for_Message;
      . . . . .
      Send_Message_or_Access_Resource;
      . . . . .
      Send_Message_or_Access_Resource;
      . . . . .
  end loop;
```

Each process waits for a message (event), and then can send any number of messages to other processes or output devices, or can access any number of resources in order to perform its functions.

An important aspect of the PC model is that application workloads can be analyzed to determine if all deadlines can be satisfied. This is possible because an optimal scheduling algorithm has been developed, assuming that worst case generation and arrival rates for all messages are known. Several operating systems kernels supporting the PC scheme have been built. Applications include conferencing with live video and audio [Jeffay_et_al92], and satellite control and communications [Mostert94]. ♦

2.5.2 General Object Classes

Other more general versions of objects have also been proposed as basic building blocks for real-time systems. These are typically extensions and adaptations of such object-oriented (OO) ideas as inheritance, attributes, and polymorphism, and always include the ADT ideas of encapsulation, classes, and instances discussed above. In most of these, the active objects, processes and threads, are also treated as instances of classes.

Inheritance is arguably the most useful addition to ADTs. The basic notion is to allow the definition of new classes, the "child" classes, as particular modifications of more general "parent" classes; a child class inherits the properties—the operations (also called *methods*) and attributes—of its parent, and can augment or change these properties. A hierarchy of classes can be defined in this manner.

▶ Inheritance Example

For our ATC example (Section 1.1.2), one could define a class *Aircraft* with the appropriate behavior common to all aircraft. Commercial passenger planes and private planes both share many aircraft properties, but also have some unique behaviors; for example, a passenger plane may be required to have advanced radar or collision avoidance equipment, and private planes may communicate over different channels than do commercial aircraft. It would thus be natural to define two classes, say *Air_Com* and *Air_Priv*, respectively, that both inherit *Aircraft* but are suitably modified to reflect these differences. Commercial planes, in turn, have many properties that are shared by long-haul passenger planes and short-haul or commuter aircraft; these specializations could be defined in *Air_Com* child classes, say *Long_Haul* and *Commuter*, respectively. The class hierarchy is shown in Figure 2.7, where each node in the tree (except the root node) has an "inherits from" relation with its parent. ♦

Object-oriented methods have proven benefits in conventional systems, particularly for code reuse and portability among applications. There is much activity, and some controversy, in applying the ideas to real-time systems; and one sees prominent OO projects and tools, such as OO operating systems, OO programming languages, and executable OO specifications for design [PD96;Shaw00]. However, the main arguments against OO architectures are that they are inherently inefficient and unpredictable. Of course, similar arguments have been used against virtually every interesting abstraction

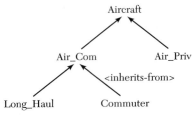

Figure 2.7 Aircraft class hierarchy.

introduced into computing, including the notion of processes; we only note that whenever an abstraction has been found useful, a sufficiently efficient implementation has been eventually discovered.

One example of a difficult and awkward type of problem that can occur in concurrent and real-time OO systems is the *inheritance anomaly* problem. When a child class defines a new operation or overrides an inherited one, the changes often affect the other elements of the class. The "anomaly" is that the changes are not isolated or opaque to the rest of the inherited object; unfortunately, it is frequently necessary to make many other changes in the child class. In particular for real-time systems, when new synchronization or timing constraints are defined for a child class, all of the affected operations must be modified to reflect the additional constraints.

▶ **Bounded Buffer Inheritance Anomaly**

Consider a class definition for a standard bounded buffer, say *BB*, with two operations, *Deposit* and *Remove* [Bic&Shaw88]. Suppose that a real-time bounded buffer, say *RTBB*, is now specified as a child class by inheriting *BB* and adding the following additional synchronization and timing constraints:

every *Remove* must be directly preceded by at least one *Deposit*, and there must be a minimum time delay, say *dt*, between any two successive operations on *RTBB*.

In order to realize these constraints, the class and the operations must be rewritten to include some history information—the name and time of the last operation that was invoked—and some constraint checking with this history information. ◆

OO mechanisms for solving the inheritance anomaly problem are discussed in papers by Bergmans and Aksit and by Ren et al. in [PD96]. More straightforward solutions can also be obtained if a system provides support for time-stamped event histories, such as functions to store and access the most recent events where an event is a triple (name, value, occurrence_time) [Shaw98].

2.5.3   OO For Everything: The Unified Modelling Language

This is an extremely ambitious attempt to provide a single framework for modelling, specifying, documenting, and constructing all aspects of software systems development, ranging from requirements through architecture, design, implementation, testing, and release. The Unified Modelling Language (UML) project started about 1994 and resulted in a standard "language" in 1997. In addition to modelling conventional applications, it is also being promoted for the real-time domain. There exist several books and many articles devoted entirely to UML (e.g., [Booch_et_al99; CACM99; Selic99]). We will only introduce briefly some of the main ideas and concepts.

UML is a set of notations held together or integrated by an overall object orientation. A system is described by a variety of views of objects and their relations, represented graphically by nine different kinds of diagrams—class, object, use case, sequence, collaboration, statechart, activity, component, and deployment diagrams. These views basically specify the *structure* and its *behavior* of some aspect of a system, such as its architecture.

▶ **Example: A Class Diagram For ATC Communications**

A recommended method for portraying the structural relations among a set of objects is through a class diagram. Figure 2.8 contains such a diagram for the architecture of the communications component of a hypothetical ATC as described in Section 1.1.2. (The inspiration for this example is the structure for the *Internode messaging* collaboration given in Figure 27-2, page 373, of [Booch_et_al99].) Informally, the diagram indicates that an *ATC_Communication* object uses a *Bounded_Buffer* object and *Message* objects, and that the *Input* and *Output Mailboxes* are specific versions or subclasses of *Bounded_Buffer*.

The boxes, such as *Bounded_Buffer*, represent object classes. A given class has a name (*Bounded_Buffer*), a list of attributes (*full*), and a set of operations or methods (*Deposit*, *Remove*). The circle labelled *Icomm* denotes an interface object that is realized by its connected component, *ATC_Communications*.

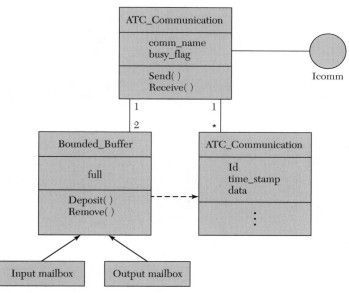

Figure 2.8 UML class diagram for ATC communications.

The lines between classes indicate associations and fulfill the same functions as relations in entity-relationship diagrams (e.g., [Ghezzi_et_al91b]). For example, there is a one-to-many relation between *ATC_Communications* and *Message* objects—any number of messages may be associated with an *ATC_Communications* object; this is indicated by the "1" and "*" labels. The arrows from the two *Mailbox* classes to *Bounded_Buffer* mean inheritance or subclassing. Finally, the dotted arrow from *Message* to *Bounded_Buffer* specifies a dependency between the two classes; the *Deposit* and *Remove* operations both use *Message* objects as parameters. ♦

The classes in the example are passive objects. Processes and threads comprise the stereotypical active classes in UML. The principal notation used to describe periodic and event-driven behaviors is a variant of statecharts [Harel87], a state-based scheme that we cover in detail in Section 4.2. Collaboration and sequence diagrams offer notations for describing the dynamic interactions among objects. Each can show a single flow of control and messages, a single "interaction," emphasizing the structures involved (collaboration) or the time ordering (sequence).

There are no particular facilities for specifying and handling timing behaviors; instead, the general UML mechanisms can be used to produce time models for a given application. There is a hook, and an associated language, for adding arbitrary constraints to UML elements. This feature may be employed for timing constraints; in principle, it could also assist in dealing with inheritance anomaly problems (Section 2.5.1).

In summary, UML is an impressive synthesis of much technology, with some software support for many of its parts. The methodology requires that the designer "buy into" a complete OO approach and adhere to a particular discipline throughout the development process. This may be too much to ask, especially given the size and complexity of UML.

▶ EXERCISES 2.5

1. Define at least two other abstract data types (ADTs) that might be used by the processes in the ATC example (Section 2.1.1 and Figure 2.2). For each object, describe a list of operations (procedures, functions) that could represent its interface.

2. Describe an inheritance hierarchy for a bounded buffer, where the root class is a standard bounded buffer

BB with the two procedures *Deposit* and *Remove*. Assume that the buffer will contain real-time data, such as temperature or position information obtained from a sensor. An inherited class should declare different or more restricted synchronization and timing constraints from its parent. Define at least three levels in the tree with at least two classes at each level.

3

Requirements and Design Specifications

The particular notations that are selected to express requirements or designs can have a very important impact on the construction time, correctness, efficiency, and maintainability of the target system. One desirable property for these languages is that they be precise and unambiguous, so that clients and implementors can agree on the required behaviors and recognize them in operation; the need for this feature, often called "formality," eliminates natural languages, such as English, as candidates, at least when not employed in conjunction with some other more formal schemes. The notation should also be easy to use by the involved parties. For example, many designers prefer graphical languages over textual ones for documentation purposes but may need symbolic or mathematical notations for analysis.

It should be possible to state and prove properties of a system before it is built; then, if the system is constructed according to the specifications, it may be guaranteed to exhibit certain properties and behaviors. This implies that the selected notation is not only formally defined but is also amenable to formal manipulation. Unfortunately, for almost all practical cases, most required properties cannot be proven a priori, mainly because of the complexity and scale of actual systems.

However, correct behaviors for many scenarios of interest can frequently be demonstrated through simulation or prototyping. Generation of behaviors is particularly convenient to do if the specification language is executable. Executable specifications are also useful for clarifying and refining requirements and designs. Another desirable feature—one that is particularly difficult to achieve—is scalability; many systems are quite large, and notations that work well "in-the-small" often become intractable when applied to larger applications.

In this chapter, we examine some basic specification techniques, starting with a brief overview and survey. Requirements and design languages are treated together because it is often difficult to distinguish between the two phases and the same notations are frequently used for both purposes.

▶ 3.1 SURVEY AND CLASSIFICATION OF NOTATIONS

It is convenient to distinguish between imperative and descriptive languages. *Imperative* or *operational* methods specify behaviors by giving algorithmic descriptions—that is, sequences of instructions or actions to be taken by one or more agents, that generate the behaviors. Specifications are directly executable in that they translate easily into corresponding computer procedures. With these notations, it is straightforward to produce examples of the specified behaviors, either manually or automatically, and thereby debug specifications. This executability allows fast prototyping of systems; in principle, such prototypes can evolve into implementations. Operational techniques also appeal to engineers because they are trained to understand systems in these generational terms, making it relatively easy to visualize the behaviors.

Declarative, descriptive, denotational, or *assertional* notations directly specify properties that must be satisfied, rather than directly generate behaviors with the desired properties. They are based on conventional mathematics, such as set theory, algebra, and symbolic logic. Some of the descriptive schemes can also be "executed" to generate their implied behaviors. It is normally easier to state and prove properties with these languages, but more difficult to use them for design. A common approach is to describe and test a system operationally, and then use an assertional notation to express and verify its properties.

▶ Examples of Imperative and Declarative Specifications

Consider a controller for a gate at the intersection of a street and a railway track. A required behavior, expressed operationally, is that a command to close the gate must be issued whenever a train approaches the intersection. In denotational terms, a similar required property might be: the gate must be in the closed state whenever a train is on the track section near or at the intersection. (Note that these two properties are not necessarily equivalent unless a command to close the gate always results in a closed gate after a well-defined time interval.)♦

Some of the principal descriptive methods include: algebraic and set theoretic schemes such as OBJ [Goguen_et_al88] and Z [Spivey89]; language-based notations such as regular expressions and flow expressions [Shaw78]; and assertional logics such as various temporal logics (e.g., [Manna&Pnueli92; Bernstein&Harter81]) and real-time logic [Jahanian&Mok86]. Combinations of English and mathematics have also been employed.

Many of the imperative notations are similar to or derived from programming languages. Examples are CSP [Hoare84], UNITY [Chandy&Misra88], and CSR [Gerber&Lee92]. A popular, but usually informal, notation related to functional programming is data flow diagrams (DFDs) [Ghezzi_et_al91b; Ward&Mellor85]. They are used extensively in information systems applications and also for real-time specifications. One attraction of DFDs is their simple graphical representation. Variations of DFDs are often combined with state machines, using the former to describe data flow and the latter for control flow, such as the modelling language in [Ward&Mellor85] and the state/activity charts in the STATEMATE environment [Harel_et_al90].

Another popular class of operational notations is state-based and admits to natural graphical representations. Some of these are variations of the Petri-net formalism (e.g.,

[Ghezzi_et_al91]). Others, such as statecharts [Harel87], Modecharts [Jahanian& Mok94], ESL [Ostroff&Wonham87], input–output automata [Lynch&Tuttle89], and CRSMs [Shaw92], are extensions of standard state machines or automata. Tabular methods, for example, those used in the SCR project [Heninger80], are based on decision tables; they are mainly imperative and state-based, but also have a descriptive flavor. A number of prominent systems, such as ROOM [Selic_et_al94], combine state machines with OO methods, with the state machines focussing on the control aspects and the OO model describing the data objects. A representative group of languages that has proven useful for real-time applications, including DFDs, tabular, state machine, and several declarative techniques, are covered in the next three chapters.

▶ 3.2 DATA FLOW DIAGRAMS

DFDs offer an attractive graphical way to portray the required functions of a system; the input, output, and internal data consumed, produced, and stored by the functions; and the relations among the functions with respect to their inputs and outputs. It accomplishes this by diagramming the flow of data from, to, and through some basic system elements. While it can be defined quite precisely and mathematically, the main application has been for relatively informal documentation and communication rather than for formal manipulation or execution; and we will present an informal version.

There are many variations and extensions of the notation, all following from the same basic scheme. The primitive objects are drawn and illustrated in Figure 3.1 as follows:

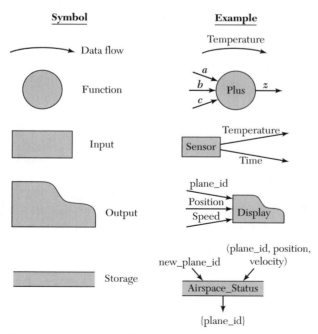

Figure 3.1 DFD symbols.

- *data flow*—This is represented by a directed edge (arrow) which shows the direction of the flow of data. The edge is labelled with the name of the data object. Thus, in the figure, the data named *Temperature* moves from the tail of the arrow to its head. The data need not be a scalar but could be any richly structured object.

- *function*—A circle with an inside label identifies a function or computation to be performed. Data flow edges denote the inputs and outputs of the function. A function can have multiple inputs and outputs. The example has a simple function *Plus* with three inputs, a, b, and c, and one output z. The function may compute, for example, the sum $z = a + b + c$, even though this is not stated explicitly in the notation. The function could be much more complicated, depending on the level of description desired.

- *input*—An object that produces or generates input, such as a terminal or a sensor, has a rectangle icon. Any number of data flow edges can emanate from an input, each edge representing a different data type. The figure has an input named *Sensor* that produces two data items, *Temperature* and *Time*.

- *output*—The graphical symbol for an output element is taken from the old data processing symbol for a printer. Here, it could represent any kind of output, for example, an actuator, a display, a printer, or a network connection. Any number of edges can flow into an output, each edge denoting an output data item.

- *storage*—The "capacitor" symbol is used to represent an internal storage area or data base. Input edges to a storage area denote data writes to the area. Output edges from the area mean that data are read from the storage. The storage *Airspace_Status* could be updated (writes) from data *new_plane_id* and (*plane_id, position, velocity*); a read of the data set {*plane_id*} could denote access of the identifiers of the planes currently stored.

To see how the symbols fit together, let's use all of them in a simple setting. Consider a billing application, similar to one at a supermarket check-out stand. For each customer transaction, a running itemized bill is computed. The total cost of a particular item, such as bottles of beer, is the unit cost times the number of items. Figure 3.2 presents a DFD representing these requirements.

The input *Transaction_Control* provides the control data for the start and end of each transaction, denoted by *start_trans* and *end_trans*, respectively. The itemized bill is maintained in the *Bill* storage area. At the end, the itemized bill, named *bill*, is read from *Bill* and then output by the *Print_Bill* function. The *Compute_Cost* function computes the total cost of an item and sends the result to *Update_Bill* which then updates the *Bill* data. (The dotted line bubble around the two functions will be discussed shortly.) A more interesting real-time application is our running air traffic control (ATC) example.

▶ Example: Partial DFD for ATC

Some of the data and functional requirements for monitoring the entry, exit, and traversal of planes in an airspace is specified in Figure 3.3. The description is at a very high level, an "in-the-large" description; however, many high-level elements and many lower-level details are omitted.

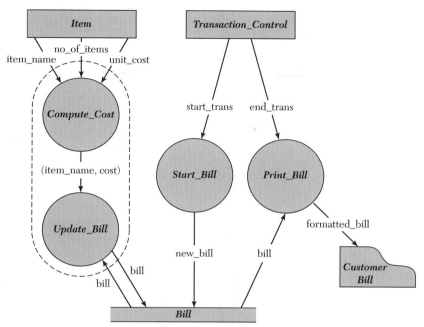

Figure 3.2 Billing application DFD.

Planes entering the space are sensed by the *Radar* input; the *Comm* input identifies planes that leave the space. The current contents of the space are maintained in the data area *Airspace_Status*. A log or history of the space is kept in the *Airspace_Log* storage. An air traffic controller can request the display of the status of a particular plane through the *Operator* input. ◆

The DFD scheme, even when used informally, forces the writer to focus upon and define the fundamental needs of an application in terms of fairly universal basic elements: inputs, outputs, internal data stores, functions, and data; and the data flow throughout these elements. There are great benefits in just listing, elaborating, and constructing DFDs with these elements. However, there are some problems and issues associated with their use, some of which are inherent to DFDs, that require some resolution or thought.

One problem that can be handled in a straightforward manner for many situations is scalability. A high-level DFD for a large system can often be decomposed into smaller, more detailed, and perhaps partial, DFDs; and small DFDs can be composed together to provide larger descriptions. As an example, the *Compute_Cost* and *Update_Bill* functions with their connecting data in Figure 3.2 could be composed into one large function, say *Compute_and_Update_Bill*, as indicated by the dotted bubble; and the *Status_Insert* and *Log_Insert* functions of Figure 3.3 can be similarly composed into one larger function.

The DFD definitions given above are ambiguous in several ways, partly due to the informality of the presentation. Are the input data consumed by the functions or are they always available until overwritten by other input? Must all of the input to a func-

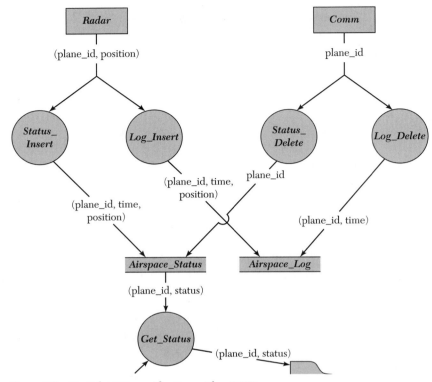

Figure 3.3 Partial ATC specification with a DFD.

tion arrive at the same time? For example, in Figure 3.3, it's clear that the *Get_Status* function requires the operator input *plane_id* before it can retrieve the plane's status from *Airspace_Status*. The meaning of reads and writes on the data stores also should be clarified. What, for example, does the *new_bill* input do to the *Bill* data store in Figure 3.2? Presumably, it clears and initializes the store for the new transaction, but this is just our reasonable interpretation applicable only to this particular write operation.

The most serious inherent problem with DFDs is the absence of control. When should a function be triggered or invoked? Some of the problems mentioned are really control problems. Another control issue is conditional execution of functions. Depending on input values, it may or may not be correct to perform a given function. A general solution here is to employ a state machine to provide control or triggering inputs to the DFD functions.

► EXERCISES 3.2

1. Draw a data flow diagram (DFD) that specifies a reasonable set of functions, data stores, inputs, outputs, and data flows for part of a credit card system that handles transactions for retail stores. For example, a transaction might consist of buying a backpack and cross-country skis at your favorite outdoors store. Your part should include functions for retrieving and checking a credit card record for a customer, approving and recording each transaction, and maintaining a log of transactions for each retail outlet. The system should maintain files of credit card holders, current transactions, and accounts payable (approved transactions) for each outlet.

2. Draw a DFD for part of an automatic teller system (ATM). Your part of the ATM handles requests to disburse cash from a given bank account and to display the balance of an account. The system should maintain records for the current cash inventory of the location, for customer accounts, and for a transaction history of the ATM.

3. Suppose that a vending machine dispenses champagne and fois gras, costing 25 euros and 50 euros, respectively. The machine accepts 10 and 25 euro bills as input, and returns change in units of 1, 5, 10, and 25 euro bills. Draw a DFD that expresses the required functionality and data flow for this system; include several internal data stores. Euro bill inputs are *ten-in* and *twenty-five-in*; selection inputs are *champagne-request*, *fois-gras-request*, and *cancel*. Item outputs are *champagne* and *fois-gras*; money outputs are *one-euro*, *five-euro*, *ten-euro*, and *twenty-five-euro*; the sound output *beep* is an indicator that more money must be inserted for the particular selection made. Comment on any problems or issues with your DFD, especially those related to control flow.

▶ 3.3 TABULAR LANGUAGES

Tables are a broadly accepted way to express and communicate information among humans in a relatively precise and concise manner. From the early days of computing up until the present time, they have also been employed for requirements, designs, and even programming of computer software systems. Our emphasis is mainly as an informal language for requirements specification.

One of the most common tabular representations for computer applications is *decision tables* [Metzner&Barnes77; Hurley83]. In its simplest form, a decision table structure is sketched in Figure 3.4.

The upper half lists n rows of conditions $C_1, \ldots, C_n$. The lower half defines m rows of actions $A_1, \ldots, A_m$. Each column describes a rule which is a *guarded* set of actions— a set of actions to perform provided that the specified combination of conditions, the "guard," hold. A condition is some assertion or Boolean expression over the state variables of the system, that evaluates to true or false; examples are

$$System\_In\_TakeOff\_Mode,$$
$$(\text{ } time > 10 \text{ }), \text{ and}$$
$$(\text{ } Landing \text{ and } (\text{ } altitude < 2000 \text{ }) \text{ }).$$

An action could be some sequence of computations and input-output operations.

A condition entry c_{ij} may contain Y (yes) or N (no). An action entry a_{ij} may be either X (do it) or $-$ (don't do it). The meaning of the jth action column or rule is then:

$$\text{if } Conditions_j \text{ then } Action_j.$$

$Column_j$ is a guard that evaluates to true or false according to the value of the expression

$$(\text{ } (\text{ } (c_{1j}=\text{"Y" and } C_1) \text{ or } (c_{1j}=\text{"N" and not}(C_1)) \text{ }) \text{ and } \ldots \text{ and}$$
$$(\text{ } (c_{nj}=\text{"Y" and } C_n) \text{ or } (c_{nj}=\text{"N" and not}(C_n)) \text{ }) \text{ }).(^*)$$

$Action_j$ is the conditional action sequence

$$\text{if } a_{1j}=\text{"X" then do } A_1 ; \ldots ; \text{ if } a_{mj}=\text{"X" then do } A_m;$$

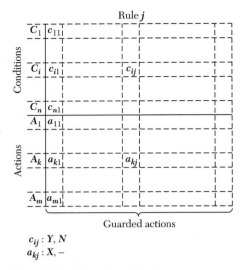

$c_{ij} : Y, N$
$a_{kj} : X, -$

Figure 3.4 A decision table form.

▶ Example: Highway Entry Control

An entry point to a highway is metered by a set of lights, so that the frequency of vehicles entering the highway can be controlled when the highway traffic is high. If the average highway speed is below a given threshold, say 30 mph, then the meter lights are activated. The metering should not be enabled if the speed exceeds the threshold. Traffic may queue up at the entrance; if the vehicle line becomes too large, say greater than 100, then the local traffic police should be alerted.

From the above description, we define the following conditions and actions:

Conditions
C_1: *Average_Vehicle_Speed* > 30
C_2: *Meter_Lights_Activated*
C_3: *Entry_Queue* > 100

Actions
A_1: *Activate_Meter_Lights*
A_2: *Deactivate_Metering*
A_3: *Alert_Police*

Figure 3.5 contains a decision table describing the requirements for this hypothetical system. As an example, the 4th rule in the table states that if both C_1 and C_2 are false, and C_3 is true, then actions A_1 and A_3 are to be executed. ◆

The columns normally cover all possible combinations of conditions. The three conditions in Figure 3.5 thus generate eight rules. Generally, if there are n independent conditions, there are 2^n possible rules. This result is useful for both checking and testing. One can easily check that there exists a rule for each of the 2^n combinations, provided of course that n is not too large. Similarly, one can test or debug a specification by providing a separate set of test cases for each rule.

C_1	Y	N	Y	N	Y	N	Y	N
C_2	Y	Y	N	N	Y	Y	N	N
C_3	Y	Y	Y	Y	N	N	N	N
A_1	–	–	–	X	–	–	–	X
A_2	X	–	–	–	X	–	–	–
A_3	X	X	X	X	–	–	–	–

Figure 3.5   Highway entry control.

Combinations of conditions that are irrelevant because they cause no actions or that are impossible are usually omitted, such as the sixth and seventh rule in Figure 3.5. In many practical situations, especially for event-driven applications, there may be irrelevant combinations of conditions that should cause no activity; that is, the underlying system is required to wait until one of the relevant conditions is satisfied. A "don't care" condition is often used to save space when a rule is satisfied for both truth values ("Y" and "N") of the particular condition; that is, the condition itself is irrelevant for the rule. A "don't care" condition entry will be designated by the "/" symbol.

▶ Example: Railway Crossing Gate[1]

Suppose that there is a road crossing a railway track, and a gate that opens and closes over the road. When a train approaches the crossing, the gate should close. More than one train can be in the crossing area at once, for example, a convoy of trains, each with a single engine and no cars. When the last train has left and the area is empty of trains, the gate should open. A single decision table describing this required behavior is given in Figure 3.6.

The condition *Train_Entering* becomes true when the first part of a train enters the area; *Train_Leaving* becomes true when the last car of a train leaves the area.[2] *count* keeps track of the number of trains in the crossing area. The last two conditions, *count*=0 and *count*=1, are not independent; for example, they can't both be true ("Y") at the same time. The notations, *count*++ and *count*− −, denote the incrementing and decrementing, respectively, of the variable *count*.

Not included in the table are the rules for the cases where both *Train_Entering* and *Train_Leaving* are "Y"; in both cases, there are no actions to be performed. (One might want to insert these rules so that the designer is assured that no significant cases are omitted.) Initially, assume that *count*=0 and the gate is open. The required control behavior is obtained by repeatedly executing the table, triggered by either or both of the sensing events. ◆

Generally, many tables are employed to describe a system or subsystem. The flow from table to table may be controlled implicitly by events or it may be given explicitly by an action, such as a branch "go to Table n." One can also encapsulate a decision table as a procedural action, such as "Execute Table n," with parameters if desired; after the called table is executed, control returns to the calling table. Thus, there is an implicit

---

[1]Variations on this application have become "classic" real-time examples, ever since the application was used in [Leveson&Stolzy87].
[2]Shortly after these events are sensed, the corresponding conditions are set to false. Alternatively, these conditions could be set to false by actions in another table.

Train_Entering	Y	Y	N	N
Train_Leaving	N	N	Y	Y
count = 0	Y	N	N	N
count = 1	N	/	Y	N
Open_Gate	–	–	X	–
Close_Gate	X	–	–	–
count^{++}	X	X	–	–
count^{--}	–	–	X	X

Figure 3.6   Railway crossing gate control.

executable machine represented by a table, where one enters from the top and exits or returns from the bottom.

In one complex real-time application, the requirements for an aircraft collision avoidance system were expressed in a state-based language called RSML; within the language, a tabular notation was used to describe assertional guards on state transitions [Heimdahl&Leveson96]. A transition T from a state U to a state V has the components

$$\text{if } guard \text{ and } event \text{ then perform } action^3$$

with the meaning: the transition T can occur provided the assertion *guard* is true and *event* occurs; if T is taken, *action* is performed and the system enters state V.

The guard is written in a form identical to the upper half of a decision table. It has the meaning:

$$\text{guard} = Column_1 \text{ or } Column_2 \text{ or } \dots \text{ or } Column_k,$$

where there are k columns in the table. The authors call these "and/or" tables since the row elements within each column are logically *and*ed together and the columns are *or*ed.

▶ Example of a Tabular Guard (taken from [Heimdahl&Leveson96])

A simple example is presented in Figure 3.7. Note that the table is not a complete decision table, but only the condition part. The guard in the figure represents the assertion

$$(C_1 \text{ and } C_3) \text{ or } (C_1 \text{ and } (\text{not } C_2)). \blacklozenge$$

An interesting variation of decision tables was developed in a project started about 1977 under the leadership of David Parnas. The aim of this project, called the Software Cost Reduction project (SCR) and sponsored by the U.S. Department of Defense, was to illustrate how computer science techniques could be applied to real-time software. The investigators proposed to accomplish this by completely redoing a working computer program, part of the weapons delivery and navigation control system for a Navy fighter airplane. We describe some of the most influential results of this work, mainly concerned with modelling and specifying requirements, as reported in [Heninger80] and [Faulk&Parnas88].[4]

---

[3]The RSML notation differs from this, but the ideas are the same.
[4]Some liberties have been taken with the notation, and many details have been omitted. The table language has since been formalized (e.g., [Janicki_et_al95]).

C_1	Own_Air_Status = On_Ground	Y	Y
C_2	Traffic_Display_Permitted	/	N
C_3	Mode_Selector = Standby	Y	/

Figure 3.7   A guard in table form.

The basic objects in the SCR requirements methodology are *modes, conditions, events*, and *actions*. Modes are named groups of states as discussed in the last chapter. Conditions are assertions or predicates on the state variables of the system. At any time, a condition is either true or false. It has the same form and interpretation as a Boolean expression in a programming language. An example of a condition is

$$(altitude < 500) \text{ and } (radar\_mode = standby).$$

Changes in the system are manifested by changes in its state variables, typically caused by input to the computer system from its environment. As a result, conditions switch from true to false or vice versa. Such changes are defined as events: an *event* is the occurrence of a condition becoming true or false. Events can also be viewed as higher-level or logical interrupt signals. It is convenient to associate a second "enabling" condition or guard with an event definition; the event can only occur if it is enabled. Notationally, we write either

$$\uparrow C1 \text{ when } C2 \qquad \text{or} \qquad \downarrow C1 \text{ when } C2$$

to mean, respectively, the event when condition *C1* turns true ($\neq$) provided that the condition *C2* holds at that time, or the event when *C1* becomes false ($\varnothing$) provided that *C2* is true. Actions are lists of instructions that change the values of state variables, typically the values of computer output.

▶ **Example of an Event**

$$\uparrow(aircraft\_airborne \text{ or } inertial\_switch=\text{ON}) \text{ when } (altitude > 80). \blacklozenge$$

Software requirements are documented using these basic objects as table entries. Two forms of tables are proposed—one for periodic functions, and the other for sporadic functions. Figure 3.8 sketches the form for a periodic function.

The initiation and termination events specify the start and stop conditions for the function. The interpretation of a particular row, column, and entry is

Name:
Initiation and termination events:

Modes	Conditions		
M		*C*	
⋮			

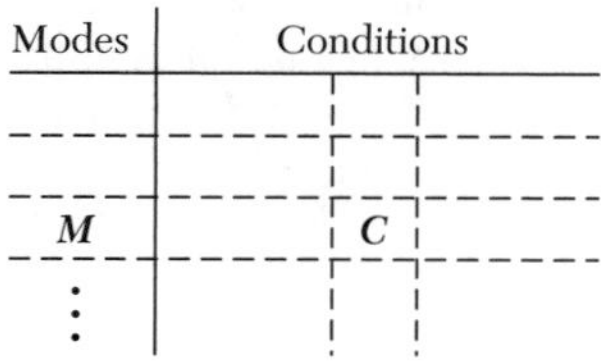

Figure 3.8   SCR periodic function.

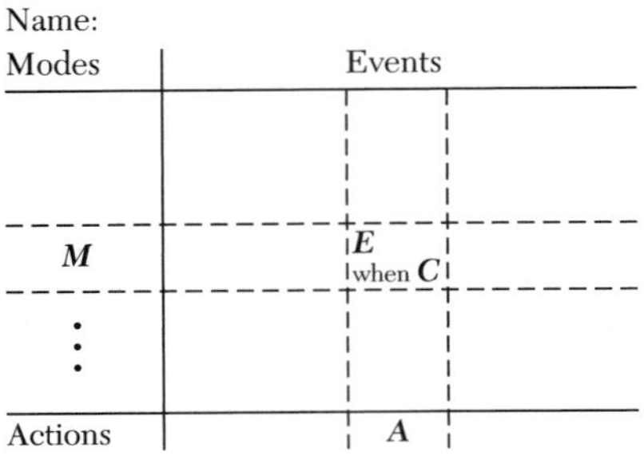

Name:

Modes	Events	
M	E when C	
⋮		
Actions	A	

Figure 3.9   SCR sporadic function.

If the system is in mode M and condition C is true, then perform action A during the period. Sporadic functions, as shown in Figure 3.9, contain guarded events rather than pure conditions in the tables. The meaning is

If the system is in mode M and event E occurs when condition C holds, then perform action A.

About 100 such functions were used to describe the logical functionality of the subsystem for the Navy airplane. Timing constraints are listed separately from the logical correctness requirements in this version of the method. One could, however, argue that they should be treated together, because timing correctness and logical correctness are often intertwined.

Many variations of tabular description methods have been proposed or used. Several common extensions, so-called "extended entry" decision tables, permit more complicated expressions in the condition and action entry portions. For example, a condition row might be named *temperature* with one entry denoting a value, say

$$15 < temperature < 40$$

and another entry being

$$(temperature < 0) \text{ or } (temperature > 50).$$

The rectangular format and structure of tables, while natural for some specifications, is awkward for many applications. There also does not appear to be any obvious way to include concurrency, communications, and timing requirements in these notations. Tables can be interpreted as state machines, which have been extended to include these additional features and which have a more flexible graphical form.

▶ EXERCISES 3.3

1. Some columns are missing in the decision table example of Figure 3.6, for example, the column corresponding to the four conditions, "N," "N," "N," and "Y," for C_1, C_2, C_3, and C_4, respectively. For each column that is missing, explain why the conjunction of conditions is either impossible or irrelevant.

2. The following describes part of a hypothetical controller, revised from the one in [Jaffe_et_al91]. The goal is to maintain the coolant temperature in a reactor tank at a given $C°$ Celsius. The temperature T is sampled periodically, every p units of time. If $T > C$, a rod in the tank is moved up a constant amount by initiating an action MU. If $T < C$, then the rod is moved down with an MD action. If no rod movement has occurred for n successive periods, i.e., $T = C$ for n periods, the temperature is considered stable and the system enters a new phase, called *keep_stable*. A potential sensor failure is indicated if either $T \leq -273$ or $T > 500$ for three successive periods; when this happens, the *error_action* is performed. Express the controller logic and actions in decision table form.

3. A computer controls two pair of traffic lights at the intersection of a street and an avenue, one pair for each. The lights can be red or green, but both pairs can never be green at the same time (else the lights will cause car collisions!). Under normal processing, the lights change, via *turn_red* and *turn_green* commands, whenever the event *change_lights* occurs, say every 45 seconds; the changes are such that one pair is red while the other is green. When an ambulance nears the intersection, a sensor signals an *amb_enter$_{road}$* event, where *road* is either

avenue or *street* depending on the location of the road location of the ambulance. The controller then must ensure that the lights on the ambulance road are green, while those on the other road are red. When the ambulance leaves the intersection area, signalled by an *amb_exit* event, the lights resume their normal sequencing. Write an SCR sporadic function that reacts appropriately to the timer and ambulance events, using the tabular format of Figure 3.9. Let there be two modes, *N* and *A*, denoting normal and ambulance processing, respectively.

▶ 3.4 STATE MACHINES

Various forms of state machines have traditionally been the language of choice for modelling and designing computer systems. They are natural notations for describing and reasoning about switching circuits, and many event-driven algorithms and software; and have an appealing graphical representation. In addition, a major part of computer science theory, automata theory, is based on these machines [Hopcroft&Ullman79]. The systems model that we defined informally in Section 2.1 is in fact a state machine.

The standard *finite state machine (fsm)* contains a finite number of *states*, and a *transition* or *next-state* function that maps states and *events* (inputs) into states. At any point, the system is in a given state. The occurrence of an event causes the system to change state according to the transition function definition. A machine normally has one *start* state and zero or more *halt* states. An fsm starts executing in its start state, changing states according to the input that it receives, until it reaches a halt state and/or exhausts the input. The graphical form of an fsm is a *state diagram*; this is a directed labelled graph where the vertices denote states and the edges represent transitions.

▶ FSM Example: Gate Sensing and Control

Consider the behavior and associated events of a gate at a train crossing. (See the railway crossing gate example presented in Section 3.2.) The gate could be in one of four states: *open, closed, opening,* and *closing*. The relevant events are: *cg* and *og* which are commands to close and open the gate, respectively; and *o-o* and *c-c* indicating from sensor input that the gate has completed opening (and thus changed from the *opening* to the *opened* state), and that the gate has completed closing, respectively.

Figure 3.10 is a finite state machine description of this behavior given in state diagram form. The initial (start) state is *closed* and there are no stop (halt) states.

This fsm accepts the *cg* and *og* commands in all of its states; thus, for example, the gate may be commanded to close while it is opening. Another kind of gate may reject these two commands while *opening* or *closing*; to model that situation, we might add another state, say *Reject*, that is entered when either of these commands are input at these points. We have omitted *o-o* and *c-c* transitions from those states where the input should not be present; for example, the *o-o* event should not appear while in state *Closing* and neither *o-o* nor *c-c* should be input while in *Open*. For completeness, these

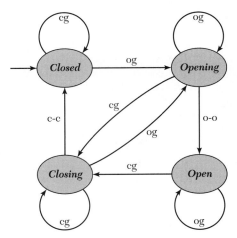

Figure 3.10 FSM for a train crossing gate.

transitions could be included with a next state, say *Error*. Error or reject states are sometimes omitted and assumed to be present implicitly. ◆

Fsms are also called *finite automata*, especially when treated theoretically. The input to any fsm is considered a sequence or string of symbols from a finite set. The symbols could be interpreted in many different ways, for example, as characters, events, commands, input data, or words. When a transition occurs, the associated input symbol is consumed.

An fsm M is defined mathematically as a five-tuple

$$M = (Q, I, f, q_0, F),$$

where Q is a finite set of states, I is a finite set of input symbols, f is a transition function, the next-state function, that maps states and inputs to states

$$f : Q \times I \rightarrow Q ,$$

q_0 is the start state, and F is a subset of Q, the set of halt states. An input sequence or string $x_0 x_1 \ldots x_n$, x_i in I, is said to be *recognized* or *accepted* by M if it takes q_0 to some state in F; that is,

$$f(f(\ldots f(f(s_0, x_0), x_1) , \ldots) , x_n) \text{ in } F.$$

Note that the input is assumed to enter the system from left to right. The set of all input strings recognized by a machine M is called the *language* recognized by M.

▶ FSM for Buffer Constraint

In the bounded buffer example at the end of Section 2.5, there is the constraint that every *Remove* operation must be directly preceded by at least one *Deposit*. Figure 3.11 expresses this constraint as an fsm M in graphical form, where R and D denote *Remove* and *Deposit*, respectively, and the halt states have double circles. Essentially, the machine does not "accept" any string containing two R's in a row. Thus, D

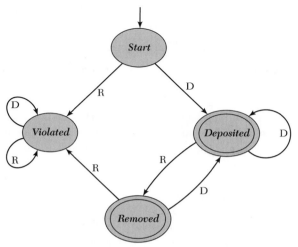

Figure 3.11 Buffer constraint machine.

$R\,D\,D\,R\,D\,R\,D\,D\,D$ and $D\,D\,D\,D\,R\,D\,R\,D\,R$ are accepted, but not $D\,R\,R$ or $D\,D\,R\,D$ $R\,R\,R\,D\,R$.

The formal definition of M is

$S = \{\ Start,\ Deposited,\ Removed,\ Violated\ \},\ I = \{\ D,\ R\ \},\ q_0 = Start,$
$F = \{\ Deposited,\ Removed\},$ and f is given by:
$f\,(Start,\ D) = Deposited, f\,(Start,R) = Violated,$
$f(Deposited,\ D) = Deposited, f(Deposited,\ R) = Removed,$
$f(Removed,\ D) = Deposited, f(Removed,\ R) = Violated,$
$f(Violated,\ x) = Violated$ for x in I.

Note that our machine assumes at least one operation, that is, that the input is non-empty. If the empty input is also permitted, then a simpler machine can be constructed by deleting *Start*, making $q_0 = Removed$, and $F = \{Removed,\ Deposited\}$. ◆

Our fsms are actually *deterministic* fsms—the next state is always uniquely defined by the next state function with its two arguments, current state and current input symbol. There also exist the more general and sometimes more convenient *nondeterministic* fsms. For these machines, the next state function maps a current state and current input into a *set* of next states (including the empty set). The meaning is that a state transition with a given event or symbol can occur to any one of the states in the next state set, but the particular one selected is arbitrary. A string is accepted if there is some path through the machine that ends in a halt state. It is noteful that every nondeterministic fsm can be transformed into an equivalent deterministic fsm that recognizes or accepts the same input. Other kinds of nondeterminism appear naturally when modelling concurrent systems; we will examine some of these in the next chapter.

Fsms are extremely useful and practical for some problems, and there exists a large body of theory that allows their manipulation and analysis. However, they are also limited in several ways. As a pure recognition mechanism, their descriptive power is not universal. For example, they are unable to recognize a set of simple balanced parentheses

$$\{(^n\ )^n\ ,\ n > 0\} = \{\ (),\ (()),\ ((())),\ (((()))),\ \dots\ \}.$$

A variation of this problem is a buffer constraint (see preceding example) that requires the number of D's to equal the number of R's—a constraint that is impossible to express as an fsm. In fact, unless a modelling language is universal, for example, with the power of a programming language or a Turing machine, there will always be some features that are impossible to model. One way to achieve this universality is to permit computations as part of the transitions. The result is still an executable notation, but not as easily manipulated as the much simpler fsms.

Another restriction of the pure fsm notation is that it has no output; one cannot directly model components where output commands or data are produced, such as the generation of cg and og in Figure 3.10. Finite state machines with output have been defined in a clean manner (Mealy machines). We remove all of the above restrictions with the general state transition system presented next.

A completely powerful version of the state machine model allows guards, inputs, outputs, and actions on transitions. A transition between states U and V is defined by the expression

$$g \rightarrow i\ /\ a\ /\ o\ ,$$

where g is a guard, that is, a Boolean expression, assertion, or condition; i is an input, such as an event; a is a sequence of actions; and o is an output. The meaning is

> If the machine is in state U, the guard g is true, and input i occurs, then perform actions a, generate the output o, and enter state V.

The actions are usually computations, but they could also denote physical activities such as opening a valve. The guard can be interpreted as an enabling or firing condition for the transition.

▶ Example: Gate Controller

Figure 3.12 contains the state diagram for an extended fsm specifying a simple controller for our train crossing gate (Section 3.3). Input events are *Train_Entering* and *Train_Leaving* signals; the output events are *Open_Gate* and *Close_Gate* commands, the latter being equivalent to the og and cg commands in Figure 3.10. The state variable *count* keeps track of the number of trains in the crossing area. The guards (*count*=1 and *count*>1) determine which transition is taken on a *Train_Leaving* event; a guard is omitted when its value is always *true*. Note the similiarity between the controller here and the decision table version given in Figure 3.6. ◆

These state machine models need to be extended further in order to handle specifications for real-time systems more completely. The principal required additional features are concurrency and time. An fsm and the generalizations described above all "run" sequentially, one transition at a time; this works well for specifying a single sequential component. Concurrency is modelled by permitting several fsms to run in parallel. Suitable intermachine communication and synchronization mechanisms must be

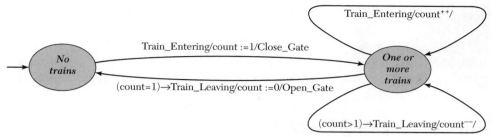

Figure 3.12   Extended FSM for gate controller.

defined; also, an appropriate parallel model needs to be selected, for example, a variation or combination of a distributed or shared memory model. For describing timing constraints and behaviors, some means of specifying transition firing times, the times for a machine to reside in each state, and/or clocks and timing events are also necessary.

All state machine techniques, including those for conventional sequential systems, suffer from a "state explosion" problem: large systems tend to have unmanageably large numbers of states. This problem is exacerbated with the additions of concurrency and time. Candidate state machine systems that directly address these issues of concurrency, time, and scalability are presented in the next chapter.

▶ EXERCISES 3.4

1. Complete the fsm in Figure 3.10 by adding a *Reject* state and "error" transitions to this new state as discussed in the text.

2. Give a finite state machine (fsm) in a state diagram form that distinguishes among the three input objects: *identifiers*, *unsigned integers*, and *other strings*. The input alphabet or set of events is $I = \{l, d, b, \$\}$, where l denotes an alphabetic character, d is a digit, i.e., d in $\{0, 1, \ldots, 9\}$, b is the "blank" or space character, and $\$$ represents any special character, such as @, #, or !. An *identifier* is any string of alphabetic characters and digits, starting with an alphabetic character and surrounded by one or more blanks. Your fsm should have a separate halt state for each of the three possible input objects.

3. Consider the following constraints on the D and R operations on a bounded buffer: there cannot be more than two D operations in a row, there cannot be more than two R operations in a row, and the system must start with a D. Define an fsm that expresses these constraints.

4. A simple digital watch maintains, displays, and permits the setting of time as a triple (*hour*, *minute*, *second*). In its normal mode, a *tick* event occurs every second; the time is

then updated and output to the watch screen. The watch has two external buttons, labelled a and b. Whenever a is pressed in normal mode, the watch enters set mode, starting with *minute* update. Each depression of the b button will then cause the *minute* field to increment by 1 (mod 60). Pressing the a button will then cause the watch to enter *hour* update; each successive depression of b then increments the *hour* field by 1 (mod 24). On depressing a again, the watch reenters its normal mode. Define an extended fsm that describes the watch reactions to the *tick*, a, and b events.

5. Draw the state diagram of an extended fsm for the traffic light controller defined in Question 3 of the Exercises of Section 3.3.

6. A single button mouse is used for generating messages in a code similar to Morse code, an old coding scheme employed for telegraph communications. A *dot* is defined by a depress-button event (D) followed by a release-button event (U) separated by no more than td time units. A dash is a D followed by a U separated by more than td. Write an extended fsm for a dot/dash recognizer. Input events are D, U, and a *tick* every unit of time. Outputs should be *dot*, *dash*, and *eol*. The *eol* output is an end-of-line indicator and should be generated after every 40 dots and dashes have been recognized.

CHAPTER 4

Systems of State Machines

The state machine model and notation have been extended in several directions in order to describe, analyze, and simulate behaviors for larger, multicomponent real-time systems. In this chapter, we present two interesting, different, and useful language extensions, *communicating real-time state machines* and *statecharts*. It is also our purpose to use these languages to specify and discuss a number of more complex examples of real-time behaviors. The two languages differ significantly in the ways that they handle concurrency and communications, time, and machine structuring and composition.

▶ 4.1 COMMUNICATING REAL-TIME STATE MACHINES

The communicating real-time state machine (CRSM) notation [Shaw92] was designed as a single, complete, and executable specification language. They have a distributed model of concurrency. Parallel components are encapsulated and isolated; they can interact only through message passing using synchronous one-to-one message communications. Time is an essential part of the language and is involved in every state transition. Some statechart ideas are incorporated in the CRSM structuring methods, but the latter are not as general.

4.1.1 Basic Features

A system specification with CRSMs will normally be *closed* in that both the environment and the computer system are described and that senders and receivers of all messages or events are included. Consequently, a complete specification will consist of at least two CRSMs, one for the external environment and one for the computer system.

A single CRSM is a state machine with guarded commands for transitions. The gate controller of Figure 3.12 is a CRSM if we change the syntax slightly to distinguish between input and output events and to delimit transitions. For example, the following code denotes three CRSM transitions in sequence:

$$(count=1) \rightarrow Train\_Leaving? \mid count := 0 \mid Open\_Gate!$$

In this notation, "?" denotes receiving a message, which is considered synonymous with an input event; "!" means sending a message, an output event; and transitions are separated by the "|" symbol.

The general form of a transition is

$$g \to c \; [\tau] \; .$$

g is a Boolean guard over the variables of the machine; c is a command, which could be either an input-output (IO) command or an internal one; and τ is a timing constraint. Internal commands may be any computation, expressed in some programming language, or they can designate the performance of some physical activity, such as opening a valve or a gate. There are no restrictions on the size or complexity of an internal command, except that it terminate. The guard may be omitted, indicating a default value of *true*.

The IO notation and meaning is taken directly from Hoare's communicating sequential processes (CSP) [Hoare78,85]. When CRSMs communicate, they do so synchronously and instantaneously over unidirectional *channels* that connect pairs of machines. A connecting channel can be thought of as a one-directional "wire." A channel has a message or event type associated with it; the message type defines the permissible message structures that may be transmitted over the channel. A channel is also given a unique name or identifier. To designate or declare the existence of a channel named *name* with message type *type*, we adopt the notation *name(type)*.

► **Examples of IO Channels**

Position(x_y_coordinates)
Calendar_Clock(calendar_time)
Deposit(character)
Open_Gate
Train_Leaving

Thus, the channel named *Position* can carry messages of type *x_y_coordinates*, such as pairs of integers or real numbers; and the *Deposit* channel transmits messages of type *character*. The last two channels, *Open_Gate* and *Train_Leaving*, are "pure" events with no data message; parentheses are omitted in these cases. ♦

Instances of communications over the channels will have actual message components instead of the event type.

► **Examples of Channel Instances**

Position((14.5, 2.87))
Calendar_Clock(((Mon, Feb, 11), (10,15,PM)))
Deposit("h")
Open_Gate ♦

An input command receives a message or event over a channel and has the syntax:

name(target)?

where *name* is a channel name and *target* is a variable that is compatible with the event type. To send a message, i.e., generate an event, over a channel, an output command with the following form is employed:

$$name(message)!$$

where name is the channel identifier and *message* is the actual message instance. IO can only occur if the sender and receiver channel names match and if the target and message types are compatible. If IO does indeed take place, this IO event occurs instantaneously, and both communicants continue execution concurrently. The effect is identical to an assignment statement at the receiver, given by

$$target := message,$$

and to a *null* operation at the sender.

Messages and events are synonymous: a message IO is an event and an event is a message IO. Sending and receiving messages constitute the only event types in CRSMs.

▶ Real-Time Bounded Buffer Example

Consider a real-time version of a producer process and a consumer process interacting through a bounded buffer. (See, for example, [Bic&Shaw88] for the standard non-real-time version.) The producer will insert or deposit data elements into the buffer, while the consumer removes them in first-in-first-out order. The data is stored in a buffer array, one data element per array element.

We use three CRSMs, one each for the producer, consumer, and buffer, as Figure 4.1(*a*) illustrates. There is a *Deposit* channel directed from the *Producer* to the *Buffer* and a *Remove* channel from the *Buffer* to the *Consumer*. The message type *m* for both channels is identical. The channel is drawn as a wavy line in the figure to indicate communications.

The CRSM details are given in Figure 4.1(*b*). Ignore the timing specifications on the transitions for now. For the example, assume that *Producer* is a physical device that generates signals through its *Generate(data)* transition, that are then sent to *Buffer* by a *Deposit(data)*! output. If the *Deposit* IO doesn't occur in time (discussed below), the *Clock* transition is taken to state P_2 and an error message is sent on an *Error* channel.[1] *Consumer* is a software task that removes and processes the data; it invokes *Remove* to obtain the next input signal.

The CRSM *Buffer* implements an *n*-slot buffer between the two other machines, using an array *Buf*[0..*n*-1] to store the data items. The *Deposit* IO may occur if *Producer* is in state P_1, *Buffer* is in state B_1, and *full* < *n* which means that the *Buf* array isn't full. If this IO takes place, the corresponding transitions occur simultaneously on both machines with the effect

$$Buf[in] := data$$

on the CRSM *Buffer*. Similarly, the *Remove* IO may occur if *Consumer* is in state C_1 and *full* > 0, the latter indicating that there is some unremoved data in the array. This

---

[1]For simplicity, we do not show the *Error* channel or the error handling machine to which this channel would be connected.

(*a*) Buffer and clients

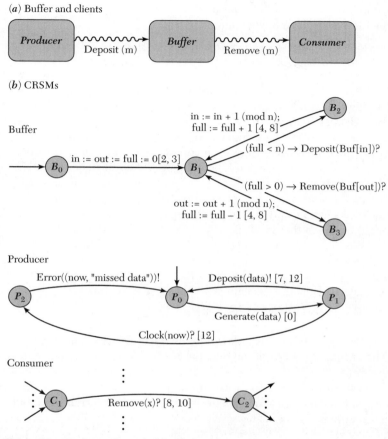

(*b*) CRSMs

Figure 4.1   Real-time bounded buffer.

IO, if it occurs, would cause *Consumer* to enter state C_2 after executing the *Remove* transition with the effect

$$x := Buf[out] .$$

Simultaneously, *Buffer* would enter state B_3. ◆

4.1.2 Timing and Clocks

The timing constraint $[\tau]$ on a transition is a pair of expressions constructed from constants and variables of the particular CRSM. The values of the expressions give lower and upper bounds on the execution duration of the transition

$$[\tau] = [exp_l, exp_u].$$

Let these expressions evaluate to $[t_{min}, t_{max}]$. If the expressions contain any variables changed by the transition action, then the values used are those before the action is executed. The specification is considered incorrect unless $0 \leq t_{min} \leq t_{max}$. Then, if the command c on the transition is an internal one, the execution time d of c is somewhere in the interval defined by the pair, i.e.

$$0 \le t_{min} \le d \le t_{max}.$$

One reason for allowing an interval rather than an exact time is the uncertainty associated with the execution time of an internal action, particularly a computation where looping and conditionals may be present. (This issue, and related ones, are treated in some detail in Chapter 7.)

IO timing is more complicated because there are two communicants involved, the sender and the receiver. For each communicant, its pair of time bounds, $[t_{min}, t_{max}]$, defines an IO time interval; the bounds are the earliest and latest times that the IO can occur *relative* to the time that the machine last entered its current state. The intersection of the sender and receiver intervals gives the time of possible communications. If the IO is possible and it occurs, it happens at the earliest possible time, that is, the start or t_{min} of one of the intervals.

We describe the IO action more precisely. Suppose machines M_1 and M_2 are in states U and X, respectively, where they may communicate over a channel ch [Figure 4.2(a)]. Let t_U and t_X be the times that machines M_1 and M_2 enter states U and X, respectively. Then, if IO occurs, it will happen at the time

$$t = \max(t_U + a, t_X + c).$$

However, if the intervals do not intersect, IO is not possible. This condition is true when t satisfies either of the relations $t > t_U + b$ or $t > t_X + d$. Figure 4.2(b) contains two examples.

Transitions are fired or executed on an *earliest-time-ready-first* basis, provided of course that their guards evaluate to true. Consider a transition with command c from

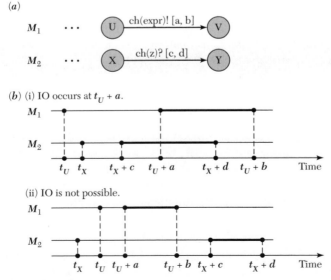

Figure 4.2 Timing on IO.

state U to V. If c is an internal command, the transition is defined as ready at the time that the CRSM enters U. If c is an IO command, the transition is ready at the earliest possible communications time as defined by the algorithm above. In the case of ties, when several transitions from a given state are ready at the same earliest time, IO takes precedence over internal commands; if there are remaining ties (the ready transitions are either all IO or all internal commands), the transition that is executed is selected arbitrarily, i.e., nondeterministically. The standard practical example of this nondeterminism occurs when several IO instances, each involving different partner machines, are simultaneously ready to execute in the same machine.

Abbreviations are employed for two of the most common types of timing constraints. When a sender or receiver is ready for IO at *any* time after entering a given state, the IO transition would declare an infinite time interval $[0, \infty]$. We omit the timing constraint field entirely in this case. When an interval evaluates to a scalar, such as $[a, a]$, we use the shortened form $[a]$.

▶ Real-Time Bounded Buffer Revisited1

Consider again the real-time bounded buffer example of Figure 4.1 which was introduced in the last section. In the *Buffer* machine, the internal computation transitions have times of $[2,3]$ and $[4,8]$, indicating for example that the initial transition from B_0 to B_1 takes somewhere between 2 and 3 time units to execute. (These times were chosen arbitrarily for the example.) The *Deposit* and *Remove* transitions have omitted timing fields, the abbreviation for $[0,\infty]$, denoting that IO could occur at any time after entering state B_1 provided the relevant guard evaluates to true. *Consumer* can execute a *Remove* sometime in the interval $[8,10]$ after entering C_1 and *Producer* can perform a *Deposit* IO only in the $[7,12]$ interval after entering P_1.

Thus, if *Producer* enters P_1 at time 1000, *Consumer* enters C_1 at time 1005, and *Buffer* enters B_1 at time 1004, the *Deposit* IO will occur at time 1004 provided that the guard *full*<n is *true*. On the other hand, if *Consumer* instead entered C_1 at time 1003, then both *Producer* and *Consumer* with their *Buffer* partner would be ready for IO at time 1004; the IO choice, *Deposit* or *Remove*, would then be made nondeterministically, assuming both guards are true. ◆

The timing constraint part of transitions permits the specification of durations for internal commands and relative intervals for IO. To make the notation a complete one with respect to time, some means of accessing absolute or real-time is also necessary. Every CRSM M has its own *real-time clock machine*, a CRSM denoted RTC_M, that performs this function. RTC_M will send the current value of real-time, rt, over a clock channel $Clock_M$ to its host M on demand. rt is the only global shared variable in the sys-

RTC_M

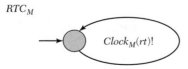

Figure 4.3   Real-time clock machine for M.

tem and is read-only by any CRSM through its clock machine. Each RTC_M is a single-state machine with one transition $Clock_M(rt)!$ (Figure 4.3).

Each real-time clock machine acts as a perfect time server to its host, providing both time values and timeout signals. An IO command

$$Clock_M(x)? \; [y]$$

executed by a host M in state U will result in the assignment $x := rt$ at the time y relative to the time that M entered U. The value for x gives an absolute "time-stamp" for the time-out event at relative time y. If the time field is omitted (implicitly equal to $[0,\infty]$) or $y=0$, we get a time-stamp for entering state U. If x is ignored, we get a pure timeout; for this use, the message field and parentheses will be omitted, i.e., $Clock_M? \; [y]$. The machine subscript M on the $Clock$ channel will normally be omitted for simplicity.

▶ Real-Time Bounded Buffer Revisited2

The remainder of the real-time bounded buffer example (Figure 4.1) can now be explained. Upon entering P_1, *Producer* has between 7 and 12 time units to issue a *Deposit* to *Buffer*. At relative time 12, a timeout occurs and the transition is taken to P_2, with the current time stored in variable *now*. A message is then sent on the channel named *Error*, perhaps to an error-logging machine (not shown), and *Producer* starts its *Generate/Deposit* cycle again.

One sequence of events leading to a timeout could occur as follows:

1. *Buffer* is in B_1, $0 < full < n$, and *Consumer* is in C_1 at time 0, say.

2. *Producer* enters P_1 at time 2.

3. *Consumer* issues *Remove* at time 8 which is successful.

4. *Producer* tries a *Deposit* at time 9 and is blocked because *Buffer* is still executing the computation between B_3 and B_1 for *Consumer*.

5. The computation completes sometime between times 12 and 16, say at 15.

6. At time 14, *Producer* is then still blocked on *Deposit* and executes a timeout on its *Clock* channel ($Clock_{Producer}$ is always ready to serve its host.) ◆

(*a*) Standard deadlock

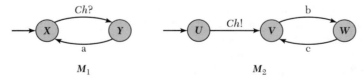

M_1 M_2

(*b*) Timed deadlock

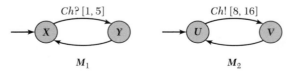

M_1 M_2

Figure 4.4   Deadlock in CRSMs.

A CRSM is *deadlocked* if it can never leave its current state. A set of interacting CRSMs can deadlock in the standard fashion for communicating processes. For example, a machine M_1 could be blocked forever waiting for IO with a partner M_2 that cannot reach a state wherein it could communicate with M_1. This case is illustrated in Figure 4.4(*a*). In the figure, *a*, *b*, and *c* are arbitrary internal commands. Machines M_1 and M_2 will initially execute the IO on channel *Ch* from states *X* and *U*, respectively. M_2 never returns to state *U*, but M_1 returns to *X* where it remains forever, thus deadlocked.

There is also a new form of deadlock that is possible due to timing. If a machine *M* reaches a state *S* where one or more of its IO transitions cannot be executed because of non-overlapping time intervals with its IO partners (e.g., Figure 4.2(b)(ii)), and if these IO transitions are the only ones leading from S, then *M* is blocked forever, that is, deadlocked, in S. A simple example appears in Figure 4.4(*b*). Assume that both machines M_1 and M_2 enter their initial states, *X* and *U*, at the same time, say time 10. Then the input on channel *Ch* in M_1 is possible only in the absolute time interval [11,16], while the corresponding partner output from M_2 can only occur in [18,26]. The intervals do not overlap. Hence, IO can never occur and the pair of machines immediately deadlock in their initial states.

4.1.3 Some CRSM Examples

Several detailed examples are presented to illustrate the real-time features of CRSMs in interesting and useful settings.

1. Periodic Process Control and a Discrete Time Clock

One important application that uses both the timeout and the current time (rt) access provided by the clock machines is timing control for a periodic process. Suppose that a state machine Q with start state S and halt state H is to executed with period p, that is, Q is to be activated every p time units. Figure 4.5 gives a CRSM that implements this control. The variable y contains the absolute time at which the next complete period starts. If the time to execute Q were zero, then y and x would always be identical at state S and neither would be necessary; $Clock?[y - x]$ could then be replaced by $Clock?[p]$. The execution time of Q is (approximately) $p - (y - x)$, using the values of the variables at state S.

The control works correctly provided that the execution time of Q doesn't exceed the period p, i.e., that $y \geq x$. (We are implicitly assuming here that the period equals the

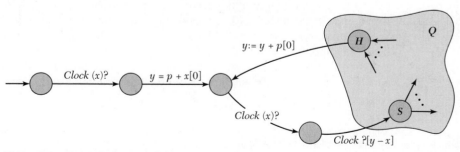

Figure 4.5   Control of a periodic activity.

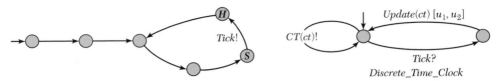

Figure 4.6   Discrete time clock.

deadline.) Otherwise, one could modify M with guarded transitions—one for the normal case and one for the fault case ($y < x$); in the latter situation, a procedure or machine for handling the timing exception should be invoked.

The periodic control mechanism can be used as the basis for a discrete time computer clock or digital watch. Discrete time is updated by the clock upon receiving "tick" messages from a periodic CRSM, say *Ticker*, that emits ticks every second. (Imagine that *Ticker* is a clock chip.) *Ticker* is presented in Figure 4.6. It has exactly the same control as in the previous figure, and only one internal transition from S to H, namely *Tick* . The *Discrete_Time_Clock* machine updates the current time *ct* with the *Update(ct)* command, upon receiving a *Tick* message. *ct* could be a triple (hours, minutes, seconds). Clients or users of this clock service would ask for the current time by sending a request *CT(now)*? and then receiving *ct* in the variable *now*.

Provided that u_2, the worst case update time, is not too large, that the period is sufficiently large, and that a client doesn't starve *Tick* IO by emitting too many *CT* requests in a single tick period, the system should keep perfect time. *Tick* starvation can be avoided by modifying *Discrete_Time_Clock* so that the *Tick* has a higher priority than the *CT* transition.

2. Mouse Click Classification

Consider a single button mouse, similar to those available on many personal computers. Single clicks, double clicks, and selections are defined based on the times between depressing and releasing the button. The purpose is to specify a recognizer that distinguishes among these three types of click input. This application is interesting, not only because it is ubiquitous, but also because the solution deals exclusively with IO signals (no internal activities) and the relative time between events.[2]

The event associated with depressing the mouse button is called a D event (for "down"); releasing the button is a U event (for "up"). A single click is defined when the time between D and the next U is less than a given duration t_{SC}. A double click (DC) is two single clicks separated by a time interval less than a given t_{DC}. We distinguish between an isolated single click (SC) and one that is part of a double click. When the time between D and U is greater than t_{SC}, a selection is defined; D then generates a selection start (SS) and U a selection end (SE). A global view of the mouse clicker system is sketched in Figure 4.7(a). M models the user who depresses and releases the button, and R is the recognizer machine. None of the channels have message data—they all transmit pure signals.

---

[2]The example was originally inspired by the double clicker description and program in [Cardelli&Pike85] and then later developed in [Shaw89a].

(*a*) Global view

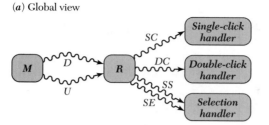

(*b*) CRSMs for *M* and *R*

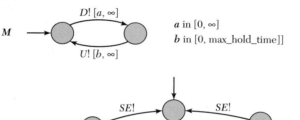

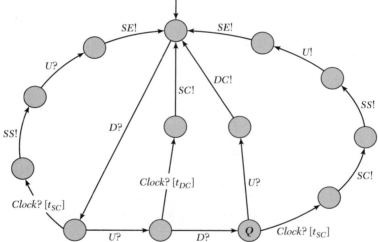

Figure 4.7 Mouse clicker system.

For the user machine *M* [Figure 4.7(*b*)], it is assumed that the button is depressed at an arbitrary time (*a* in [0,∞]) and released within some finite bounded time (*max_hold_time*). *M* also defines unbounded intervals within which *R* can sense the *D* and *U* events, by specifying infinity (∞) as the upper bound for both *D*! and *U*!. If these were finite rather than infinity, then a bounded rendezvous on the IO would be necessary. Such a rendezvous might not always be possible; for example if one of the handlers did not respond quickly enough, the result would be a deadlock.

The most complex part of the *R* CRSM is the logic leading to and following state *Q*. At that point, a single click and the start of a double click have been recognized—the events *D*, *U*, and *D* in sequence with appropriate separation times. If the second *U* occurs within t_{SC}, then a complete double click has been input and a *DC* signal is emitted; otherwise, *SC* is output to signal the previous single click and the second *D* is identified as the start of a selection, causing the generation of an *SS* event.

This CRSM has several straight-line chains of transitions; for example, there are two leading from Q to the start state, corresponding to the two situations described above. It is often convenient to abbreviate such chains by a single transition; we use the "|" symbol as a separator within this "compound" transition. In machine R, the farthest right path from Q to the start state can be thus described by the single abbreviated transition:

$$Clock? \, [t_{SC}] \mid SC! \mid SS! \mid U? \mid SE!$$

3. Alarm Clock

A useful specification utility is an alarm clock that can be set to "ring" at a given time. Facilities for resetting or disabling the alarm and for adjusting the interval over which the alarm rings are also convenient. Our alarm clock AC will have the IO interface depicted in Figure 4.8(a). The *start* channel initiates its operation and *stop* terminates it. A *Reset* message disables AC. *Wake_Me(t)* will enable AC and cause it to generate a *Wakeup* IO in t time units, provided that a *Reset* was not received in the interim. The *Wakeup* IO remains ready to execute for up to *ring_time* time units after t; if a partner (client) doesn't engage in *Wakeup* IO within that time, AC resets.

The alarm clock CRSM of Figure 4.8(b) implements these features. A similar CRSM could be designed for an absolute time alarm that generates a *Wakeup* signal starting at a particular given value of real-time.

4. Asynchronous and Multicast Communications

The CRSM model assumes that all communications are synchronous, one-way, and have a unique sender and receiver. Other standard forms of communications can also

(a) Interfaces

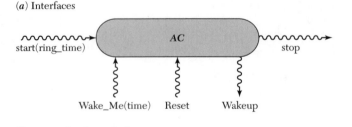

(b) CRSM for alarm clock

Figure 4.8 Relative time alarm clock.

be modelled easily by placing an appropriate handler or controller between the sender(s) and receiver(s).

One form of *asynchronous* communication between senders and receivers has a non-blocking send operation that transmits immediately regardless of the receiver state and a blocking receive that waits until a message is available. The real-time bounded buffer CRSM *Buffer* introduced earlier implements this type of asynchronous communications between a producer and a consumer. A non-blocking "send" operation is just an output by a producer on the *Deposit* channel, assuming a large enough buffer bound n; a "receive" message operation corresponds to an input by a consumer on the *Remove* channel. A variation of this would never block the sender even if the buffer were full, but instead have some buffer overflow policy such as overwriting.

A *multicast* facility allows a message or event to be broadcast to a designated set of possible receivers. Our facility will use the alarm clock utility defined above and has the organization given by Figure 4.9(*a*).

(*a*) Global view and interfaces

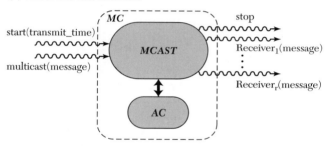

(*b*) Multicast CRSM

MCAST

Figure 4.9 Multicast communications controller.

After initialization through *start*, the machine *MCAST* is ready to respond to communications requests through the *multicast* channel. A message will be broadcast to *r* potential receivers on the *Receiver_i* channels for a period given by the *transmit_time* parameter. The *stop* channel is used to terminate operation of the facility, similar to its use in *AC*.

Several features of the CRSM for *MCAST* [Figure 4.9(*b*)] are noteworthy. To distinguish between the channels on *AC* and *MCAST* with the same names (*start* and *stop*), we use the standard method of prepending the machine name when necessary; thus *AC.start* refers to the *start* channel connected to *AC*. The alarm clock is employed to provide a timeout signal (through *Wakeup*) after a message has been available for the transmit time duration. The notation C_i, $i := 1,..,r$ on a transition between two states U and V is an abbreviation for r transitions $C_1, ... , C_r$ between U and V. The Boolean variables R_i are used to ensure that a particular message is received at most once by a receiver on *Receiver_i*.

A more efficient implementation would not always wait for the entire *transmit_time* interval before returning to state S. If all receivers have collected a message, then an earlier return is possible. One can accomplish this by resetting the alarm clock using the following transition between T and S:

$$((\text{not } R_1) \text{ and } \ldots \text{ and } (\text{not } R_r)) \rightarrow Reset!$$

One application of *MCAST* in real-time systems is in specifying the behavior of a subsystem on receiving power-on and power-off signals. A signal could be multicast to each of the subsystem components, represented as a CRSM. The value of the *transmit_time* parameter might reflect the physics of turning power on or off, the complexity and nature of the components, and systems requirements.

4.1.4 Semantics, Tools, and Extensions

Time bounds and global real-time (*rt*) are assumed to be "dense" real numbers in the original CRSM model. There is no unit of time or tick time. One could alternatively define a discrete time version of CRSMs, as is done either implicitly or explicitly in any (digital) implementation or simulation. The principal advantage of the dense time assumption is conceptual simplicity. There is no need to worry about the size of a tick interval, about synchronizing all machines to a global click, or about relating ticks to standard units. For example, with discrete time, it would be difficult to have a tick time of 1/3 of a second (0.3333....) that produces exactly 3 ticks a second.

Another set of issues relates to how long a machine remains in a state and how long a transition takes. It is natural to permit commands to execute immediately and with zero durations, as is done for statecharts (next section) and as we have done using time bounds of [0] and [0,∞]. Normally, the intent is to describe a command that takes negligible time compared with other activities in the system. However, zero-time transitions may lead to at least two unpleasant logical problems.

First, it becomes possible and too easy to specify an infinite amount of work that takes no time! A CRSM with a single state having a single transition to itself, say *null* [0], would accomplish this. If the durations on *Buffer* and *Producer* in Figure 4.1 were all changed to [0], the same unfortunate result occurs, with time never advancing.

Using nonzero time for transitions, one could still specify an infinite amount of work performed in finite time, but not quite so easily. For example, consider a transition leading from a state back to itself:

$$t := t/2 \; [t].$$

If t is initially 1, then an infinite number of transitions are executed in $1 + 1/2 + 1/4 + \ldots = 2$ units of time. Some care must be exercised in defining time bounds that don't violate the properties of time and physics.

The second problem with zero-time transitions is one of causality. If an event A "causes" an event B, then it is often desirable and assumed that the time of occurrence of B be greater than that of A. However, if two transitions on the same machine, each having zero duration, occur in sequence, their occurrence times would be identical—implying that they happened simultaneously.

One common method of handling this problem is to show or prove that it cannot happen for each particular system. For example, it is easy to argue that the discrete time clock system of Figure 4.6 will not loop forever in zero time, provided that the tick period is positive and that a *Discrete_Time_Clock* client does not have an infinite loop on a *CT* IO transition. A second solution avoids the problem entirely by assuming that every machine will spend a minimal nonzero amount of time δ in each state that it enters or, equivalently, that every transition takes at least δ time. More formally, the time bound values $[t_{min}, t_{max}]$ of every transition, where $0 \leq t_{min} \leq t_{max}$, is interpreted as $[t_{min} + \delta, t_{max} + \delta]$. This solution was used in the Timed CSP language [Reed&Roscoe86] and adopted in our original paper defining CRSMs.

The precise semantics or meaning of CRSMs can be given operationally by describing an algorithm that simulates their behavior [Shaw92,93]. Given a set of CRSMs, the basic output of the simulation algorithm is a timed trace or history of the IO events of the system

$$((ch,v)_0, t_0), ((ch,v)_1, t_1), \ldots, ((ch,v)_i, t_i), \ldots,$$

where $(ch,v)_i$ is the (channel_name, message_value) pair for an IO event that occurred at time t_i, $t_i \leq t_{i+1}$ for all i, and the first IO occurs at time t_0. Initially, all CRSMs are in their start states.

The simulation algorithm iterates through the following three phases:

Phase 1: Construct a list of possible next events for each machine. The possible next events are the start or end of the execution of an internal command, or an IO execution, depending on the machine's most recent activity. For each machine, the *earliest* next event or events are determined. Ties are possible when more than one transition leaves the same state and they are ready at the same time. Since IO requires two machines, there is some work involved in checking the possibility and time of an IO event. The global earliest next time t_{next} is then defined as the smallest of the local earliest times; t_{next} becomes the time of the next events in the simulation.

Phase 2: Select the subset of CRSMs and corresponding events for execution. Events occurring at t_{next} are selected for execution. In case of ties, the choice is made nondeterministically. If an IO event on machine M is selected and the partner machine has already been selected for a different event occurring at t_{next}, then another transition on M is chosen if possible; if there does not exist another eligible transition, then machine M is not selected.

Phase3: Execute the machines to the selected events. The next step of the simulation is made by executing up to the selected events on their CRSMs. If IO events are executed, output the trace element $((ch,v)_i, t_i)$ for each IO, where $t_i = t_{next}$. Simulated real time is updated to equal t_{next}. When the start event for an internal command is executed, its end event time is chosen arbitrarily from its timing interval.

The algorithm is implemented in a software environment that includes tools for constructing, executing, checking, and (to some extent) verifying CRSMs [Raju&Shaw94;Raju94]. The construction tool is a graphical editor that permits a user to interactively specify state diagrams for individual CRSMs and to describe systems of CRSMs with their connecting channels. The simulator tool uses a discrete time model, executing the system following the above algorithm. The simulation can be checked during execution using an assertion checker tool based on real-time logic (Section 5.4). Finally, a verifier allows some reachability analysis and assertion checking for a restricted version of CRSMs.[3] The system is written in C/C++. A set of tools for specifying and checking CRSMs, but written in Java and generating Java code, has also been implemented [Fortino&Nigro00].

In order to specify a wide variety of faults, exceptions, and possible interruptions, it is convenient to have a uniform mechanism for interrupting and reentering a CRSM as a unit. Our scheme is inspired by the statechart method for exiting and entering superstates, as presented next in Section 4.2.1.

The interrupt scheme is not a change or addition, but merely a useful notational convention. An IO transition i entering and exiting a CRSM is interpreted to mean that *every* state in the machine has an i transition to the machine's start state (Figure 4.10). An example with our bounded buffer machine is diagrammed in Figure 4.11. Thus, to interrupt *Buffer* and force it to reenter its start state, another machine would issue the IO *int*!

The channels of a CRSM are its interface to the outside "world" of other CRSMs. Two CRSMs are said to be *connected* if they communicate through a common channel.

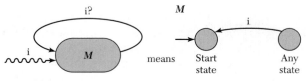

Figure 4.10   Interrupts.

---

[3]The purpose of reachability analysis is to determine all possible states that can be reached from a start state of a system. Unfortunately, performing this analysis is not computationally possible or feasible, in general, especially when the state includes a time component.

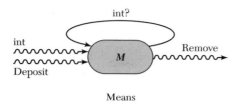

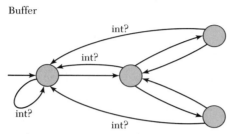

Figure 4.11   Interrupting the Buffer CRSM.

In order to connect two CRSMs, it may be necessary to rename channels; from another point of view, one can interpret the channel names as parameters that are instantiated when machines are connected. Of course, the message types for sender and receiver must be compatible.

A set of CRSMs that may have some internal connections to each other via IO channels can be identified and labelled as a higher-level object. The unconnected channels of this object are its interface. Hierarchical system structures can be constructed using these simple conventions. An example is the multicast communications structure illustrated in Figure 4.9(a). This higher-level component, surrounded by dotted lines and named *MC*, consists of two connected CRSMs, *MCAST* and *AC*, with an interface equal to a subset of that of *MCAST*.

Using these ideas, one can also define in-the-large specification architectures and "patterns," including conventional control for large components, such as sequential, parallel, guarded selection, and looping; and scalable encapsulated data objects that handle shared data. Interrupts for these structured objects can be implemented by successively broadcasting interrupt messages to lower level structures and using the interrupt mechanism for the lowest level CRSMs. These notions are developed in [Shaw94]. Another approach to hierarchical CRSMs appears in [Fortino_et_al00].

► EXERCISES 4.1

1. Modify the *Discrete_Time_Clock* CRSM (Figure 4.6) so that starvation of *Tick* IO by a client is avoided. Hint: Check for a *Tick* transition before looking for a *CT*.

2. Change the *Buffer* CRSM (Figure 4.1) so that a send on a *Deposit* is asynchronous. Assume that the buffer is overwritten when overflow occurs. (See Example 4 in Section 4.1.3.)

3. Construct a CRSM for an absolute-time alarm clock. The machine should have three input channels, *start*(*ring_time*), *Wake_Me*(*t*), and *Reset*, and two output channels *Wakeup* and *stop*(*ring_count*). The argument *t* to the *Wake_Me* channel gives the absolute time at which the clock will try to send a *Wakeup* message. The channels have the same functions as in the relative-time clock presented in the text (Figure 4.8). When the alarm clock stops, the *ring_count* parameter contains the number of times that the clock has been rung since it was last started.

4. Construct two interacting CRSMs, M1 and M2, according to the following specifications. M1 is a dot/dash recognizer. M2 constructs a message from the output of M1 and transmits it to some client.

M1 has 3 input channels, *D*, *U*, and *dstart*, representing the down and up events from a single button mouse and the start message event, respectively. A dot is a *D* followed by a *U* separated by no more than *td* time units. A dash is a *D* followed by a *U* separated by *td* or more time units. M1 has 4 output channels, *dot*, *dash*, *mstart*, and *mend*, representing the recognition of a dot, a dash, the start of a new message, and the end of a message, respectively. A *mend* is generated whenever no *D* event is received for *teom* time units after a preceding event ($teom \gg td$).

M2 is connected to M1 through the 4 output channels of M1. It builds a message consisting of a dot/dash sequence, keeps track of the length of the message, and time stamps the message with the current value of real time after *mend* has been received. The dot/dash message along with a header containing its length and time stamp is output on the channel *message*. Assume the following routines in M2 for constructing a message:

Im(m) : Initialize message *m*, with header and data components.

Am(m, d) : Add *d* (dot or dash) to data part of *m*.

Ah(m, L, ts) : Add length *L* and time stamp *ts* to *m*'s header.

5. Extension of the Railway Crossing Gate Example:
A gate, a pair of lights, and a computer controller are located at the intersection of a road and a railway track. The gate operates according to the fsm of Figure 3.10. The controller assures that the gate is closed whenever a train is in the intersection area (Figure 3.12), and also controls the lights. If there are no trains in the area, the lights are green. When a first train enters the area, the lights turn to flashing red, and remain flashing until the last train leaves and the gate has completely opened. Describe this system with at least four CRSMs, one each for the gate, lights, and controller; and at least one that simulates the train behaviors.

6. Describe the behavior of a simple computer using CRSMs. The computer contains four functional units:
(i) a *console* for input,
(ii) a *control unit* that performs a standard fetch-decode-execute cycle and contains an instruction register *instr*, a program counter *pc*, and an accumulator *ac*,
(iii) a *storage unit* containing 1000 cells, designated S(0) ... S(999), and that responds appropriately to read and write commands, and
(iv) an *arithmetic-logic unit* (ALU) that, given two arguments and an operation, executes the requested operation and returns the result.

Your specification should have at least four CRSMs, one for each functional unit. Assume that a storage write takes 2 time units to complete, a storage read takes 1 time unit, and that all operations performed by the ALU complete in 2 time units. Make up reasonable times for other functions in each unit.

The user can input commands from the console to stop or *halt* the machine, to *start* the machine at a particular given location, and to *enter* data or instructions, one cell at a time, into specified storage addresses. The computer must first be halted before it can be started or before data can be entered. The computer is a single address machine and can execute the following instructions internally (in addition to the console commands): *halt*, *load*, *store*, *add*, *subtract*, *and*, *or*, *branch_unconditional*, and *branch_if_ac_greater_than_zero*. Assume that functions exist for decoding an instruction, for example, operation(x) and operand(x), where *x* is an instruction.

7. A VCR can operate in three different modes:
(i) Play: Commands or buttons are available to *play*, *pause* or *stop*, *rewind*, or *eject* a tape.
(ii) Program: A user can set the machine to record the TV signal on tape from a given *channel*, starting at a particular *time*, and for a given *duration*.
(iii) Record: The TV signal from a given channel can be recorded on tape, either *manually* in real-time or *automatically* as specified by a program [(ii) above].

Define a system of CRSMs describing the behavior of the VCR.

8. Consider the Real-Time Bounded Buffer example (Figure 4.1) and assume that the *Remove* transition from state C_1 of the *Consumer* is the only transition leaving that state. Show how the *Consumer* can deadlock in C_1 by giving a finite sequence of events and their times such that the *Consumer* remains in C_1 forever.

9. Consider once again the traffic light controller specified in Question 3 in the Exercises 3.3. Using the interrupt mechanism suggested in the text (Figure 4.10), construct a set of CRSMs with the required and given behaviors. Employ a separate CRSM for normal processing (*N*), for ambulance processing (*A*), and for a controller that switches between the two, for example, by interrupting *N*. In addition, describe the environment, that is, ambulance and lights, with CRSMs.

► 4.2 STATECHARTS

A major breakthrough in extending state machine ideas for use in realistic real-time applications was made by Harel and his colleagues. This work was started in the early 1980s, and culminated in the statechart notation and an associated software development environment named STATEMATE [Harel87; Harel_et_al90]. The language was invented originally for the development of the avionics system for an Israeli aircraft, and has seen widespread use since then (e.g., [Leveson_et_al94]). It is also one of the major components of UML (Section 2.5.3).

The principal innovations in statecharts lay in their techniques for defining the structure of state machines through superstates. Statecharts may be composed in series or in parallel. The formalism has efficient ways to specify transitions into and out of superstates and the composed machines. Communication among machines occurs by broadcasting events. Relative timing constraints among events can be described by translating them into timeout events. The notation is essentially graphical—the creators term it a "visual language." This visual aspect is especially significant because it provides a natural, compact, and easy-to-use interface.

4.2.1 Concepts and Graphical Syntax

At the lowest level, a statechart is a state diagram as described in the last chapter. Transitions between states are similar to those in the more general extended fsms, with the same form

$$guard \rightarrow input\_event \ / \ action \ / \ output\_event.^4$$

For example,

$$(count=1) \rightarrow Train\_Leaving \ / \ count:=0 \ / \ Open\_Gate.$$

Similarly, true guards and empty fields are omitted. Thus, the examples in Figures 3.10, 3.11, and 3.12 from Section 3.4 are simple statecharts.

Sets of related states can be collected into named *superstates*, which can themselves be grouped further into superstates. Conversely, a superstate can be refined into its component states or superstates. A superstate has a default start or entry (sub)state. Transitions between superstates denote their potential execution in sequence. They also model "interrupts" in the following clever but natural manner.[5] Suppose two super-

---

[4] We have modified the statechart transition notation slightly, in order to be consistent with the rest of the book.

[5] This idea was borrowed for the CRSM interrupt scheme that was proposed in Section 4.1.4.

Figure 4.12   Superstates.

states S_1 and S_2 are connected by the transition i as shown in Figure 4.12. The meaning of this visual form is that *all* states in S_1 are connected by transition i to the entry state of S_2. This simple convention saves an enormous amount of space, otherwise taken up by identical transitions, and substantially enhances the clarity of a diagram.

The interrupt transition is used in many applications, for example, S_1 could describe the normal operation of some subsystem, S_2 the emergency operation, and i the fault event causing the transition between normal and emergency modes. Figure 4.13 illustrates this application. The *fault* event causes a transition from the *Normal* superstate into *Emergency*, entering at its default start state E_0. All of the states in the figure could themselves be superstates.

▶ Watch Example[6]

Consider a simple digital watch with time, date, hourly chime, and alarm clock functions, and 4 buttons, a, b, c, and d, for user control (Figure 4.14).

Suppose, for now, that there are three main modes of operation:

Normal_Display wherein either the time or date is displayed;
Clock_Update within which a user can update the time and date; and
Chime_Alarm_Set where the chime and alarm clock are set.

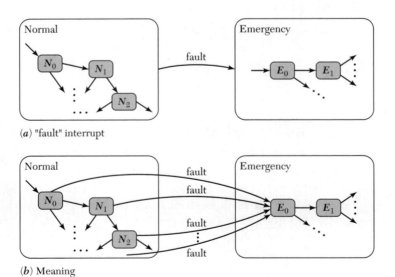

(*a*) "fault" interrupt

(*b*) Meaning

Figure 4.13   Statechart interrupt.

---

[6]Our digital watch examples are variations of and inspired by the one given in [Harel87].

(a) Time display

(b) Date display

Figure 4.14   Digital watch.

The statechart of Figure 4.15 shows a possible behavior for parts of these modes and for the interactions among them.

Input events caused by pressing one of the four buttons are represented on the transitions by the button identifiers. Thus, the watch is normally entered through the *Normal_Display* superstate and into the *Time* state (or superstate, since *Time* could also be refined). Button *a* could then be used to move the system to and from *Date*. Pressing *c* while in any state in *Normal_Display* will result in a transition to the entry state (*min*) of *Update*; upon pressing button *d* while in any state inside *Update*, a transition back to the entry state of *Normal_Display* occurs. Without the exit and entry conventions for superstates, these two transitions would have to be replaced by (at least) 7 transitions, 2 leaving *Normal_Display* and 5 leaving *Update*. A similar behavior results between *Normal_Display* and *Chime_Alarm_Set* using buttons *b* and *d*.

Within the *Update* superstate, the transitions fired by button *b* cause the updating of internal variables, m, h, D, M, and Y, denoting the current minute, hour, day, month, and year, respectively. The notation x_n^{++} means:

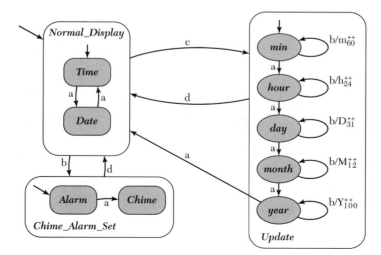

Figure 4.15   Three modes of the watch.

$$x := x+1 \bmod n. \text{ [7]}$$

Note the use of the *a* transition from the *year* state; it is still possible to easily express a superstate exit from a single inside state. One can similarly override the default entry state by simply drawing the transition arrow through the superstate box into the desired state. ◆

It is occasionally desirable to "save" the state when leaving a mode and subsequently restore the old state when reentering. Statecharts provide such a facility with a transition type called "entry with history" (*H*) which enters a superstate at the (first-level) state that it last left. *H* only specifies reentry to the superstate at the same level that the *H* designator appears; lower levels are reentered at their default normal entries. A "deep history" entry, denoted H^*, is also defined; it restores state down to the lowest level, i.e., down to the level at which no further decomposition of states is defined.

A general timeout mechanism is provided. The notation

$$timeout(E, \delta t)$$

designates an event occurring δt time units after the event *E*. *E* is often the event associated with the entry to the superstate within which the *timeout* transition appears. For this common case, a labelled "resistor" squiggle and a timeout exit have been suggested as illustrated in Figure 4.16(*a*). Alternatively, a timeout exit of the form *timeout(entered(S)*, δt) could be employed, where *entered(S)* is the event associated with entering state *S* [Figure 4.16(*b*)]. The figure also shows how an entry (*i*) with history is drawn.

A statechart with these features (Figure 4.17) specifies the behavior of the nuclear power plant monitor outlined in Section 2.3. The *T*, *F*, and *S* tasks, and some of the *B*

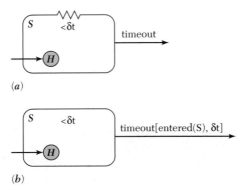

(*a*)

(*b*)

Figure 4.16 History and timeout.

---

[7]Note that we are potentially guilty of causing a "Y2K" problem because 2-digit year abbreviations are being used. As long as our watch is set manually and accessed visually by humans only (not by computers), there should be no resulting difficulties.

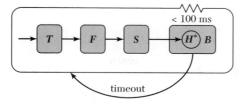

Figure 4.17 Statechart for coolant monitor.

tasks are repeatedly executed every 100 ms. Note that B is entered with deep history. Thus, during each cycle, the background processes in B are continued starting from their point of interruption during the previous cycle.

It is interesting to compare the periodic control exhibited here using statecharts with that using CRSMs (Example 1, Section 4.1.3). The statechart produces a much more compact description at the expense of a more complex timeout primitive (*timeout*) and event defintions (*entered*(S)).

The history and timeout features also appear in Figure 4.18 which adds alarm ringing to the watch behavior described earlier in Figure 4.15. The triggering event

$$\uparrow(ct = t_{alarm})$$

occurs when the condition ($ct=t_{alarm}$) becomes true ($\uparrow$). The SCR notation for general events defined when conditions change to true or false and given in Section 3.3 is used; ct denotes current time and t_{alarm} is the time to which the alarm clock is set. Pressing any button (the *any_button* event) will cause the alarm to stop ringing; otherwise, the ringing will stop after 30 seconds. In either case, the *Main* superstate is reentered at the same point where it was interrupted by the alarm (H entry); that is, at the default entry of one of the three substates of *Main*. The *a* transition from inside of *Update* to *Normal_Display* indicates that the transition only occurs from some, but not all, of the states of *Update*.

The concurrent operation of two statecharts is represented by attaching their boxes with a dashed common edge, as shown in Figure 4.19. The watch, as we have so far de-

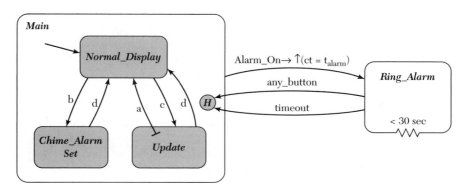

Figure 4.18 Ringing the watch alarm.

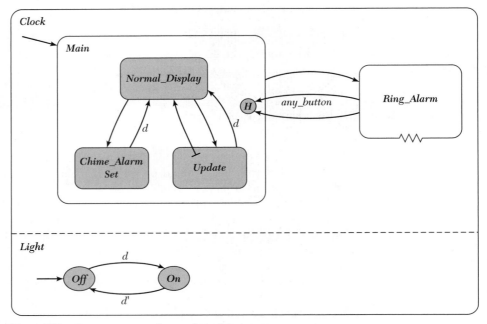

Figure 4.19 Concurrency and event broadcasting.

fined it, is encapsulated in a superstate named *Clock*. In parallel with this is a machine, *Light*, which specifies that the light can be turned on or off with the *d* button. *d'* is the event associated with letting go of the button. (If we let *d* be a condition which is true while the button is depressed and false otherwise, then we could use the SCR notation, ↑*d* and ↓*d*, to represent *d* and *d'*, respectively.)

Statecharts can be arbitrarily composed both sequentially and concurrently. For example, *Ring_Alarm* might consist of two concurrent components, each of which is composed further of sequential ones, which in turn could be composed of sequential and concurrent charts, and so on, until reaching the lowest basic state level.

When events are generated, they are broadcast throughout the system. This is the principal way that machines interact and communicate directly. Thus, in the figure, the depress button event *d* is broadcast to both the *Light* and the *Clock* superstates. In *Light*, the event causes a transition to the *on* state. At the same time, if the *Clock* machine were in either *Chime_Alarm_Set* or *Update*, *d* would also cause a transition back to *Normal_Display*; if the *Clock* machine was in *Ring_Alarm*, the transition back to *Main* would be fired instead.

Events are not the only object type that is "shared" across machines. Statecharts implement a shared storage model of parallelism. Variables may be shared among parallel and sequential superstates; and conditions and events can refer to states. The events *entered*(*S*) and *exit*(*S*) are associated with entering and leaving state *S*, respectively; in the timeout mechanism discussed above, we showed one application of *entered*(*S*). *in*(*S*) is a condition stating that some component of the system is in state *S*.

For example, if there is a requirement that the light not be turned on if the *Clock* is in *Update*, the transition from *off* to *on* in *Light* should be changed by inserting a guard:

$$not(in(Update)) \rightarrow d$$

Statecharts have several other features, similar to those in programming languages, that simplify their construction. There is a "scoping" convention that associates identifiers, e.g., for variables and superstates, with superstate blocks so that they are hidden outside of the block. Another useful mechanism is an array-like scheme to define many parallel instances of the same machine. Recall the air traffic monitoring (ATC) example presented in Section 1.1.2. The behavior of an aircraft *i*—entering the airspace, travelling through it, and departing—could be specified by a statechart $AC(i)$; the notation $AC(i: 1 \ldots n)$ represents *n* instances: $AC(1), \ldots, AC(n)$, as shown in Figure 4.20.

The notation has a variety of other mechanisms that appear useful, but complex. For example, there are facilities to define actions that are executed inside a state and terminated when the state is exited; these actions are called *static reactions*. Transitions may have different priorities. And chains of transitions can be connected through conditional "or" connectors.

4.2.2 Semantics and Tools

The precise meaning (semantics) of statecharts is quite complicated [Harel& Naamad96], and is only introduced here briefly and informally. The behavior of a statechart is explained operationally by tracing through or simulating a "step" of its execution. One or more events trigger the start of a step. These could be external events produced from the environment or internal events generated during a previous step.

The execution of a step involves first selecting a maximal set of *compound* transitions to fire from the set that are enabled in the current state, where a compound

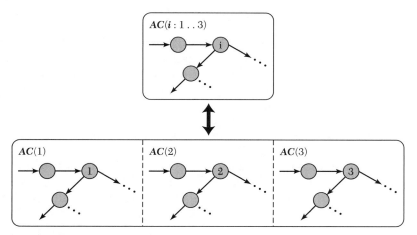

Figure 4.20   Arrays of statecharts.

transition is a chain of executable transitions. This selection may require some nondeterministic choices. The selected transitions are then taken by performing their actions and moving to the next states following each compound transition. (We are ignoring the execution of any static reactions.) All events that are enabled at the beginning of a step are consumed by the step, even if not used. Events that are generated in a step are not handled or accepted until the next step.

One interesting aspect of the semantics is that all activities executed during a step or a transition are performed logically in parallel using data values at the beginning of the step. Thus if a transition had the action

$$a := a + 10; x := a + 1 ;$$

and a was 3 initially, then x would have the value 4 after execution. However, if instead, two assignments were made to a, such as in

$$a := a + 10; a := a + 1;$$

the resulting value of a would be unpredictable—a race condition because both statements are executed in parallel.

Transitions take zero time in the original statechart notation. Time passes inside states while the system is waiting for external events to occur. In one version, a step is executed at the end of every unit of time, handling all events that were generated during the previous unit. Another model waits until at least one external event occurs before reacting; at that point, a sequence of steps is executed (in zero time) until the system reaches a stable state where there are no outstanding events with enabled transitions.

It is instructive to compare statecharts with the CRSM language presented in Section 4.1. Both notations start with the same extended state machines, but extend them in different ways to handle multiple machines. Statecharts are based on a shared memory model where all states are known globally, while CRSMs use a distributed model where the state of each machine is private and local. CRSMs communicate over one-to-one channels by synchronous message passing; the only events are message communications events.

In statecharts, there are a variety of possible types of events, both internal and external; events are broadcast to all statecharts. CRSMs assume a closed world and have no notion of external environmental events; all events (messages) are generated by CRSMs in principle. On the other hand, statecharts could be used to represent the environments, and thus model a closed world; and CRSMs could be written to send and receive messages from an unmodelled external world.

Statechart superstates and their series-parallel composition, interrupts, and history entries have no comparable analogs in CRSMs, beyond the simple techniques described at the end of Section 4.1.3. Another main difference between the two notations is how they handle time. CRSMs have an elaborate and complete scheme with time bounds on transitions and clock machines for accessing real time. Statecharts assume zero-time transitions and have no built-in method to access time, but do have an elegant timeout event mechanism. Finally, a much more elaborate set of software tools has been developed for statecharts as discussed next.

Statecharts are part of an integrated set of software tools, called the STATEMATE environment [Harel_et_al90], and available through the i-Logix Corporation. The tools are meant to aid requirements, design, and implementation of both hardware and software systems for "reactive" (i.e., real-time) applications. They include software packages for editing, simulation, testing, code generation, project management, and data base control and maintenance.

Requirements and designs are specified through statecharts and a variant of data flow diagrams (DFDs) called activity charts. A system's data flow and functionality is described by DFDs. The sequential and parallel activation of the DFD functions, with any timing constraints, are specified by accompanying statecharts.

▶ EXERCISES 4.2

1. Consider the digital watch example and the statechart of Figure 4.18. Augment the figure to include the behavior of the *Chime*. Assume that the chime will ring on the hour every hour for one second, provided of course that it is "on." Your augmented chart should have a new superstate, say *Ring_Chime*, and appropriate transitions to and from *Main* and *Ring_Alarm*.

2. Modify and extend the Coolant Monitor statechart (Figure 4.17) to handle timing errors. In particular, if *T*, *F*, and *S* are not completed within 100 ms, the system should be interrupted and control passed to a *Fault* component. The *Fault* component may either terminate in a Shutdown state or reenter the main component to complete its {*T*, *F*, *S*} cycle.

3. Draw a statechart for the mouse clicker recognizer (*R*) described in Section 4.1.3, Example 2. Assume that the button click events are generated by an external environment (*M*) which need not be specified.

Questions 4, 5, 6, and 7 refer to questions in Exercises 4.1. In each case, answer the question with statecharts instead of CRSMs.

4. Question 5, Railway Crossing Gate System. There should be at least three superstates, one each describing the gate, light, and controller behaviors. Assume that the train signals are events generated from an unspecified external environment.

5. Question 9, Traffic Light Controller System. Your statechart should have at least two superstates, one for normal processing (*N*) and another for ambulance processing (*A*).

6. Question 7, VCR.

7. Question 6, Simple Computer. Ignore the timing requirements, and use at least 4 superstates, one for each of the functional units.

8. Consider the ATM briefly described in Question 2, Exercises 3.2. Write a statechart that specifies the required behavior. Compare the statechart with a DFD description.

CHAPTER 5

Declarative Specifications

Assertions and declarations are used to describe directly the required properties of a system. This is in contrast to operational techniques such as state machines which generate behaviors that satisfy or exhibit the required characteristics. Properties are specified in terms of system events, time, or the values of state variables. The properties are asserted to hold at various times during systems execution, such as for all time, eventually, before or after a given time, within a given time interval, or before or after some function is performed; assertions for the latter are called pre- and post-conditions, respectively.

Safety and liveness were mentioned briefly in the software engineering discussion in Section 1.4. Essentially, any system property can be classified as either a *safety property* or a *liveness property*. Safety is concerned with the "invariants" of a system: every state satisfies the property. An alternative definition is that a system is safe if it never enters an undesirable (unsafe, faulty, bad, . . .) state. Liveness or progress describes the responsiveness of a system: a particular good state is reached eventually.

▶ Examples of Safety and Liveness

1. Consider a system controlling two pairs of traffic lights at the intersection of a street and an avenue. The street and avenue lights should never be green at the same time. This mutual exclusion requirement is a safety property since it must be satisfied in all states. One could maintain this property by, for example, permanently keeping one pair of lights red, say the street, or both pairs red. Liveness properties might be: from any state, the street lights will eventually turn green; and from any state, the avenue lights will eventually be green.
2. Meeting a deadline is a safety property. For example, a shutdown must be initiated within 10 seconds of sensing an out-of-range temperature in a process control system. ♦

The concepts of safety and liveness have been defined more precisely and mathematically (e.g., [Manna&Pnueli93]), but we will use them in an informal way. Most properties of interest in the real-time domain are safety properties.

Applications of declarative methods include documentation; informal reasoning; verification of requirements, designs, and implementations; as well as debugging and monitoring of executable specifications and implementations. This chapter discusses three different and useful classes of declarative or descriptive techniques: regular expressions and their extensions, which have a straightforward and formal relationship with state machines; some conventional formal logics—propositional, predicate, and temporal—that deal generally with the truth values of expressions; and a particular logic, real-time logic, that explicitly includes time and events.

► 5.1 REGULAR EXPRESSIONS AND EXTENSIONS

There is a natural formal correspondence between state machines or automata, on the one hand, and formal languages, on the other [Hopcroft&Ullman79]. Here, we define a formal language to be the set of strings generated by a grammar. For each of various well-defined classes of machines, there exists an equivalent class of grammars such that the symbol or event sequences accepted by the machines are identical to those in the languages generated by that class of grammar.[1]

Finite state machines correspond to *regular grammars* in this classification, and regular grammars can be represented elegantly as *regular expressions* (REs). Because of their straightforward relationship with state machines and because they describe sequences directly, REs and their extensions are useful notations for specifying behavioral properties. We review the definition of REs using the fsm for the Train Crossing Gate presented in Figure 3.10.

Assume that the state *Closed* is both the start and halt state of the machine. One set of paths through the states goes from *Closed* to *Opening*, then back and forth through *Closing* and *Opening*, and finally through *Closing* to *Closed*. Ignoring the self loops at these states, the possible sequences of events tracing these paths are the set

$$E = \{og\ cg\ c\text{-}c,\ og\ cg\ og\ cg\ c\text{-}c,\ og\ cg\ og\ cg\ og\ cg\ c\text{-}c,\ \dots\}.$$

This unbounded set can be represented by the RE

$$G_1 = og\ cg\ (og\ cg)^*\ c\text{-}c,$$

where the notation α^* means zero or more instances of sequences or strings taken from α. The set of strings represented by a regular expression S is called a *regular set* and will be represented by $L(S)$. Thus, for the above expression and set, $L(G_1) = E$.

Not including the self loops, the complete RE G for the fsm is

$$G = og\ (cg\ og)^*\ (cg \cup ((o\text{-}o\ cg\ og)^*\ o\text{-}o\ cg\ (og\ cg)^*\ ))\ c\text{-}c.$$

The "union" symbol $\cup$ means a selection of a string or sequence from one of its arguments. G represents all event sequences accepted by the Gate, except those produced by self loops. Each self loop can be characterized as a "starred" expression, for example, og^* at state *Open*.

Let Σ be a given set of basic symbols. An RE S and its corresponding regular set $L(S)$ is defined precisely from Σ as follows:

1. (a) For any x in Σ, x is an RE. $L(x) = \{x\}$.
   (b) $\varnothing$ and λ are REs. $L(\varnothing)$ = the empty set. $L(\lambda) = \{\lambda\}$, where λ is the empty string.

---

[1]A machine M *accepts* or recognizes a sequence or string s if input of s to M causes M to terminate in a halt state.

2. Let S, S_1, and S_2 be REs.
    (a) The concatenation $S_1 S_2$ is an RE.
        $L(S_1 S_2) = \{z = xy: x \text{ in } L(S_1) \text{ and } y \text{ in } L(S_2)\}$.
    (b) The union $S_1 \cup S_2$ is an RE.
        $L(S_1 \cup S_2) = \{z \text{ in either } L(S_1) \text{ or } L(S_2)\} = L(S_1) \cup L(S_2)$.
    (c) The Kleene closure S^* is an RE.
        $L(S^*) = \cup \, S^i = \{\lambda\} \cup L\{S\} \cup L(SS) \cup L(SSS) \cup \ldots$

The RE definitions can often be used directly to formally manipulate expressions in order to prove various properties of event sequences, such as set membership or set inclusion.

▶ Analysis Example: The Train Crossing Gate

The RE G above for the Gate has the form

$$G = A \, (\, B \cup C) \, D,$$

where $A = og \, (cg \, og)^*$, $B = cg$, $C = (\, (o\text{-}o \, cg \, og)^* \, o\text{-}o \, cg \, (og \, cg)^*)$, and $D = c\text{-}c$. The "normal" event sequence s starting from the closed state is

$$s = og \, o\text{-}o \, cg \, c\text{-}c.$$

We want to show that s is in $L(G)$. This can be done by first simplifying G. G is equivalent to the RE

$$G' = ABD \cup ACD,$$

in the sense that $L(G) = L(G')$. The manipulation to G' works because RE concatenation distributes over union;

that is, $L(A(B \cup C)) = L(AB \cup AC)$ and $L((B \cup C)D) = L(BD \cup CD)$.

If s is in $L(G)$, then it must also be the case that s is in $L(G')$. We now show that s is in $L(ACD)$ and hence in $L(G')$. The desired string from $L(ACD)$ is obtained simply by selecting the empty string from each of the starred terms in A and C, leaving $\{og\}$ in $L(A)$ and $\{o\text{-}o \, cg\}$ in $L(C)$. ◆

There is also a straightforward algorithm to convert an RE S into an accepting or equivalent nondeterministic fsm M_S. The halt states of M_S correspond to input strings of $L(S)$. The basic idea is to follow the formal definition above. For each of the regular expression forms, x, $\varnothing$, λ, $S_1 S_2$, $S_1 \cup S_2$, and S^*, there is an equivalent fsm that can be constructed that recognizes or halts on the associated regular set.

Given fsms M_1 and M_2 for REs S_1 and S_2, respectively, the fsm for the concatenation $S_1 S_2$ is obtained by connecting the halt states of M_1 with the start state of M_2 using a λ transition. The λ transition is an event-less one that is always ready to fire; in simple cases, the halt states of one machine can be directly identified with the start state of its concatenated machine, eliminating the empty transition. An fsm for any element x in Σ is a two state machine, a start state and a halt state, with a transition x from the start to the halt. The other forms can be handled in a similar manner, using empty transitions where necessary to connect machines.

► **Buffer Example**

Consider again the buffer constraint example given in Section 3.4. One RE expressing the constraint that every R must be preceded by at least one D is

$$B = (D\,(D^* \cup R)\,)^*.$$

The accepting fsm for $L(B)$ is given in Figure 5.1. The machine has three halt states. Note that a simpler machine with only two halt states can be obtained by eliminating the two empty transitions and making the *start* state into a halt state also. ♦

Discrete time can be included in REs in a straightforward way by assuming the existence of a clock that generates *tick* events periodically. Let t be the symbol for a tick event. Then, two events a and b that are separated by n ticks can be represented by $a\,t^n\,b$. (The expression actually specifies an interval between a and b bounded by $(n-1)$ and $(n+1)$ ticks.)

► **Mouse Clicker**

Recall the mouse clicker example described in Section 4.1.3 and Figure 4.7. The user M's events with time included are represented by the RE

$$(t^x\,D\,t^y\,U)^*,$$

where $x \geq a$ and $y \geq b$. (Integer discrete time is assumed here.) The recognizer R can be specified as the union of four REs, one corresponding to each path through the CRSM. The simple selection path is defined by the RE

$$t^*\,D\,t^s\,t^*\,SS\,t^*\,U\,t^*\,SE$$

with s equal to a discrete integer approximation to t_{SC}. A simple single click has an associated RE

$$D\,t^{<s}\,U\,t^d\,SC,$$

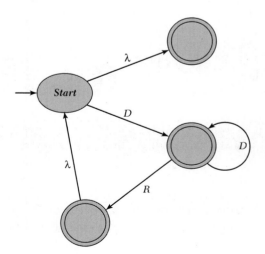

Figure 5.1   RE for the buffer constraint.

where $t^{<s}$ means less than s events of type t in sequence[2] and d is a discrete version of t_{DC}. These REs clearly describe the desired behavioral properties. ◆

A convenient way to describe event sequences that may occur in parallel is through an *interleaved* model. For example, the sequence a b in parallel with the sequence c d can be represented by the set of all possible interleaves or shuffles of the two sequences:

$$A = \{a\,b\,c\,d, a\,c\,d\,b, a\,c\,b\,d, c\,d\,a\,b, c\,a\,b\,d, c\,a\,d\,b\}.$$

REs are extended with a shuffle operator, denoted ⊕, so that the set above is represented by the expression: $(a\,b) \oplus (c\,d)$; that is,

$$L((a\,b) \oplus (c\,d)) = A.$$

Expressions with this operator and additional ones to be mentioned are called *flow expressions* (FEs) [Shaw78, Chi&Shaw86].

In general, $S_1 \oplus S_2$ will mean the set of strings or sequences obtained by performing all possible interleaves of an arbitrary string from S_1 with one from S_2, where S_1 and S_2 are FEs. More formally,

$$L(S_1 \oplus S_2) = \cup L(x \oplus y) \text{ for all } x \text{ in } L(S_1) \text{ and } y \text{ in } L(S_2).$$

▶ Traffic Light Example

Suppose that there are two pairs of traffic lights at the intersection of a street and an avenue, one pair to control the street traffic and one for the avenue. Each pair runs through a green-yellow-red sequence cyclically. The unrestricted operations of the pairs can be specified by the FE:

$$(rs\,(gs\,ys\,rs)^*) \oplus (ra\,(ga\,ya\,ra)^*),$$

where the g, y, and r refer to the colors green, yellow, and red, respectively, s denotes street, a means avenue, and each symbol designates the event of turning the light to the indicated color. It is assumed that the first event for each light after "power-on" turns the light red, hence the initial rs and ra.

In order for this system to be safe, the pairs of lights should never be green or yellow at the same time—when one pair is green or yellow, the other pair must be red. Thus the set of interleaves of events must be restricted so that the unsafe cases are eliminated. Globally, the system must then satisfy the constraint or property given by the following simple FE:

$$(rs \oplus ra)\,((\,gs\,ys\,rs\,) \cup (ga\,ya\,ra\,))^*. ◆$$

The shuffle operator doesn't make the notation more expressive theoretically. It does allow more convenient and less complex descriptions. More power, formally and practically, is obtained if the closure of the ⊕ operator is added. The shuffle closure operator, denoted ⊗, is the interleave equivalent of the * operator. The notation $S^{\otimes}$ will

---

[2] $t^{<s}$ is an abbreviation for $(\lambda \cup t \cup t^2 \ldots \cup t^{s-1})$.

represent zero or more interleaves of strings from S, that is, any number of interleaves of S with itself including none:

$$S^{\otimes} = \lambda \ \cup \ S \ \cup \ (S \oplus S) \ \cup \ (S \oplus S \oplus S) \ \cup \ \dots .$$

The shuffle operator and its closure were first defined and applied to message sequences in [Riddle72].

► **Gate Controller Example**

Consider again the extended fsm for the Gate Controller presented in Section 3.4 (Figure 3.12). Let *cg*, *og*, *te*, and *tl* be the events *Close_Gate*, *Open_Gate*, *Train_Entering*, and *Train_Leaving*, respectively. Assume that *No_Trains* is both the start and halt state for the machine. Following is an FE that specifies exactly the possible sequences of events recognized by this machine:

$$((te \ cg(te \ tl)^{\otimes} \ tl) \ og)^{*}.$$

Every string s from $L((te \ tl)^{\otimes})$ has the desirable characteristic that in any initial substring of s, the number of *te*'s is greater than or equal to the number of *tl*'s. It should be evident from the FE that the open gate command *og* is issued only after the last train has left and the area is empty. This property is guaranteed in the fsm by using the *count* variable. ♦

The flow expression notation also has some operators, similar to locks and binary semaphores, that permit the specification of arbitrary restrictions on interleaving of symbols. In fact, the complete notation is computationally universal. A survey of various extensions of regular expressions, such as path expressions, event expressions, and message transfer expressions, and their applications in non-real-time software appears in [Shaw80]. A similar notation called constrained expressions has also been used for representing and analyzing the behavior of distributed systems [Dillon_et_al88] and real-time systems.

REs and their extensions are particularly appealing because of their close connection with state machines and because they deal directly with events and sequences of events. However, it is also frequently desirable to make direct statements regarding the truth or falsity of various required properties and their relations. Assertional logics provide notational support for this kind of specification.

► **EXERCISES 5.1**

1. Look up the definitions of *identifiers*, *unsigned integers*, and *other strings*, in Question 2 of Exercises 3.4. Specify each of these objects as REs.

2. Treat the *Watch* machine (Section 4.2.1, Figure 4.15) as a finite state machine where each lowest level node (circle or bubble) in the figure represents a simple state. The machine states are thus

{*Time, Date, Alarm, Chime, min, hour,*
day, month, year}.

Assume that every legitimate input sequence of button presses terminates at the *Time* state. For example, the RE given by $(aa)^{*}$ defines all direct paths between *Time* and *Date*; and the sequence *a b a d a* denotes the path

Time - Date - Alarm - Chime - Date - Time.

Write an RE that describes all legitimate paths through *Watch*.

3. Consider the valid sequences of *Deposit* and *Remove* operations handled by the *Buffer* CRSM in the Real-

Time Bounded Buffer example (Section 4.1.1, Figure 4.1). If there is only one buffer ($n = 1$), then this sequence is specified by the RE:

$$(\textit{Deposit Remove})^*.$$

(a) Suppose that $n = 2$. Give a flow expression (FE) specification for the valid sequences of *Deposit* and *Remove* operations.
(b) Repeat (a) for the case when n is unbounded.

4. The text gives extended REs for two of the four paths through the mouse clicker recognizer CRSM (R). Describe the remaining two paths with the same notation.

5. Derive an fsm that accepts the same set of strings as the language generated by the following RE:

$$\textit{Open (Read ((Update Write) } \cup \textit{Print}))^* \textit{ Close.}$$

6. Show by a diagram how the expression, $a \ t^n \ b$, represents any of $(n - 1)$, n, and $(n + 1)$ ticks between the events denoted by a and b.

Hint: A tick event can occur simultaneously with either an a or a b event.

▶ 5.2 TRADITIONAL LOGICS

Logics are formal notations that deal with the truth or falsity of statements and relations. They provide precise methods for specifying, checking, manipulating, and verifying properties and behaviors. In this section, we introduce and evaluate three mainstream logics. The train crossing gate application is employed as an example to illustrate each language.

5.2.1 Propositional Logic

The simplest logic is the propositional calculus. It defines a system for expressing and reasoning about the truth values of statements or *propositions* that are composed of basic objects and logical connectives. The basic objects are the constants T and F, for *true* and *false*, respectively, and a set of variables that can take on the values T or F. Such a variable or constant is often called propositional or Boolean.

The standard logical connectives include *and, or, not, equivalent,* and *implies*; these will be denoted by the symbols $\wedge, \vee, \neg, \Leftrightarrow,$ and $\Rightarrow$, respectively. We define the syntax and semantics of propositional logic more precisely, in a manner similar to that used for regular expressions in the last section. Let Σ be given set of symbols representing propositional variables.

1. (a) Any x in Σ is a proposition. x can take either of two truth values, *true* or *false*.
   (b) The constants T and F are propositions, denoting *true* and *false*, respectively.
2. Let S, S_1, and S_2 be propositions.
   (a) The "or" or disjunction $S_1 \vee S_2$ is a proposition. It's value is *true* if either S_1 or S_2 evaluates to *true*, and *false* otherwise. This is an inclusive "or" since it is also *true* when both S_1 and S_2 are *true*. (An exclusive "or" is *true* only if either, but not both, is *true*.)
   (b) The "and" or conjunction $S_1 \wedge S_2$ is a proposition, with value *true* only if both S_1 and S_2 evaluate to *true*.
   (c) The negation $\neg S$ is a proposition, with value *true* if S is *false* and *false* if S is *true*.

(d) The equivalence $S_1 \Leftrightarrow S_2$ is a proposition. It's value is *true* only if S_1 and S_2 have the same truth values. It is read "S_1 is equivalent to S_2."

(e) The implication $S_1 \Rightarrow S_2$ is a proposition. It is *true* only if S_1 is *false* or S_2 is *true*. It is read "if S_1 then S_2."

The propositional forms defined above are almost identical to Boolean expressions used in programming languages and to the guards that we have employed on transitions in state machines. Propositions can often be transformed into more convenient forms by applying some basic laws or equivalences. Examples of these laws are

$$(S_1 \wedge \neg S_1) \Leftrightarrow F$$

$$(S_1 \Rightarrow S_2) \Leftrightarrow (\neg S_1 \vee S_2)$$

$$(S \vee S_1) \vee S_2 \Leftrightarrow S \vee (S_1 \vee S_2) \text{ (Associative law)}$$

$$S \vee (S_1 \wedge S_2) \Leftrightarrow (S \vee S_1) \wedge (S \vee S_2) \text{ (Distributive law)}$$

$$\neg(S_1 \wedge S_2) \Leftrightarrow \neg S_1 \vee \neg S_2 \text{ (De Morgan's law)}$$

Let *Trains_In* and *Gate_Closed* be Boolean variables whose truth values denote whether or not there are trains in the crossing area and if the gate is closed, respectively. Then, the global requirement for a gate system can be expressed as a proposition that must evaluate to *true*:

$$(\textit{Trains\_In} \Rightarrow \textit{Gate\_Closed}) \wedge (\neg \textit{Trains\_In} \Rightarrow \neg \textit{Gate\_Closed}) \,(*).$$

The first term is a safety assertion—if there are trains in the area, the gate must be closed. Using the second law above, this term can be transformed into an equivalent one:

$$(\textit{Trains\_In} \Rightarrow \textit{Gate\_Closed}) \Leftrightarrow (\neg \textit{Trains\_In} \vee \textit{Gate\_Closed}).$$

Thus, for example, the property expressed by the first term can be satisfied if *Gate_Closed* is always *true*, regardless of the value of *Trains_In*. The second term in (*) is a statement about the progress or liveness of the system, assuming that the gate is open when the condition ¬*Gate_Closed* is *true*.

The original expression (*) can be manipulated into the equivalent expression

$$(\textit{Trains\_In} \wedge \textit{Gate\_Closed}) \vee (\neg \textit{Trains\_In} \wedge \neg \textit{Gate\_Closed}).$$

Here, the safety property given by the first term requires that *Gate_Closed* be *true* only when *Trains_In* is *true*.

The statements can be interpreted as conditions that change truth values as a result of state changes in the system; the state changes are triggered by events. However, the logic does not support any explicit notion of events. Alternatively, any state S can be represented by an expression E such that E is *true* whenever the system is in state S and *false* otherwise. One serious limitation of propositional logic is that it doesn't provide any more detailed way to say what it means to be in a given state. For example, the variable or state *Trains_In* could be true or false, but it may be more useful to describe its meaning more elaborately.

5.2.2 Predicates

Predicate logic is a major extension of propositional logic that adds facilities to elaborate propositions in a more complete fashion. This more powerful logic allows *predicates* which are assertions containing variables and functions that may range over general domains such as integers, strings, or sets. There are also universal and existential quantifiers, denoted $\forall$ ("for all") and $\exists$ ("there exist(s)"), respectively.

A predicate in n-variables $P(x_1, \ldots, x_n)$ is a truth-valued function of the variables. For one variable, say x, the expression

$$\forall x\, P(x)$$

has the meaning as a proposition:

For all x in its universe of discourse, the function $P(x)$ is *true*.

x's "universe of discourse" is the set of all possible values of x.

Thus, for example, if the the universe of discourse is {boat, plane, train} and P is the function

$$P(x) = x \text{ weighs more than 100 lb,}$$

then the expression $\forall x\, P(x)$ is equivalent to the propositional expression

$$(boat \text{ weighs more than 100 lb}) \wedge$$

$$(plane \text{ weighs more than 100 lb}) \wedge$$

$$(train \text{ weighs more than 100 lb}).$$

An expression with an existential quantifier

$$\exists x\, P(x)$$

has the following meaning:

There exists an x in its universe of discourse such that $P(x)$ is *true*.

Thus, using the same universe of discourse for x and $P(x)$ as above, the expression $\exists x\, P(x)$ is equivalent to the proposition

$$(boat \text{ weighs more than 100 lb}) \vee$$

$$(plane \text{ weighs more than 100 lb}) \vee$$

$$(train \text{ weighs more than 100 lb}).$$

Consider the train crossing application again, as in Figure 3.12. The variable *count* ranges over the nonnegative integers and contains the number of trains in the crossing area. Then the proposition *Trains_In* that was used in the expression (*) in the last section can be refined and restated as the predicate $count > 0$. A predicate logic expression of the gate requirement is

$$\forall count\, ((count > 0 \Rightarrow Gate\_Closed\,) \wedge (\,count = 0 \Rightarrow \neg Gate\_Closed\,)). \quad (+)$$

In general, if there is more than one variable in the expression, multiple quantifiers are used. These are interpreted from the outside in, in a manner similar to nested loops in a programming language.

▶ **Examples**

1. Let the function *Separation*(x, y) compute the separation distance between two aircraft *x* and *y*. (Assume that the data record for an aircraft contains its current location, updated sufficiently often.) Then, a statement in the predicate calculus asserting that all planes maintain a minimum separation distance *dmin* is

$$\forall x \ \forall y \ (Separation(x, y) > dmin).$$

2. Let *C*(h) be the predicate "the worker *h* is an air traffic controller," and *CA*(m, p) denote the predicate "controller *m* controls aircraft *p*." The requirement that every plane have a designated controller can be expressed

$$\forall a \ \exists h \ (C(h) \land CA(h, a)).$$

The universe of discourse for *h* is the set of all workers. The expression is then read "for all *a* there exists an *h* such that *C*(h) and *CA*(h, a)." ◆

While more powerful than propositional logic, the predicate calculus notation still has some of the same limitations. One major problem is that the logic has no convenient way to express ordering. For example, the intent in the requirement (+) is that ¬*Gate_Closed* be true (the gate is to be open) sometime after *count* becomes zero, since the gate should be closed at the moment that the gate area becomes empty.

5.2.3 Temporal Logic

Temporal logic is an interesting extension of the predicate calculus [Manna&Pnueli93], but without some of its limitations. It is particularly applicable to concurrent and reactive systems. Despite its name, temporal logic does not deal directly with time, but only with the ordering of events and states in a system.

The operation of a system is characterized by sequences of states, each sequence representing a possible execution or path through the system starting from a given initial state. Assertions on properties of the sequences and states can be made with temporal logic, which consists of the predicate calculus plus some new *temporal* operators.

The most widely used operators are the two unary operators, □ and ◊. They have the meaning:

□*A*: The assertion *A* is *true* for all future states.

◊*A*: The assertion *A* is eventually *true*.

The meaning is interpreted relative to some given state or "time" *S*, such as an initial or a current state. Usually, the state *S* is omitted under the assumption that the formula applies to all states starting from the initial state.

Thus, the statement □ *P* asserts that *P* is *true* for all states including and after some specified state *S*; *P* is an invariant for all future execution sequences starting from *S*.

Similarly, the assertion ◊P at some state S specifies that every sequence of reachable states starting from S (and including S) will eventually contain a state where P is *true*. An example is

$$\Box \ (Temperature\_Out\_of\_Range \Rightarrow \Diamond \ Plant\_Shutdown).$$

The meaning is that for any state S in the system, if *Temperature_Out_of_Range* is *true* at S, then *Plant_ShutDown* will be *true* at some future state starting at S.

Another basic unary operator is the *Next-State* operator O. The assertion

$$O \ A$$

states that at any state S, the next state immediately following S will satisfy A.

Using these operators, we express some of the requirements for the train crossing gate. An apparently natural safety assertion is

$$\Box \ (count > 0 \Rightarrow \Diamond \ Gate\_Closed).$$

This assertion could be made relative to the start state or any intermediate state. It declares that every state with *count* > 0 coincides with or is followed eventually by a state such that *Gate_Closed* is *true*. However, the assertion is flawed—there may be any number of intermediate states between the time that *count* > 0 and *Gate_Closed* where either ¬*Gate_Closed* or *count* = 0 holds.

A more satisfying statement is

$$\Box \ (count > 0 \Rightarrow O \ Gate\_Closed) \wedge (count = 0 \Rightarrow O \ \neg Gate\_Closed).$$

In this case, the requirement is that the gate be closed or open *at least* by the next step after the area becomes nonempty or empty, respectively.

Yet another useful temporal operator is the binary *until* operator, denoted ʊ, which is defined for the assertions A and B:

A ʊ B: A holds (at least) until the first occurrence of B and B will eventually occur.

Using this operator, an alternative statement that allows more than one state change to occur before the gate is closed or opened is

$$\Box \ (count > 0 \ \text{ʊ} \ Gate\_Closed) \wedge (count = 0 \ \text{ʊ} \ \neg \ Gate\_Closed) \, .$$

Other operators, such as *Unless* and *Previous-State*, are also defined. Temporal logic is a very powerful extension of conventional logic, and has proven quite effective for reasoning about concurrent programs. However, it does not specify time or describe events directly. For example, it would be desirable to specify a deadline, such as the maximum amount of time permitted to close the gate once a train enters the crossing area. Some extensions with time intervals and absolute time have been proposed, but none seem as useful as the real-time logic presented in the next section.

▶ EXERCISES 5.2

1. Let the states of a gate be as in Figure 3.10: *Closed*, *Closing*, *Open*, and *Opening*. State the following requirements as an expression in propositional logic: Whenever trains are in the area, the gate must be either closed or closing; if there are no trains in the crossing area, the gate must be open or opening.

2. Let *srt_green*, *str_yellow*, *srt_red*, *ave_green*, *ave_yellow*, and *ave_red* be Boolean state variables representing in an obvious way the colors of the street and avenue lights at any time in the Traffic Light Example of Section 5.1. For example, if the street light is green, then *srt_green* is *true*; otherwise, *str_green* is *false*. A safety requirement is that the street and avenue lights must never be green at the same time. One progress requirement is that the lights are never red or yellow together. Express both the safety and progress requirements in propositional logic. What would be another progress property?

3. Consider the coolant controller described in Question 2 of the Exercises at the end of Section 3.3. Let T_i be the temperature sampled in period i, $i = 1, 2, \ldots$. The system should be in one of three phases, represented by Boolean state variables, depending on the T_i values obtained in the most recent periods:

Moving: Temperature is not stable.

Stable: System has entered the *keep_stable* phase.
Error: System has entered the *error_action* phase.

Specify this requirement in predicate logic.

4. Let the predicate *Inspace(a)* be *true* if aircraft *a* is in a given airspace, and *false* otherwise. Using temporal logic, state the requirement that all planes inside a given airspace should leave the space at some future time.

5. We use the same example and variables as in question 3.

(a) Explain in words the meaning of the following temporal logic expression.

$$\Box \, (\forall i \, ((\, T_i = C \,) \land \, (T_{i+1} = C)) \Rightarrow \Diamond \, stable)$$

(b) A required behavior for the system is as follows: Whenever $T_i \neq C$, and T_i is a valid value, the rods will be moved, eventually resulting in $T_i = C$ and entering the *keep_stable* phase, provided that the *error_action* is not invoked. Describe this behavior in temporal logic.

▶ 5.3 REAL-TIME LOGIC

Real-time logic (RTL) was invented by Jahanian and Mok in the 1980s (e.g., [Jahanian &Mok86]). RTL was designed specifically as a logic for reasoning about the timing properties of real-time systems. This was accomplished through a very simple but clever addition to predicate logic—a function for describing events and their occurrence times.

This function, denoted @, is called the *occurrence* function. @ maps event types and positive integers into nonnegative integers, with the interpretation:

@(*E*, *i*) yields the time of the *i*th instance of an event of class *E*.

Here, an event name *E* designates a class of events whose occurrences are ordered both by *instance* (*i*) and by *time* (@). Instances of events in the same class cannot occur simultaneously; consequently, the (*i* + 1)st instance of an event from a given class occurs, if at all, after the *i*th instance. Time is discrete and is translated to the nonnegative integers 0, 1, 2, 3, ...

With the @ function, one can talk about the time of the tenth depression of button *a*, @(*a*, 10), or the time of the 43rd clock tick, say @(*tick*, 43). Thus, if the first instance of event *E* occurs at time 16, the second at time 23, the third at time 24, and no further instances of *E* have occurred, we have @(*E*, 1) = 16, @(*E*, 2) = 23, @(*E*, 3) = 24, and @(*E*, *i*) undefined for *i* > 3.

It is also convenient to define initiation and termination events for actions or computations. The start of an action of type *A* will correspond to an event class ↑*A*; the completion of *A* will correspond to an event ↓*A*. Another way of stating this that is consistent with our previous event notation starts with the notion that *A* is a condition that is true when *A* is executing and false otherwise; then ↑*A* corresponds to the event defined when A changes from false to true, and $\downarrow A$ is the event when A changes from true to false.

▶ Examples

1. Let a train crossing gate (Figure 3.10) operate so that the gate will always close within five time units of receiving a close command. The transition events are classes in the RTL sense. This behavior may be stated precisely in terms of these events:

$$\forall i \; @(cg, i) = t_1 \Rightarrow \exists j \; @(c\text{-}c, j) = t_2 \wedge (t_1 < t_2 \leq t_1 + 5).$$

2. Using the gate example again (Figure 3.10), let *Train_Entering* be the event associated with a train entering the area and *Train_Leaving* be the event occurring when a train leaves. The following RTL expression gives the conditions for at least one train in the area at some time between times t_1 and t_2:

$$\forall t \; ((t_1 \leq t \leq t_2) \Rightarrow \exists i \; \neg \exists j \; ((@(Train\_Entering, i) \leq t) \wedge$$
$$(@(Train\_Leaving, j) \leq t) \wedge (j = i \;))).$$

The assertion states that between t_1 and t_2 there always exists at least one previous train entering event without a subsequent matching exit.

3. Suppose that upon pressing Button a, a computation *Test* must be completed within 30 seconds. This requirement can be expressed in RTL as

$$\forall x \; (@(a, x) < @(\uparrow Test, x)) \wedge (@(\downarrow Test, x) \leq @(a, x) + 30).$$

Note that the a and *Test* events are matched; the xth a has a corresponding xth *Test*.

One particular subtlety about the @ function is ignored here and in subsequent examples. Namely, it is only a *partial* function, defined possibly only for a finite number of instances of the event. Thus, one should really specify that for each (a, x) that is defined (rather than for all x), there exist corresponding $(\uparrow Test, x)$ and $(\downarrow Test, x)$ events that meet the constraints. This can be expressed as follows:

$$\forall x \forall t_1 \; (\; @(a, x) = t_1 \Rightarrow \exists t_2, t_3 \; (\; @(\uparrow Test, x) = t_2 \wedge$$
$$@(\downarrow Test, x) = t_3 \wedge t_1 < t_2 \wedge t_3 \leq t_1 + 30 \;) \;).$$

4. Two actions A_1 and A_2 are to be mutually exclusive; that is, during the execution of A_1, A_2 cannot be executed, and vice versa. This standard constraint can be stated in RTL using the start and end events of the actions:

$$\forall i, j \; ((@(\downarrow A_1, i) < @(\uparrow A_2, j) \;) \vee (@(\downarrow A_2, j) < @(\uparrow A_1, i))).$$

5. Consider a standard sporadic timing constraint [Jahanian&Mok86]: On event E with minimum event separation p, execute A with deadline d. An RTL specification of these constraints is

$$\forall i \; \exists j \; ((@(E, i) \leq @(\uparrow A, j)) \wedge (@(\downarrow A, j) \leq (@(E, i) + d)))$$
$$\wedge \; \forall i \; ((@(E, i) + p) \leq @(E, i+1)).$$

In this specification, other instances of A are possible. It is required only that there exist one instance, a "jth," associated with each E. Note also that a unique A does not necessarily correspond to each E; the specification is satisfied, for example, if two successive E's are followed by a single associated A and d is sufficiently large. This problem cannot occur if $d \leq p$. ◆

RTL has been used by its creators for some manual and automatic theorem proving of properties of specifications; in their methodology, they translate Modecharts, a state-based scheme similar to statecharts, into RTL formulas for subsequent analysis [Jahanian&Mok94]. RTL has also been applied to proving the correctness of computer programs, where the actions are program statements.

Some recent more practical applications include using RTL as the assertional language for run-time monitoring of timing constraints in distributed programs [Jahanian_et_al94] and for checking the behavior of CRSMs (Section 4.1) during simulations [Raju&Shaw94; Fortino&Nigro00]. One variation of this type of monitoring and checking includes the program form

```
when <event_class> {assert( <RTL_constraint>)}.
```

The semantics is that the <RTL_constraint> is checked whenever an instance of <event_class> occurs. If the check fails, an error exception is raised.

The <RTL_constraint> contains an expression in RTL without quantifiers and referring to the past history of events. It is most common to refer to the most recent event of a given class, the second most recent, and so on, rather than to the events starting from the first occurrence. The notation $@(E, -i)$, $i > 0$, will denote the time of the ith most recent event of class E, where $@(E, -1)$ returns the time of the most recent E event. Thus, if n instances of E have occurred with times $@(E, 1), \ldots, @(E, n)$, then

$$@(E, -i) = @(E, n-i + 1), (i > 0).$$

► **Examples of RTL Constraint Checks**

1. Suppose that a traffic light controller at an intersection gives special service and priority to emergency vehicles, such as ambulances or police cars. When such a vehicle approaches the intersection, the controller switches all lights to red with enough time so that the area can be cleared safely before the emergency vehicle arrives. Let the vehicle send two types of messages (events) to the controller—an *approaching* event indicating that the vehicle will be crossing the intersection shortly, and a *before* event when the vehicle is just at the intersection. There must be at least five seconds between these events, in order for the controller to switch the lights and for the intersection to clear. To check that the system adheres to this constraint, the following statement can be used:

```
when before {assert(@(before, -1) ≥ @(approaching, -1) + 5)}.
```

Each time an instance of the event *before* occurs, the assertion is checked.

2. Recall the mouse clicker example presented in Section 4.1.3. A *DC* message (event) is emitted every time that a double click is recognized. The correctness of an implementation or of an executable CRSM specification can be checked on each instance of *DC* with the following:

```
when DC
    {assert( (@(U,-1) - @(D,-1)) ≤ t_SC ∧
             (@(D,-1) - @(U,-2)) ≤ t_DC ∧
             (@(U,-2) - @(D,-2)) ≤ t_SC }.♦
```

▶ EXERCISES 5.3

1. An alarm clock is defined with the following property:

When the alarm event occurs, a bell should ring for either 30 seconds or until a stop button is pressed, whichever happens first.

Express this property in RTL. Let AC, $\uparrow BELL$, $\downarrow BELL$, and $STOP$ be the names of the alarm event, start_bell_ringing, stop_bell_ringing, and stop button events, respectively.

2. Specify the following mutual exclusion constraint in RTL:

In the Traffic Light system (Section 5.1), the street and avenue lights can never be green simultaneously.

Assume that each of the commands gs, ys, rs, ga, ya, and ra are event classes.

3. Let the train crossing gate (Figure 3.10) operate so that the gate will close within five time units of receiving a close command, *provided* that an intervening open command has not been issued. Describe this behavior formally in RTL.

4. Recall the Nuclear Power Plant Monitor example of Section 2.3. Every 100 ms, the T, F, and S actions are to be executed in sequence in the order shown in Figure 2.5, and completed before the end of the 100 ms cycle. Express this requirement in RTL.

5. Let SC, DC, SS, SE, D, and U be event classes in the Mouse Clicker example of Section 4.1.3. Using RTL, describe the relations that must hold among instances of these events.

Hint: Examine a history of instances of these events, ordered by time of occurrence.

6. Consider the following additional constraints on a standard bounded buffer with *Deposit* and *Remove* operations:

Every *Remove* must be preceded by at least one *Deposit*, and there must be a time delay of at least dt time units between the start of one operation and the end of a previous one.

Express these constraints in real-time logic (RTL).

CHAPTER 6

Deterministic Scheduling

The previous chapters have discussed the importance of time in real-time systems, developed several systems models that included time, presented many examples of timing properties, and described methods for specifying behaviors involving time. This chapter and the next one are concerned with analyzing and predicting the timing behavior of software. At the systems level, time is treated explicitly as a resource in the form of hardware processors that must be allocated to real-time computations. The purpose is to determine whether or not a set of computations are schedulable, and if so, how. A set of computations is said to be *schedulable* on one or more processors if there exist enough processor cycles, that is, enough time, to execute all the computations.

This subject is called deterministic scheduling—*deterministic* because the input data and results are not statistical. Many of the ideas originated years ago in job-shop or assembly-line problems related to factory scheduling. We first examine some scheduling methods and theory, using a very simple model and assumptions. The assumptions are then relaxed and more general situations are investigated, including the effects of process interactions. The final section discusses how the theory and models can be used in practice.

▶ 6.1 ASSUMPTIONS AND CANDIDATE ALGORITHMS

We are given one or more processors and a set of tasks with information and constraints about their behavior and requirements. Such information usually includes task activation times, deadlines, and execution times. The problem is then to devise a policy for allocating the tasks to the processors. Such a policy or its implementation is called a *scheduler* or *scheduling* algorithm, and the detailed assignment of tasks to processors is termed a *schedule*. If the algorithm is able to allocate the processes so that all constraints are met, the resulting schedule is said to be *feasible*. An *optimal* algorithm is one that will produce a feasible schedule if it exists.

▶ Example 1

Let P_1 and P_2 be periodic processes, characterized by the (compute_time, period, deadline) triples $P_1 = (1, 2, 2)$ and $P_2 = (2, 5, 5)$. They share a single processor. Suppose that the processes have fixed scheduling priorities, π_1 and π_2, respectively, such that $\pi_1 > \pi_2$; that processes are scheduled when ready according to priority, highest priority first; that both processes are activated for the first time at time 0; and that processes are not preempted during execution. The last assumption means that once a process is allocated to the CPU, it retains the CPU until completing its computation for that cycle.

Then, a feasible schedule is produced as shown in Figure 6.1(a). The cross-hatched areas indicate execution on the processor; an arrow denotes the start of a period. The entire schedule can be repeated at time 10. Note that the processor is idle (not utilized) between times 9 and 10, since neither process is ready then.

On the other hand, if the priorities are reversed ($\pi_1 < \pi_2$), a feasible schedule is no longer possible. P_2 would start at time 0 consuming two units of time. P_2's execution will thus consume the first cycle of P_1, causing it to miss its deadline.

Another possibility is to do "round-robin" scheduling with preemption at fixed time intervals. Suppose that at every time unit, the currently executing process (if any) is preempted by the other process if ready. Then the schedule of Figure 6.1(b) results if P_2 starts first. As before, the schedule is repeated at time 10, and there is one unit of idle time at time 9. ◆

For this and the next section, we make a number of assumptions about the system and scheduler. The effects of relaxing or changing these assumptions are discussed in Section 6.3. The analysis is restricted initially to a single processor and a set of periodic processes

$$\{P_i = (c_i, p_i, d_i): p_i = d_i\},$$

where c_i is the execution time, p_i the period, and d_i is the deadline. Note that the deadline is the same as the period. Sporadic processes are not directly included; they can be

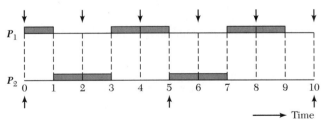

(a) P_1 has higher priority.

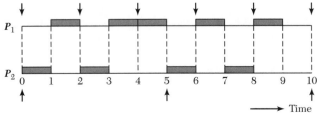

(b) Round-robin scheduling with preemption.

Figure 6.1 Two feasible schedules.

treated separately or translated into equivalent periodic ones. Processes are independent and have no interactions. They all start at the same time, say $t = 0$, ready to execute their first cycle; the terminology is that there is no *phasing*. Finally, unless stated otherwise, we assume that a process may be preempted from the CPU by another process during any of its executions. Normally, a preempted process is later resumed.

When a process is released at the beginning of its cycle, it becomes *ready* and remains ready or running until it has completed its execution. A scheduling decision can be made when a process becomes ready, when a process completes its execution, or as a result of a timer interrupt. (Because we are ignoring process interactions for the moment, blocking is not included.) There exist a large number of scheduling algorithms that have been used or proposed for both real-time and conventional computations. Several of the most common and plausible ones are described.

One appealing approach is *First-Come, First-Served* (FCFS), also sometimes called *First-In, First-Out* (FIFO). In its purest form, a process is inserted at the end of a ready list when it is released, and processes are allocated from the front of the list; once running, a process completes its cycle (no preemption). If more than one process becomes ready at the same time, they are inserted at the end of the ready list in an arbitrary order. Figure 6.1(a) is also an FCFS schedule. However, if the orders of P_1 and P_2 happened to be reversed when placed on the ready list, a schedule would not be possible; this case is identical to the one above where the priorities are reversed. FCFS is actually the same as round-robin but *without* preemption.

Round-Robin (RR) with fixed time intervals and preemption is another scheme that has proven effective in conventional systems. As its name indicates, RR works by allocating from the front of the ready list, and by inserting timer-interrupted or newly released processes at the end of the list. RR produces a feasible schedule for the example of Figure 6.1(b). However, it isn't always guaranteed as the following example shows.

▶ **Example 2**

Let $P_1 = (3, 4, 4)$ and $P_2 = (2, 8, 8)$. Figure 6.2(a) shows what happens when attempting to schedule using RR with one unit time intervals. At time 4, P_1 has only received two units of processor time and therefore misses its deadline. However, if P_1 is given a higher priority than P_2, a feasible schedule results [Figure 6.2(b)]. P_2 is preempted by P_1 at $t = 4$; the preemption is indicated by a thick arrow in the figure. The schedule is repeated at time 8. ◆

For real-time systems, most of the most interesting and useful approaches are either based directly on priorities or can be described conveniently in terms of priorities. The general policy is to ensure that at all times, the highest priority ready process receives the CPU. Normally, this requires that lower priority processes are preempted, that is, interrupted and replaced during execution. At one extreme, one can have a *fixed* or *static* priority system, where a process's priority is assigned before the system starts executing and doesn't change. With the exception of the RR, all of the above examples use static priority assignment and scheduling.

The question, of course, is how to assign the priorities. Initially, we will examine priorities that are based on the quantitative characteristics of the process, namely c, p,

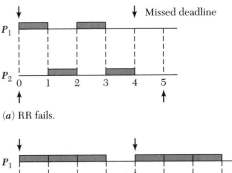

(a) RR fails.

(b) P_1 has higher priority.

Figure 6.2   Example 2.

and d. Other features that could determine priority, such as blocking and the importance or criticality of a task, are introduced later.

The *rate monotonic* method (RM) assigns fixed priorities in reverse order of period length: the shorter the period, the higher the priority. Formally, for any two processes P and Q with periods p and q, if $p < q$ then $\pi_P > \pi_Q$, where π_P and π_Q are the priorities given to P and Q, respectively. The intuition underlying the appeal of RM is that processes requiring frequent attention (smaller periods) should receive higher priorities; for example, imagine a process with a period of 1 hour competing for a CPU with a process having a period of 1 second. In Examples 1 and 2, RM would assign $\pi_{P1} > \pi_{P2}$. Figure 6.2(b) is an RM schedule. Figure 6.1(a) is not considered RM because it is non-preemptive.

Another fixed priority method is *least compute time* (LCT), which assigns priorities in reverse order of compute times. The intuition here is that tasks with smaller compute times should receive higher priorities because they will finish relatively quickly. For the Example 2 processes, LCT would give P_2 a higher priority than P_1. Unfortunately, a schedule is not possible with this assignment; P_1 would miss its first deadline.

The more complicated policies permit *dynamic* priorities, that is, priorities that change during execution; or use a combination of static and dynamic schemes where priorities may be fixed except for some well-defined places that require dynamic changes. Three common dynamic priority schemes are *shortest completion time* (SCT), *earliest deadline first* (EDF), and *least slack time* (LST). All three potentially recompute priorities at period boundaries.

The SCT policy ensures that the ready process with the smallest remaining compute time is allocated to the CPU. The schedule of Figure 6.1(a) is an SCT schedule. Initially, P_1 requires less compute time than P_2 (1 unit vs. 2 units) and runs; at $t = 2$ and $t = 6$, there are ties which could be broken arbitrarily. However, the processes of Example 2 cannot be scheduled with the SCT method. P_1 will miss its first deadline at $t = 4$, in exactly the same way as in the LCT case.

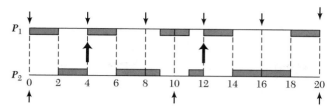

Figure 6.3 An EDF schedule.

EDF looks at deadlines rather than compute times. The ready process with the earliest (future) deadline has the highest priority at any point. Figure 6.2(*b*) is also an EDF schedule. Initially, P_1 has the earliest deadline (4 vs. 8); at $t = 4$, both processes have the same deadline, and either one could be selected.

The LST policy examines the amount of free or slack time for each process. The slack time for a process is defined as

$$(d - t) - c',$$

where d is its deadline, t is the real time since the start of the current cycle, and c' is its remaining compute time. The process with the smallest slack time is given the highest priority.

▶ **Example 3**

Let $P_1 = (2, 4, 4)$ and $P_2 = (5, 10, 10)$. An EDF schedule for these two processes is drawn in Figure 6.3. Preemptions are marked by thick arrows. P_1 starts at $t = 0$ because its deadline at $t = 4$ is earlier than P_2's ($t = 10$). At $t = 4$, P_2 is preempted because P_1 has an earlier deadline at $t = 8$. There is no preemption at $t = 8$ since P_2's deadline is 10 while the new cycle of P_1 has a deadline of 12. At $t = 16$, both processes have deadlines of 20, so either choice is possible. The same schedule can be repeated starting at time 20. Using SCT, an identical schedule would be produced for these same processes. ◆

▶ **EXERCISES 6.1**

1. Define two periodic processes $P_1 = (1, 6, 6)$ and $P_2 = (3, 4, 4)$. Suppose that they have fixed scheduling priorities π_1 and π_2, respectively. Assume nonpreemptive scheduling.
(a) Show a feasible schedule when $\pi_1 > \pi_2$. Your schedule should cover 12 time units.
(b) Repeat (a) using $\pi_1 < \pi_2$.

2. Consider the two periodic processes $P_1 = (15, 20, 20)$ and $P_2 = (10, 40, 40)$.
(a) Assume the round-robin (RR) scheduling policy with one unit time intervals. Show that a feasible schedule does *not* exist.

(b) Exhibit a feasible schedule using the rate monotonic (RM) method. Your schedule should cover 40 time units.
(c) Repeat (b) using the EDF policy.
(d) Assume the LCT scheduling policy. Does a feasible schedule exist? Prove the correctness of your answer by either giving an LCT schedule or showing where the policy fails.

3. Assume three periodic processes $P_1 = (3, 9, 9)$, $P_2 = (5, 18, 18)$, and $P_3 = (4, 12, 12)$.
(a) Show that the RM method does not produce a feasible schedule.
(b) Give a schedule following the EDF policy.

▶ 6.2 BASIC RM AND EDF RESULTS

Since the 1970s, researchers have produced an enormous number of publications with many interesting theorems in the field of deterministic scheduling. One paper and set of results, however, has dominated all others and provided the basis for real-time scheduling—the article [Liu&Layland73]. We present and discuss the most significant results from this paper, but without formal proofs.

Consider first the problem of assigning priorities in a *fixed* or static priority system. The most important theorem for fixed priorities in [Liu&Layland73] states:

> *Rate monotonic RM is an optimal priority assignment method.*

In other words, if a schedule that meets all the deadlines exists with fixed priorities, then RM will produce a feasible schedule.

Informal Argument for the Theorem

The theorem can be proven by first showing that it holds for two processes (n = 2). Suppose that processes $P_1 = (c_1, p_1, d_1)$ and $P_2 = (c_2, p_2, d_2)$ can be scheduled with a fixed but non-RM priority assignment where P_2 has the highest priority, that is, $p_1 < p_2$. Suppose that the two processes are released at the same time; that is, each starts one of their periods at the same time. It can be shown that this is the worst possible case, leading to the greatest response time, for the lower priority process. However, at this point, in order for both processes to be schedulable, we must have $c_1 + c_2 \le p_1$; otherwise P_1 could not meet its period or deadline. Because of this relation between the compute times and the period (deadline) of the first process, we can also obtain a feasible schedule by reversing priorities, thereby scheduling P_1 first, that is, with an RM assignment.

The general case, n > 2, can then be proven as follows. Suppose that processes $P_1, \ldots, P_n$ are schedulable and in ascending priority order. Furthermore, the priority assignment is not RM. Let P_i and P_{i+1}, $1 \le i < n$, be the first two tasks with non-RM priorities, that is, $p_i > p_{i+1}$. The proof proceeds by interchanging the priorities of these two processes and showing that the set is still schedulable, using the n = 2 result above. One then continues interchanging non-RM pairs in this fashion until the assignment is RM. Therefore, if a fixed priority assignment can produce a feasible schedule, so can the RM assignment. ◆

The next important question is concerned with feasibility. Under what conditions is a schedule possible in the static priority case? To answer this and other questions, it is necessary to define the notion of *processor utilization*, denoted U, as follows:

$$U = \sum_{i=1}^{n} (c_i/p_i).$$

U is a measure of what fraction of the processor is used over all periods. For the process groups in the last section, we have the following utilizations:

Example 1: $U = 1/2 + 2/5 = 0.9$

Example 2: $U = 3/4 + 2/8 = 1.0$

Example 3: $U = 2/4 + 5/10 = 1.0$

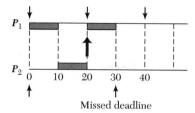

Missed deadline

(a) P_1 = (10, 20, 20) P_2 = (15, 30, 30)

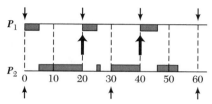

(b) P_1 = (6, 20, 20) P_2 = (15, 30, 30)

Figure 6.4 RM scheduling.

Note that $U \leq 1$ is a necessary condition for feasibility regardless of the scheduling policy. Informally, the reason is that a schedule with $U = 1$ is guaranteed to completely pack the time line (Figures 6.2, 6.3, and 6.4). With $U > 1$, any attempt at a schedule will fail at or before the least common multiple (lcm) of the periods.

The significant result on feasibility is the following sufficient condition:

Scheduling with static priorities is feasible if $U \leq n\,(\,2^{1/n} - 1)$.

This means that whenever U is at or below the given bound, a schedule can be made with RM. In the limit when the number of processes $n = \infty$, we have

$$\lim_{n \to \infty} n\,(2^{1/n} - 1) = \ln 2 \approx 0.69.$$

The value of this bound for various values of n is tabulated as follows:

n	1	2	3	4	5	6	$\cdots$	∞
bound for U	1.0	0.83	0.78	0.76	0.74	0.73	$\cdots$	0.69

Schedulability is thus guaranteed whenever the utilization is less than about 0.7. Only 30% of the CPU is wasted to achieve schedules for any number of processes. This is a very strong result indeed, even though it is theoretical!

Note also that the bound is sufficient, but not necessary. One can often produce schedules with larger values of U, as Example 2 [Figure 6.2(b)] in the last section demonstrates. On the other hand, RM can fail if the bound is not met. As an example, let P_1 = (10, 20, 20) and P_2 = (15, 30, 30), giving $U = 1$. Fixed priority scheduling is not possible as shown in Figure 6.4(a); P_2 misses its deadline at the end of the first cycle at $t = 30$. However, if the compute time of P_1 is changed to, say, 6, giving $U = 0.8$, scheduling becomes feasible [Figure 6.4(b)]; P_2 is preempted by P_1 at $t = 20$ and at $t = 40$ in this RM schedule.

For *dynamic* priorities, the theory is equally interesting but the results are somewhat simpler and stronger. The first theorem is

Earliest deadline first (EDF) is optimal.

In other words, if a feasible schedule exists using dynamic priorities, then the EDF method will also produce a feasible schedule. It was later shown that LST is also optimal [Dertouzos&Mok89].

The optimality result for EDF is proven by showing that EDF can always produce a feasible schedule if $U \leq 1$, that is, 100% utilization. Thus the feasibility theorem is

Scheduling with dynamic priorities is feasible if and only if $U \leq 1$.

The condition is clearly necessary because, as we argued earlier, a feasible schedule is never possible if the utilization is greater than 1. The theorem adds that the condition is also sufficient.

Before leaving this section, we introduce a very simple but optimal scheduling algorithm that does not use priorities. Assume that the periods are integer values. Then, in every unit of time, allocate a fraction of the CPU equal to c_i/p_i to each process P_i; at the end of p_i units of time, process P_i will have received exactly c_i execution units and thus meet its deadline. For example, if $P_1 = (3, 4, 4)$ and $P_2 = (2, 8, 8)$, then 0.75 units of processor time is given to P_1 and 0.25 to P_2 in each unit interval of time. This algorithm is clearly optimal since a feasible schedule results whenever $U \leq 1$. The technique apparently first appeared in Mok's thesis [Mok83]. We will refer to it as *algorithm M*.

▶ EXERCISES 6.2

Assume that all processes are periodic.

1. Consider the process set defined in Example 1 of Section 6.1. Show that an RM schedule either does or does not exist for this set.

2. Let $P_1 = (5, 10, 10)$ and $P_2 = (20, 40, 40)$.
(a) Give the processor utilization U.
(b) Show a feasible schedule using EDF.
(c) Demonstrate that a feasible schedule based on *fixed* priorities exists or prove that one cannot exist.

3. Let $P_1 = (1, 6, 6)$ and $P_2 = (3, 4, 4)$.
(a) What is the processor utilization U?

(b) Show how algorithm M would schedule these processes.

4. Define $P_1 = (3, 9, 9)$, $P_2 = (4, 18, 18)$, and $P_3 = (4, 12, 12)$.
(a) Give the processor utilization U.
(b) Show that an RM schedule does or does not exist.

5. Let $P_1 = (3, 9, 9)$, $P_2 = (2, 18, 18)$, and $P_3 = (4, 12, 12)$.
(a) Compute the processor utilization U.
(b) Show that an RM schedule does or does not exist.

6. Prove that the utilization U must satisfy $U \leq 1$ in order for a feasible schedule to exist, regardless of the policy used.

▶ 6.3 RELAXING THE ASSUMPTIONS

We discuss briefly some results in more general scheduling situations. Consider an extension of our model of periodic processes. Instead of a three-tuple, a process is now characterized as a five-tuple,

$$P_i = (s_i, r_i, c_i, p_i, d_i),$$

where s_i is the start time or *phasing*, r_i is the *release* time, and $r_i + c_i \leq d_i \leq p_i$. In the previous sections, it was assumed that all processes started at the same time $t = 0$, that is, that $s_i = 0$, and that the kth period of P_i started at time $(k - 1)p_i$. Here, the kth period of P_i starts at $s_i + (k - 1)p_i$.

The release time gives the earliest time in the period that a process can begin execution; earlier, we assumed implicitly that $r_i = 0$. One reason for a nonzero release time is to ensure that process executions are evenly spaced from period to period; for example, it may be desirable to avoid situations such as in Figure 6.1(a) at $t = 4$ when the end of one execution of P_1 is immediately followed by the start of another execution of P_1. A nonzero r_i also provides tighter control over the allowable jitter (Section 2.1) since c_i must fit into $d_i - r_i$, rather than just d_i.

Because the worst case response time occurs when all s_i are zero, it can be shown that RM and EDF are also optimal for arbitrary start times. The feasibility results given in the last section are also valid for arbitrary s_i.

Next, assume that deadlines are not necessarily equal to periods, but that they can also be less than periods. An optimal static priority assignment method for this case is *deadline monotonic* [Leung&Whitehead82]—the smaller the deadline, the higher the priority. For dynamic priorities, EDF is still optimal but deciding feasibility is NP-hard [Leung&Merrill80]; a sufficient condition for schedulability is that $\Sigma(c_i/d_i) \leq 1$.

The theory presented so far assumes that processes may be preempted at any time. Consider the other extreme—*no preemption*. Once a process is selected for execution, it runs to completion. Examples where nonpreemption is desirable or necessary include critical sections, IO processes, timer processes, and other tasks or parts of an operating system kernel. In these cases, interrupting a running process could result in inconsistent and incorrect data. Preemption may also not be practical for processes that have tight deadlines. [Jeffay_et_al91] prove that EDF is optimal in a fairly general nonpreemptive setting that disallows inserted idle time in a schedule; they also give necessary and sufficient conditions for feasibility.

Most of the useful scheduling theory applies only to uniprocessor systems and not to *multiprocessors*—systems with more than one CPU and shared memory. For example, neither RM nor EDF are optimal for multiprocessor systems. Using our standard three-tuples, let $P_1 = (2, 4, 4)$, $P_2 = (2, 4, 4)$, and $P_3 = (5, 8, 8)$, and suppose that there are two homogeneous processors available. Then, RM would allocate both processors to P_1 and P_2 initially at $t = 0$ and also at $t = 4$, causing P_3 to miss its deadline. However, if P_3 had highest priority, a feasible schedule results. Similarly, if we changed P_3 to $(7, 8, 8)$, EDF would fail, but a static priority assignment with P_3 highest produces a feasible schedule.

Algorithm M introduced at the end of the previous section would always work here, provided of course that $U \leq m$, where m is the number of processors, and that $d_i = p_i$. A fraction c_i/p_i of processor time is allocated to each process P_i for every time unit. Note that a process may need to be allocated to more than one CPU over a single time unit in order to fit; for example, if $m = 2$ and there are three processes each with $c/p = 2/3$, then one of the processes has to be partially allocated to each of the two CPUs.

The most practical policy for multiprocessors is to pre-assign processes to CPUs using some heuristic technique, and then schedule each one independently. As one example, [Oh&Baker98] show that the assignment of periodic tasks to processors using a first-fit algorithm, followed by RM scheduling on each CPU, leads to guaranteed schedulability under worst case utilization between 41% and 66%.

One standard approach for handling *sporadic* tasks that was mentioned in earlier chapters is to translate each sporadic process $P = (c, p, d)$ into an equivalent periodic one $P' = (c, p', d')$, where ($c \leq d \leq p$). P' polls to determine whether or not the event associated with P has occurred since the last period; if so, it performs the same computation as P and meets P's deadline. Then, if a feasible schedule exists with P', one is guaranteed that the sporadic P would be handled in time. The difficult part is to ensure that no matter when the event occurs, the equivalent periodic process will poll it in time.

Assume integer values for the elements of P and P'. One such transformation [Mok83] selects any d' and p' that satisfy the following relations:

$$d \geq d' \geq c \text{ and } p' \leq (d - d') + 1.$$

Thus, for example, if $P = (2, 10, 7)$, five equivalent periodic processes P' are $(2, 4, 4)$, $(2, 3, 5)$, $(2, 1, 7)$, $(2, 6, 2)$, and $(2, 5, 3)$. Note that d' could be greater than p'.

The correctness of this transformation can be shown as follows. Suppose that an interrupt occurs at an arbitrary time t. t can be expressed in the form

$$t = ip' + \delta,$$

where $i \geq 0$ and $0 < \delta \leq p'$. Then, the equivalent periodic process P will handle it in the period starting at time $(i + 1)p'$. The interrupt processing will be completed within $d' + p' - 1$ time units after it occurs—d' in the handling period and $p' - 1$ if it occurred at the earliest possible time in the previous period. Using the second relation defining the transformation, we have

$$d' + p' - 1 \leq d' + (d - d') + 1 - 1 = d.$$

Therefore the interrupt will be processed before its real deadline d.

There is a trade-off between p' and d'. In one extreme, the deadlines are the same ($d = d'$) and P' polls every time unit ($p' = 1$). At the other extreme, $d' = c$ and p' can be its maximum size of $d - c + 1$. Generally, the polling period p' is smaller than the minimum separation time p between events. (An exception is when $p = p' = d = d' = 1$.)

▶ EXERCISES 6.3

1. Show that the deadline monotonic policy produces a feasible schedule for the two periodic processes $P_1 = (3, 10, 7)$ and $P_2 = (4, 12, 6)$. Is there a feasible schedule if the priorities are reversed?

2. Assume two processors and three periodic processes $P_1 = (2, 4, 4)$, $P_2 = (3, 4, 4)$, and $P_3 = (5, 8, 8)$.
(a) Show how algorithm M would schedule these processes on the two machines.
(b) Prove that it is not possible to produce a feasible schedule using fixed priorities.
(c) Exhibit a schedule with the minimum number of preemptions.

3. Describe in detail an algorithm to schedule a set of periodic processes on a mutiprocessor using the approach of algorithm M. Test it on paper for the case of four processes, each with $c/p = 0.75$ and $m = 2$.

4. Suppose that $P = (3, 6, 6)$ is a sporadic process. List *all* possible equivalent periodic processes P' satisfying the conditions given in the text.

5. Build (program) a library of different scheduling routines. Compare the different methods experimentally on simulated real-time programs composed of periodic and sporadic processes. Include at least the following algorithms: random fixed priority, rate monotonic, first-in-first-out, earliest deadline, and shortest completion time.

▶ 6.4 PROCESS INTERACTIONS: PRIORITY INVERSION AND INHERITANCE

Scheduling to assure timing constraints becomes more complicated when standard process interactions are included in the model. In this section, we examine the effects and problems caused by the task synchronization required to correctly maintain shared data and to utilize nonpreemptable resources. Examples of the mechanisms employed to achieve mutually exclusive use of data and resources are semaphores, locks, monitors, and rendezvous [Bic&Shaw88]. We will assume that access to these kinds of shared objects occurs in critical sections of code protected by binary semaphore locks.

The major problem is how to minimize the *blocking* that can occur when a process attempts to access a shared object in competition with other processes. The straightforward use of conventional fixed priority techniques can lead to a situation where a low priority task causes a higher priority one to be blocked for an unbounded or an excessive amount of time. This is the *priority inversion* problem.

▶ Example of Priority Inversion

Three processes P_1, P_2, and P_3 have relative priorities $\pi_{P1} > \pi_{P2} > \pi_{P3}$. P_1 and P_3 share some data or resource that requires exclusive access, and P_2 does not interact with either of the other processes. Suppose that their executions follow these code skeletons:

```
P1:: begin .... lock(S); CS1 ; unlock(S); ... end
P2:: begin ....          ...          ...  end
P3:: begin .... lock(S); CS3 ; unlock(S); ... end
```

The shared resource is accessed in critical sections *CS1* and *CS3*, and is protected by a semaphore lock S, initialized to unlocked or free. The first *lock(S)* that is executed sets S so that other processes attempting a *lock(S)* will block until the lock becomes available; *unlock(S)* resets the lock, permitting another process to enter its critical section. Instead of *lock* and *unlock*, we could equally well substitute equivalent primitives, such as *wait* and *signal*, *P* and *V*, or *Request* and *Release*.

Consider the following execution scenario (Figure 6.5). P_3 starts executing first, obtains the S lock, and enters its critical section. At time t_1 while P_3 is in *CS3*, P_2 is activated and preempts P_3 because it has a higher priority. P_1 then starts executing at time

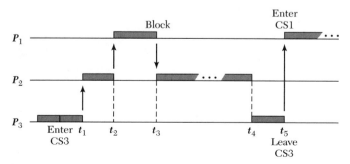

Figure 6.5 Priority inversion.

t_2, preempting P_2. At t_3, P_1 attempts to enter its *CS1* but cannot obtain the lock S which is held by P_3; it therefore blocks on *lock*(S) and the CPU is given to P_2. After P_2 completes at t_4, P_3 continues in *CS3* and unlocks S. P_1 is then unblocked and preempts P_3 at t_5. P_1 now successfully completes its *lock*(S) and enters *CS1*.

What's wrong with this sequence of preemptions and executions? It is certainly "logically" correct. However, the lowest priority process P_3 has prevented the highest priority one P_1 from executing for a time period that depends not only on the time that P_3 is in its critical section but also on the computation time of P_2. If there were other ready tasks of intermediate priority, then P_1 would have to wait for their completion also. In general, P_1 may have to wait for an unbounded period of time. The highest priority has become the lowest—a clear "inversion" of the designers' intent. It would obviously be more desirable if the blocking time of P_1 depended only on P_3 and its *CS3* execution time. ◆

The priority inversion problem was first introduced in a non-real-time setting by [Lampson&Redell80]. There are at least two simple solutions that would provide better timing predictability. Critical sections could be made nonpreemptable. Then the blocking time for a process would be the maximum of the critical section times of all lower priority processes. This solution may be practical provided that all the critical sections are short. However, more commonly, resources may be held for longer periods of time. The nonpreemptability solution would also unecessarily penalize high priority tasks; in the worst cases, a process P would have to wait for lower priority and unrelated tasks that do not share resources with P, another form of inversion.

Another solution, the one proposed in [Lampson&Redell80], is to execute critical sections at the highest priority of any process that might use it. In the example above, P_3 would execute its *CS3* at P_1's priority. This is also too strong a solution. Regardless of whether or not a higher priority process accesses a shared resource, or when it does so, the lower priority process inherits the high priority. Using this method, P_3 would not be preempted by P_2 at t_2 in Figure 6.5, even though P_2 has a higher priority than P_1 and is unrelated to it. Again, some unnecessary priority inversion remains. This would be especially bothersome if P_1 did not enter the system until much later, say, after P_3 completed.

The priority inversion problem in real-time systems has been studied intensively in recent years, particularly at Carnegie Mellon University. This work has lead to a satisfactory class of solutions for accessing shared data and resources [Sha,Rajkumar& Lehoczky90]. These solutions are called *priority inheritance* protocols. Most of the subsequent presentation is based directly on this research.

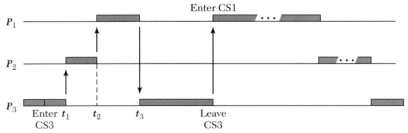

Figure 6.6 Priority inheritance.

The basic idea is to temporarily raise the priority of a process only if and when it actually blocks a higher priority one; on leaving the critical section, the process priority reverts to its original value. Thus, in our example above, P_3's priority would be raised to that of P_1 at time t_3, resulting in the execution sequence of Figure 6.6. P_1 is blocked for at most the length of $CS3$.

The protocol is defined when more than one higher priority task is competing for a locked critical section. If a process P in a critical section blocks the execution of higher priority tasks $P_1, \ldots, P_n$, then P will execute the critical section at a level equal to the highest priority of $P_1, \ldots, P_n$. The scheme also applies to nested critical sections or resource accesses. For example, in the following code skeleton, the critical section protected by $S2$ ($CS12$) is nested inside that protected by the lock $S1$.

```
begin ... lock(S1); CS11; lock(S2); CS12; unlock(S2); CS13; unlock(S1); ... end
```

A process will continue to inherit the highest priority of those it blocks. On leaving a critical section (*unlock* operation), an inherited priority may decrease. A process will always execute at its original (uninherited) priority after it exits its outermost critical section.

Blocking times using the basic priority inheritance protocol are predictable but may be large in the worst case. Provided that the processes do not deadlock (discussed below), the following results can be proven formally. A process P can block no longer than the execution times of the (outermost) critical sections of processes with lower priorities; each lower priority process can block P for at most the time to execute one of its critical sections. Also, if a task can be blocked by m semaphores, its blocking time is bounded by the time it takes to execute m critical sections of lower priority tasks.

▶ Example: Multilevel Blocking

Consider three processes with code skeletons as below and relative priorities $\pi_{P1} > \pi_{P2} > \pi_{P3}$.

```
P1:: begin ... lock(S1); CS1 ; unlock(S1); ... end
P2:: begin .. lock(S1); CS21; lock(S2); CS22; unlock(S2); CS23; unlock(S1); ..
     end
P3:: begin ... lock(S2); CS3 ; unlock(S2); ... end
```

One possible execution sequence is sketched in Figure 6.7. P_3 starts first at time t_0 and obtains S2 at t_1. P_2 enters at t_2, preempts P_3, and locks S1 at t_3. P_1 now enters at t_4 and preempts P_2. When P_1 tries to obtain S1 at t_5, it blocks. P_2 then continues after in-

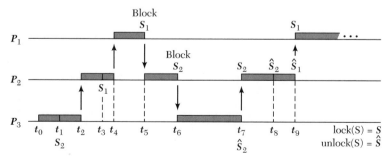

Figure 6.7 Multilevel blocking.

heriting P_1's priority. At t_6, P_2 requests $S2$ and is blocked since $S2$ is still held by P_3. The priority of P_2, the inherited π_{P1}, is then inherited by P_3 which executes until it releases $S2$ at t_7. P_3's priority then reverts back to its original value. P_2 then preempts P_3 and runs until it unlocks $S1$ at t_9, reverting back to its original priority. P_1 preempts P_2, locks $S1$, and completes its execution. Note that P_1 is blocked for the execution of most of both $CS3$ and $CS21$ through $CS23$. ◆

It would clearly be desirable if worst case blocking bounds were smaller. Also, there is nothing in the basic protocol that prevents processes from entering deadlock states. For example, suppose two processes have nested critical sections:

```
P1:: ... lock(S1); ... lock(S2); ... unlock(S2); ... unlock(S1); ...
P2:: ... lock(S2); ... lock(S1); ... unlock(S1); ... unlock(S2); ...
```

If P_1 has higher priority, then the sequence of Figure 6.8 leads to a deadlock at time t_2. P_1 has $S1$ and is requesting $S2$; P_2 has $S2$ and wants $S1$. A standard solution to this problem is to insist that all resources, that is, semaphores in our examples, are requested in the same order. However, this is not always convenient or efficient.

An elegant and clever protocol that reduces both the worst case blocking time and prevents deadlock is the *priority ceiling protocol*. The *priority ceiling* of a lock, resource, or semaphore S, denoted PC(S), is defined as the highest priority of all processes that may lock S. The protocol states that a task P that attempts to lock a semaphore will be suspended unless its priority is higher than PC(S) for all S currently locked by all tasks $Q \neq P$. If P is suspended, then the task Q that holds the lock with the highest PC is considered to be blocking P; Q then inherits P's priority, much the same way as in the inheritance protocol.

Consider the last two examples again. For the multilevel blocking example (Figure 6.7), we have these priority ceilings:

$$\text{PC}(S1) = \max(\pi_{P1}, \pi_{P2}) = \pi_{P1}$$
$$\text{PC}(S2) = \max(\pi_{P2}, \pi_{P3}) = \pi_{P2}$$

If the processes enter and request at the same times as above, we obtain the execution sequence of Figure 6.9. At time t_3, P_2 is suspended because its priority is not higher than PC($S2$); P_3, which holds $S2$, then inherits P_2's priority. This is the key step in the protocol. P_1 preempts when it enters at t_4, and executes to completion. Note that P_1 has no blocking in this scenario and P_2 is blocked for at most the length of $CS3$.

The priority ceilings in the deadlock example (Figure 6.8) are

$$\text{PC}(S1) = \text{PC}(S2) = \max(\pi_{P1}, \pi_{P2}) = \pi_{P1}.$$

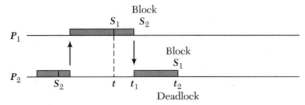

Figure 6.8 Deadlock example.

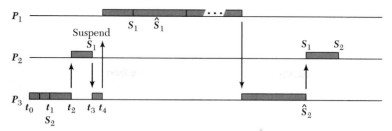

Figure 6.9 Priority ceiling: blocking.

If we now try to repeat the sequence of Figure 6.8, a different decision is made at time t (Figure 6.10). P_1 is suspended because its priority is not higher than PC($S2$), and P_2 inherits P_1's priority. When P_2 exits $S2$, it receives its original priority again, and is preempted. Thus, there is no deadlock.

A process can be blocked by a lower priority process only once and for no longer than the execution time of a critical section. [Sha,Rajkumar&Lehoczky90] also prove the following sufficient condition for feasible RM scheduling of n periodic processes under all task phasings:

$$U + \max(B_1/p_1, \ldots, B_{n-1}/p_{n-1}) \leq n\,(2^{1/n} - 1),$$

where B_i is the blocking time that process P_i can experience from a lower priority task and p_i is the period of process P_i. The processes are assumed to be ordered by priority, with P_1 highest. B_n is zero since P_n is the lowest priority process. Based on these properties, the priority ceiling protocol is clearly superior to the simpler inheritance scheme. The principal reason for also using simple priority inheritance is its less complex implementation (see next section).

This development applies directly to systems with fixed priorities, such as RM. Similar priority inheritance and priority ceiling protocols have also been adapted for dynamic priorities, particularly EDF (e.g., [Stankovic_et_al98]).

▶ EXERCISES 6.4

1. Consider the processes P_1 and P_2 described in the text and deadlocked in Figure 6.8. Trace an execution sequence in which P_1 blocks on lock S_1, deadlock does not occur, and priority inheritance is used.

2. Assume the processes and code skeletons given in the first example of the section, and the scenario in Figure 6.5 up to time t_3. Trace the execution sequence from t_3 onward using the priority ceiling protocol.

3. Code skeletons for three processes are sketched next. Assume that $\pi_{P1} > \pi_{P2} > \pi_{P3}$.

```
P1:: begin ... lock(S1); CS11; lock(S2);
     CS12; unlock(S2); CS13; unlock(S1); ...
     end
```

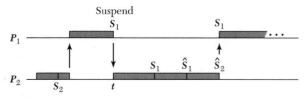

Figure 6.10 Priority ceiling: No deadlock.

```
P2:: begin ... lock(S2); CS21; lock(S3);
   CS22; unlock(S3); CS23; unlock(S2); ...
   end
P3:: begin ... lock(S3); CS31; lock(S1);
   CS32; unlock(S1); CS33; unlock(S3); ...
   end
```

(a) Exhibit an execution sequence that leads to deadlock, assuming that no priority inversion protocol is used.
(b) Show how the priority ceiling protocol would prevent your deadlock scenario in (a).

► 6.5 SOME PRACTICAL ISSUES

The theory presented in the previous sections is based on simple models of periodic processes that may be violated and that don't include certain practical system features. Here are some examples. Computation time estimates are occasionally exceeded; overloads occur; the relative importance of tasks isn't reflected by standard priority methods; tasks must also satisfy precedence relationships among each other; synchronization and blocking costs may not be accounted for; and overheads, such as context-switching times due to preemptions, may not be factored into an analysis or a simulation, and may consume too much time. However, despite many limitations, scheduling theory is surprisingly useful for analyzing and scheduling real systems.

Many engineers argue convincingly that scheduling must be done *before* run time in order to assure predictability in hard real-time systems; that is, the allocation of processors to particular tasks at each unit of time is predetermined [Xu&Parnas93]. This requires, of course, accurate knowledge of task characteristics. The cyclic executive approach described in Section 2.2 relies upon such pre-run-time scheduling. Given a set of periodic processes, a reasonable pre-run-time technique is to adopt RM, LST, or EDF as heuristics, and attempt to compute a feasible schedule over the least common multiple of the periods. A successful schedule can then be placed in a table or "hard-wired" in the code of a simple and efficient run-time dispatcher. Note that failure to produce a feasible schedule with this method does not mean that one doesn't exist, since the assumptions under which the schedule was attempted may be too restrictive or conservative.

When nonpreemptive scheduling blocks are known a priori, it is also easy to incorporate *context-switching* times, the time required to store the state of a task and resume the state of another one. Assume that this time is bounded by δ. Then, it suffices to replace the compute time c of each block by $c + \delta$, before trying to compute a schedule. In more dynamic situations where processes are arbitrarily preemptible based on priorities, simulations may be used to confirm theoretical schedulability analyses. The preemption time δ can be added in directly during a simulated execution.

Processes and their subparts often must obey *precedence* constraints that further restrict and complicate scheduling. For example, a sensor task that acquires data must precede an analysis task that manipulates the acquired data. Such task relations can be represented by a precedence graph as illustrated in Figure 6.11(a). This is an acyclic directed graph with a start node N and edges denoting processes. Starting from N, if a process P precedes a process Q on any directed path, then P must terminate before Q can start. Thus, in the figure, P_5 cannot start until both P_3 and P_4 have terminated.

Precedence relationships could exist among a set of tasks that were initially activated by some event, such as a mode change, or they could be required among a set of periodic processes or *sub*processes having the same period. They also occur naturally among distributed processes that communicate—message senders precede message re-

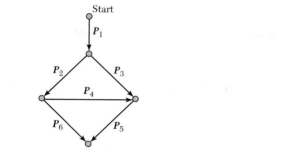

(a) Constraint graph.

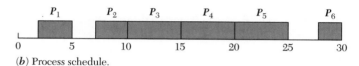

(b) Process schedule.

Figure 6.11 Precedence constraints.

ceivers. In the simplest case where all processes in a graph are released at the same time, have deadlines and known computation times, and do not interact, some straightforward heuristics can be used to determine schedulability on a single processor.

One such algorithm orders the processes by deadline and makes a schedule starting with a process P having the largest deadline and no successor [Krishna&Shin97]. P is then scheduled to complete at exactly its deadline. The algorithm then iterates over unscheduled processes that have the largest deadlines and have scheduled successors (when such successors exist) at each point scheduling the selected process as late as possible.

Figure 6.11(b) shows the results of this algorithm for the task set of (a), assuming the deadlines and execution times, d and c, respectively, are the (d, c) pairs:

$$(5, 3), (10, 3), (20, 5), (25, 5), (25, 5), \text{ and } (30, 2),$$

in the order P_1 through P_6. Thus P_6 is selected first and scheduled from time 28 through 30, then P_5 (alternatively, P_4) is chosen and scheduled to complete at its deadline 25. If the schedule works, as it does in the example, it can then be tightened by pushing it back through any idle or slack times; in our example, the three idle blocks can be filled in by moving the processes left, resulting in a feasible schedule in the interval 0 to 23. If the schedule does not meet all deadlines, and there exist idle blocks, then it is possible that the tightening phase will generate a feasible schedule by causing processes to terminate earlier.

The optimal scheduling methods presented earlier select priorities to ensure a feasible schedule for all processes. There is no relationship between the importance of a task and its assigned priority. However, in real systems, deadlines are occasionally missed. Load estimates on systems resources are often deliberately lower than absolute achievable worst cases because worst cases may occur infrequently and because designing for worst cases can be too expensive; for example, the minimum separation time estimate for sporadic processes may be deliberately higher than worst case, resulting in occasional overloads. Computation time estimates may be incorrect, perhaps deliberately, in order to obtain high CPU utilizations for most behaviors; or the system may be subjected to unpredictable sporadic or transient overloads.

In these situations, it could easily be the case that the least important processes miss their deadlines or exceed their time estimates first, and thereby cause a more important one to also fail. A clever way to take advantage of the theory and still give highest priority to the most critical processes was suggested by [Sha,Lehoczky& Rajkumar87]. They outline a *period transformation* technique to solve this problem. We illustrate their method with RM scheduling.

The basic idea is to transform a lower priority important process $P = (c, p, d)$ into a pseudoprocess $P' = (c/k, p/k, d/k)$. P' has a smaller period and hence a higher priority than P. The pseudoprocess is fictitious—instead of P being executed as one unit, it is executed as k sequential instances of P', each instance a different portion of the original P. This division of the process into smaller units is similar to that performed in the cyclic executive method (Section 2.2) when decomposing a process into scheduling blocks. The execution can be controlled by the scheduler without making any direct changes to P. The scheduler must suspend and save the state of P after executing for c/k time units; it must also keep track of which part of P is in execution, that is, the value of k.

▶ Example 1

Let the original processes be $P_1 = (6, 20, 20)$ and $P_2 = (15, 30, 30)$, and assume RM scheduling, as in Figure 6.4(b). If P_1 were the least critical of the two and occasionally missed its deadline (or even exceeded its computation time estimate by a modest amount), then P_2 would automatically miss its deadline shortly thereafter. However, if P_2 were transformed into three instances of the higher priority pseudoprocess $P'_2 = (5, 10, 10)$, it would continue to perform its function even as P_1 fails. ◆

Algorithm M has much appeal due to its simplicity, but unfortunately it does not seem directly practical in general settings. For n periodic processes, it would require n context switches for every unit of time, and would need a clock that provided an accurate tick after each c_i/p_i interval. However, there are some cases where a slightly modified version of the method is indeed useful. In particular, let r be the greatest common divisor of the periods and suppose that each rc_i/p_i evaluates to an integer. Then a tick length of one can be employed for an efficient implementation, where the allocation sequence is repeated every r units. This scheme works for both uniprocessor and multiprocessor scheduling.

▶ Example 2

Let $P_1 = (3, 5, 5)$, $P_2 = (2, 10, 10)$ and $P_3 = (3, 15, 15)$. CPU utilization is 100%. The greatest common divisor of the periods is gcd(5, 10, 15) = 5. During each five unit time interval, P_1 receives $(5 \times 3)/5 = 3$ units of CPU time, P_2 receives $(5 \times 2)/10 = 1$ unit, and P_3 is allocated $(5 \times 3)/15 = 1$ unit. ◆

Most of the other theoretical insights for multiprocessor scheduling are negative (Section 6.3), and provide little insight for actual systems. Because of this, practical scheduling schemes for these architectures are usually based on static pre-allocation of processes to each machine. A static allocation policy seems to be the most practical approach for distributed systems for the same reasons. The alternative extreme of a centralized scheduler with tasks "migrating" among computers seems to reduce both schedulability and predictability. However, there are some arguments to be made for handling sporadic processes and overloads using centralized dispatching, since unused CPU capacity can often be determined and allocated dynamically.

Much of the RM and priority inheritance theory has been applied to real-time programs, for example, [Sha,Rajkumar&Sathaye94]. It has also strongly influenced the design of real-time operating systems and the real-time "annex" in the Ada 95 language (see Chapters 9 and 10). In particular, many fixed priority systems now allow some controlled priority changes during synchronization activities to accommodate inheritance policies. A noteworthy application was in the operating software for the Pathfinder mission to Mars in 1997. A serious priority inversion occurred, but was later discovered and corrected by turning on the priority inheritance mechanism for a semaphore lock.[1]

The basic priority inheritance protocol can be implemented in a straightforward manner, local to each semaphore or lock. As part of a *lock(S)* operation, if the process would be blocked, the priority of the holder of S is raised. On an *unlock(S)*, the priority may be decreased depending on the identity of the processes blocked on S if any. The lock holding and blocked processes could all be linked through the semaphore's data structure as usual.

The priority ceiling protocol seems to require some major changes to the system data structures, replacing the standard global ready list and local blocked process list normally associated with each semaphore. [Sha,Rajkumar&Lehoczky90] suggest two global lists—a *ready+* list and a *sem_locked* list. The *ready+* list contains the currently executing process, the ready processes, and all processes that have been blocked under the priority ceiling protocol; the list is ordered by priority, so that the highest priority process is at the front and running. All semaphores that are currently locked are stored on the *sem_locked* list, in priority ceiling order.

▶ EXERCISES 6.5

1. Suppose that a system has n periodic processes $P_i = (c_i, p_i, d_i)$, $i = 1 .. n$, where $n > 1$ and $p_i = d_i$. RM scheduling is used.

(a) How many context switches (preemptions) occur in the worst case over the lcm of the periods?

Hint: Derive the worst case number of preemptions made by the highest priority process over the lcm.

(b) Let the context switch time be fixed and equal to δ. How could you use this time and the results of (a) for a more realistic RM analysis?

2. Consider the example of Figure 6.11.
(a) Change the deadlines of both P_4 and P_5 to 20. Can you make a feasible schedule following the same algorithm?
(b) Change the execution time of P_6 to 6. Can you make a feasible schedule using the algorithm of the text?

3. Give detailed algorithms for the semaphore *lock* and *unlock* operations with the basic priority inheritance protocol.

---

[1]The story behind this can be found at the following web site and its links: http://www.research.microsoft.com/~mjb/Mars_Pathfinder/Mars_Pathfinder.html

CHAPTER 7

Execution Time Prediction

A central problem of computer science is to predict the execution time of a program. More general predictive reasoning about and with time can only be performed after this problem is solved. For a real-time system, it is clearly important to know the program's timing behavior *before* it is deployed, that is, before the "start" button is pressed for the first time.

In this chapter, we present the principal techniques for predicting the deterministic timing behavior of computer software. Emphasis is on execution time prediction. Measurement and analysis methods are treated in detail after our overall framework and some general issues are discussed.

▶ 7.1 APPROACHES AND ISSUES

A major goal is to determine worst case execution times—the "c" of the (c, p, d) characterization of periodic and sporadic processes. It is also useful to have best case bounds, that is, numbers or expressions that give the earliest times that programs will terminate. Doing something too quickly is often as undesirable as doing it too slowly. For example, raising the flaps on an aircraft or applying the brakes on a vehicle too soon may be as dangerous or incorrect as doing it too late; a softer example appears in some telephone systems, where the artificial ring that a caller hears after dialing a number, indicating reassuringly that the callee's phone is ringing, is programmed to start after some minimum waiting time. Thus, one may have deadlines for both the lower and the upper bounds on computation times.

The execution of a program or statement S can be delimited by two events, a *start* execution event and an *end* event. Analogous start and end events for actions, denoted $\uparrow A$ and $\downarrow A$, were specified for assertions in real-time logic (RTL) in Section 5.3. For a particular execution of S, the time between these two events is denoted by $t(S)$. Expressed in RTL, the ith execution of S takes time

$$t(S) = @(\uparrow S, i) - @(\downarrow S, i).$$

In general, for any particular execution or for any set of executions, the best that can be predicted a priori is a set of bounds

$$T(S) = [t_{\min}(S), t_{\max}(S)] \,,$$

where $t_{\min}(S)$ is an estimate for the best case running time and $t_{\max}(S)$ is a worst case estimate.

Two desirable properties for these bounds are that they be *safe* and *tight*. $T(S)$ is defined to be safe if

$$t_{\min}(S) \le t(S) \le t_{\max}(S)$$

for all valid executions of S, where a valid execution is one with correct and specified inputs and outputs. A tight prediction is one where there exist executions at or near the predicted bounds. The bounds are perfectly tight if the best case execution is indeed $t_{\min}$ and the worst case is exactly $t_{\max}$.

For sequential programs, more general reasoning about time can be accomplished with some straightforward extensions to program logic, provided that execution times $T(S)$ are known [Shaw89a]. Standard Hoare logic [Hoare69] uses assertions P and Q around a statement or statements S, with the notation

$$\{P\} \ S \ \{Q\}.$$

The meaning is

> If P is true before the execution of S, then Q will be true after executing S, if and when the execution terminates.

The assertions are essentially Boolean functions of the program variables and state. S could be as small as a simple basic statement or as large as an entire program.

▶ Example of Program Assertions

The following statements compute a closest integer approximation to the square root of a nonnegative integer n. The assertions around the program fragment declare the intended initial and final relations among the program variables.

```
{ n ≥ 0 }
a := 0;
while (a+1)² ≤ n loop a := a+1; end loop;
{ ( a² ≤ n ) ∧ ( a + 1 )² > n } ♦
```

Let rt be perfect global real time, for example, as defined and used in Section 3.3.2. Then, with exact knowledge of timing, we could extend the above notation to

$$\{P\} < S \ ; rt := rt + t(S) > \{Q\},$$

where the brackets $(< >)$ mean that the execution of S and incrementing of rt occur simultaneously, and the assertions P and Q can now also include relations involving rt. It is assumed that the incrementing and assignment to rt takes zero time.

The axiom of assignment can then be used to prove assertions that contain time. Recall that this axiom states:

$$\{Q(expr)\} \ x := expr \ \{Q(x)\}.$$

That is, if the assertion $Q(x)$ is to hold after executing the assignment $x := expr$, then $Q(expr)$ must be true before executing the statement, where $Q(expr)$ is Q with $expr$ substituted for x. If the assertion P is a function of rt and possibly other variables, $P = P(rt, \dots)$, one can assert either

$$\{P(rt, \dots)\}S \{P(rt - t(S), \dots)\}$$
$$\text{or}$$
$$\{P\{rt + t(S), \dots)\}S \{P\{rt, \dots)\}.$$

These results are obtained by employing the axiom on the assignment $rt := rt + t(S)$. Note that the value of rt before executing S is different (smaller) than its value after S, since rt is always increasing.

▶ Example: Deadline Assertions

Let dl be an absolute time deadline on the execution of S; that is, the assertion $\{rt \leq dl\}$ is to hold after S's execution. Using the second form, one can assert

$$\{rt + t(S) \leq dl\} \ S \ \{rt \leq dl\}.$$

Stated in words with some re-arrangement, the notation means that if $rt \leq dl - t(S)$ before S, then the dl deadline holds after S. ◆

These ideas can be generalized to handle time intervals or bounds that represent our imperfect knowlege of execution times. Real time will be known only by its bounds rt_{min} and rt_{max}, so that at any time we have $rt_{min} \leq rt \leq rt_{max}$. Let $RT = [rt_{min}, rt_{max}]$. Then, the more general proof rule makes assertions about RT and has this form:

$$\{P\} < S \ ; RT := RT + T(S) > \{Q\},$$

where P and Q can include relations involving the two bounds of RT. The RT assignment is an abbreviation for the two statements

$$rt_{min} := rt_{min} + t_{min}(S)$$

and

$$rt_{max} := rt_{max} + t_{max}(S) .$$

A naming conflict problem with RT arises when statements are composed. A simple solution [Haase81] is to introduce a new local variable RT_0 for each statement and replace the above with

$$\{P\} < RT_0 := RT; S \ ; RT := RT_0 + T(S) > \{Q\} .$$

It is assumed that the first statement, "$RT_0 := RT;$" takes zero time and is executed immediately at the start of S, that is, at $\uparrow S$.

▶ Example: Deadline Bounds

Let $DL = [dl_{min}, dl_{max}]$ be absolute time deadlines such that a program S must be completed no later than dl_{max} and no earlier than dl_{min}. This general deadline and safety requirement can be expressed

$$\{(RT + T(S)) \text{ in } DL\} \ S \ \{RT \text{ in } DL\} \ ,$$

where the notation

$$[a, b] \text{ in } [c, d]$$

means that $a \geq c$ and $b \leq d$, that is, the interval $[a, b]$ is inside $[c, d]$. The assertions can be proven directly from the assignment axiom. From this, one can conclude that at $\uparrow S$, the *start* event of S, real-time rt must be bounded as

$$dl_{min} - t_{min}(S) \leq rt \leq dl_{max} - t_{max}(S) \ . \ \blacklozenge$$

A Digression on Interval Arithmetic

The bounded intervals that are employed here and in later sections are identical to the *interval numbers* defined and analyzed in [Moore66]. Arithmetic on these intervals, for example, for the expression $RT+T(S)$ above, is defined as follows for any binary operator ø in $\{+, \times, -, /\}$:

$$[a, b] \ ø \ [c, d] = [\min(u \ ø \ v), \max(y \ ø \ z)],$$

where $a \leq u, \ y \leq b$ and $c \leq v, z \leq d$. (For division, intervals that cross zero are undefined as "denominators.") Addition is straightforward, but the results for the other operators are less obvious.

An insightful way to understand this arithmetic is to treat an interval as a set

$$[a, b] = \{ x : a \leq x \leq b\}.$$

Then, the general result for these binary operators can be restated

$$[a, b] \ ø \ [c, d] = \{x \ ø \ y : x \text{ in } [a, b] \text{ and } y \text{ in } [c, d]\}.$$

► **Examples**

$$[4, 5] + [3, 70] = [7, 75]; \ [3, 6] \times [2, 5] = [6, 30];$$
$$[-3, 6] \times [-11, 5] = [-66, 33]; \ [4, 10] - [2, 6] = [-2, 8]; \ [10, 20] / [2, 5] = [2, 10]. \ \blacklozenge$$

❂   ❂   ❂

How can execution times $T(S)$ be predicted? There are at least three general approaches to this problem. The most obvious solution is to actually run the program of interest and *measure* its execution times. A second common set of methods relies on *simulation*. The program and its environment are modelled, and the model is executed or interpreted to produce performance estimates. A third standard approach is based on *analysis*. Execution time predictions are obtained by mathematical analysis of a model of the system. In practice, all three methods may be attempted for a given system.

Prediction of deterministic bounds by measurement is an attractive and important technique, but the method cannot always be applied in practice. The best and worst case paths through a program are seldom obvious, and they are often difficult to find. Unless great care is taken, it is easy to miss an extreme case and produce results that are not safe. Interferences from an operating system, from the measuring procedure itself, or from hardware, such as interrupts and bus contentions, can be unpredictable and change from run to run. Measurements, which are normally made on machine language, are not always easy to relate to source program sections; making such relations is desirable so that bottlenecks may be discovered, source language changes made, and assertional reasoning, for example in RTL or the Hoare-like logic just presented, can be done. The effects of changes in hardware and software are also difficult to predict. Finally, for truly accurate measurements, the system must be run while performing its real-time mission, which may be impractical because of the high costs associated with failures.

Simulation prevents some of the problems mentioned, but introduces new ones. It allows the engineer to abstract the system and focus on the performance of particular parts. In principle, it is possible to perform many experiments without incurring the failure costs of a real system. Simulation can be done at any of several levels of hardware or software. A typical approach is to compile the real-time software into object code, and run it on a simulated architecture and physical environment. Here, one has the same problems as in the measurement case of obtaining the correct shortest and longest paths, reasoning, and discovering the effects of changes; in addition, it is difficult to simulate computers and their environments accurately and in an error-predictable way. This approach has been studied in several research efforts, notably in the work on Real-Time Euclid (Section 9.5) [Stoyenko87] and in [Mok_et_al89].

Analytic methods permit source program reasoning about execution times and other behaviors, and a high degree of experimentation. They are the most abstract of the three approaches, and care must be taken so that important practical system properties are not excluded from the models. In the next three sections, prediction techniques first using measurements and then analysis are presented and evaluated.

Several issues and complexities need to be addressed when attempting to determine execution times of application programs. There is the underlying family of machines or architectures on which the programs are intended to run. Modern hardware systems are designed to achieve high performance *most* of the time, rather than to minimize worst case times. The result is that their deterministic timing properties are often unknown and difficult to determine. Performance enhancing features, such as instruction and data caches, translation look-aside buffers, and instruction and data pipelining contribute to this problem. The effects of concurrent activities, for example, IO processors, CPUs, and timers contending for and accessing memories, buses, and processors, are also typically nondeterministic.

An operating system that manages the computer resources resides between the hardware and the application programs. The behavior of this systems software, for example, interrupt handling, IO, and scheduling times, must also be factored into any timing measurement or analysis. Generally, there may be a substantial difference between the execution time of a program when run in isolation and its execution time when run with other system software. It is also the case that different compilers and run-time support packages produce different object codes, and hence different execution times for the same program. Some ideas on incorporating hardware and software interferences into execution time predictions are discussed in Section 7.5.

▶ EXERCISES 7.1

1. Let dl be the relative deadline for the execution of a statement S. Show informally that

$$\{(rt \leq t_{start}) \wedge (dl \geq t(S))\} \; S \; \{rt \leq t_{start} + dl\}.$$

2. Let RT_{start} and DL be real-time bounds, and S a program statement.

(a) Argue informally the truth of

$$\{(RT = RT_{start}) \wedge (T(S) \text{ in } DL)\} \; S \; \{RT \text{ in } (RT_{start} + DL)\}.$$

(b) Give bounds on rt_{min} and rt_{max} after the execution of S, assuming the postcondition of (a).

3. Compute values for x and y in the following expressions in interval arithmetic.

(a) $[x, y] = [20, 30] - [10, 15]$.

(b) $[x, y] + [10, 20] = [35, 55]$.

(c) $[x, y] - [3, 12] = [5, 20]$.

▶ 7.2 MEASUREMENT OF SOFTWARE BY SOFTWARE

Execution times of programs can be obtained by direct measurements using software probes. This might be done in order to predict execution times, to check that run-time behaviors meet requirements, to validate an analytic method, to provide data for simulations, or to track the actual performance of a system. Elements that may need to be timed include complete applications, individual programs, procedures and functions, code blocks, higher-level language constructs, and even single machine level instructions. In addition to performance data on applications software, execution times for various systems components are also typically desired or required. Examples of such systems code blocks or functions include interrupt handlers, context-switching mechanisms, schedulers, synchronization routines, clock and delay functions, and input–output programs.

Suppose that S is a self-contained body of code, containing no input–output or other system calls. To obtain the execution time for S, we need a timer or clock. Let *Clock* be a function that returns the current value of time. Then the simple way to measure the performance of S is to call *Clock* immediately before and after running S, as in the following *test* program:

```
-- Test Program 1
t_start := Clock ;
S ;
t_finish := Clock ;
test_time := t_finish - t_start ;
```

This might produce a satisfactory approximation to the desired value in the variable *test_time*. However, for many cases, regrettably, the technique is too simple.

One problem is that the overhead in computing *test_time* is not taken into account. This overhead involves at least the time of two calls to the *Clock* function and the assignments to *t_start* and *t_finish*. The overhead time can be found by running the following control program, which essentially substitutes the *null* program for S in the above:

```
-- Control Program
t_start := Clock ;
-- This line is empty. It is the null program.
t_finish := Clock ;
control_time := t_finish - t_start ;
```

The running time of S is then the difference:

```
S_time = test_time - control_time.
```

Some other sources of inaccuracy are due to interferences from the underlying operating system. Disabling interrupts during a timing run will assure that no operating systems tasks preempt the test or control tasks. However, it is not always possible to disable interrupts; for example, the clock itself is often driven by periodic "tick" interrupts. These and other hardware interferences are discussed in Section 7.5.

Finally, there may be significant errors due to the tick granularity and accuracy of the clock. Let ct be the time returned from the *Clock* function, p be the tick period or tick interval, and rt be perfect real time. Assume that ct is updated to real time at each tick, and is immediately available at that time (no overhead on the update), as illustrated in Figure 7.1.

If *Clock* is called at real-time rt, then the time ct returned will satisfy the relation

$$ct = rt - \delta p , 0 \le \delta < 1.$$

Therefore, ct will be in error and early by as much as p.[1] Consider now the difference Δct obtained from two calls of *Clock*:

$$\Delta ct = ct_2 - ct_1 = rt_2 - \delta_2 p - rt_1 + \delta_1 p = \Delta rt \pm \varepsilon,$$

where $\varepsilon < p$. Thus, the difference between two clock times will have an error bounded by p. The *S_time* will then have a maximum error of $2p$, since it is the difference between two differences. In addition, the clock's tick may not occur exactly "on-time."

To overcome these problems, it is common to time the execution of many instances of S in a loop, and eventually divide by the loop count to get a better approximation to S's time. A test program that executes n instances of S is

```
-- Test Program 2
t_start := Clock;
for i in 1 . . n loop
        S ;
end loop;
t_finish := Clock;
test_time := t_finish - t_start ;
```

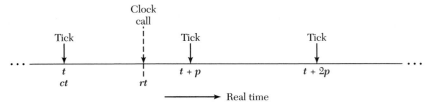

Figure 7.1   Relations among clock variables.

---

[1] One could compensate for this error by adding $0.5p$ to ct.

The control program is exactly the same as above, substituting the *null* statement for *S* in the loop. The control program now measures the *Clock* and loop overheads. We have the relation

$$test\_time - control\_time = n \times S\_time + error,$$

where *error* is bounded by 2*p*. Rearranging terms, this gives

$$S\_time = (test\_time - control\_time)/n + error/n.$$

If the loop count *n* is sufficiently large, the error term can be ignored. This is essentially the technique used in [Park92] and taken from [Clapp_et_al86], for validating an analytic technique.

[Clapp_et_al86] presents methods for measuring the performance of various constructs in the Ada language. For measuring higher-level language elements, it is also necessary to prevent the compiler from performing optimizations that might invalidate the timing data. Typical optimizations remove code from a loop or eliminate loops entirely if possible, for example, in the case of a *null* statement in the loop. A general solution to this problem is to embed *S* and the null program in procedures, say *S_proc* and *null_proc*, respectively, substitute a *while* loop for the *for* loop, and use a procedure to increment the loop index. For example, the test program may now become

```
-- Test Program 3
t_start := Clock ; i := 0 ;
while i < n loop
        S_proc ;
        Increment(i) ;
end loop ;
t_finish := Clock ;
test_time := t_finish - t_start ;
```

The presented techniques apply to a particular single execution encapsulated in *S*, and without explicit inputs or outputs. The inputs are defined implicitly by initializing variables of *S* with input values. To obtain best or worst case executions of a program, it would be necessary to select appropriate initializations (inputs) for these situations. While such a task is theoretically unsolvable in general, it can be approached in many practical instances. For example, standard software testing methods that attempt to provide control flow edge or path coverage may be employed (e.g., [Ghezzi_et_al91b]). Another approach, developed in the next sections, uses pure analytic methods to determine best and worst case paths and to predict execution times.

► EXERCISES 7.2

1. Measure the execution time of a short program (run time of a few ms) and a medium one (a few seconds). Use an optimizing compiler if possible. For each program, measure their times with both the *for* loop and *while* loop techniques; note and explain any differences.

2. Are measurements repeatable in your computer system? Run a control and test loop several times for your programs in Question 1. Why might the results not be repeatable on your or another computer system?

3. Find a computer and operating system in which the timer service is driven by a periodic tick interrupt. What is the tick period? What is the granularity of the software clock, that is, the smallest unit of time returned?

▶ 7.3 PROGRAM ANALYSIS WITH TIMING SCHEMA

The methodologies discussed in the next two sections for predicting best and worst case execution times are based on reasoning at the *source program* level. Two approaches are developed, the first using timing schema and the second based on optimization ideas. In the timing schema approach, predictions are obtained directly from the source program by tracing shortest and longest paths [Shaw89a,91; Park&Shaw90; Park93]. [Puschner&Koza89] present some similar ideas and results for obtaining worst case computation times. A related method was first proposed in [Haase81].

7.3.1 Schema Concepts

The time bounds $T(S)$ for a statement S are defined in terms of the components of S by a *timing schema* that describes the best and worst case paths through S. The schema is simply an expression or formula that can be instantiated with particular statement elements. The basic requirement is that a programming language have *compositional* timing semantics roughly corresponding to its syntactic structure and meaning. For our purposes, compositionality means, for example, that the time bounds for a statement S that is composed of two statements, S_1 and S_2, can be expressed in terms of the bounds of its constituents. This can be stated as

$$T(S) = f(T(S_1), T(S_2)),$$

for some composition function f that depends on how S_1 and S_2 are combined in S.

The components of a schema could be objects of a variety of kinds including control, data, expression, and statement types. At the lowest level are elementary objects or components that have given time bounds. The bounds may be functions of the execution-time environment and implementation for the programming language, such as the compiler, run-time system, operating system, architecture, and machine cycle time. The lowest level objects are called *atomic blocks*. A simple example is a statement S consisting of two statements in sequence

$$S = S_1; S_2.$$

A reasonable timing schema for S is

$$T(S) = T(S_1) + T(S_2).$$

This assumes that the end event of S_1 occurs simultaneously with the start event of S_2; for example, in RTL,

$$@(\downarrow S_1, i) = @(\uparrow S_2, j),$$

for particular instances, i and j, of the execution of S_1 and S_2, respectively.

A more accurate formula might also include the sequencing control time, giving

$$T(S) = T(S_1) + T(S_2) + T(;),$$

where $T(;)$ denotes this sequencing time. ($T(;)$ might be significant and nonzero in an interpreted language, such as Java.)

A conventional conditional construct

$S = $ if B then S_1 else S_2 end if;

would typically have a timing behavior obtained from tracing the two paths through S. Let

$$[t_{1b}, t_{1w}] = T(B) + T(S_1) + T(then) \text{ and}$$
$$[t_{2b}, t_{2w}] = T(B) + T(S_2) + T(else),$$

where $T(B)$ is the execution bounds for evaluating B, $T(then)$ is the control time associated with executing the "then" path through the statement, and $T(else)$ is the control time for executing the "else" path. These paths are illustrated in the control flow graph for S in Figure 7.2.

The control costs are the times to transfer either to or around S_1 and S_2 in a standard implementation. Typically, $T(then) = 2T(else)$, where the times are simply those for conditional or unconditional branches. (b and w in the bound subscripts denote "best" and "worst," respectively.) Then

$$T(S) = [\min(t_{1b}, t_{2b}), \max(t_{1w}, t_{2w})].$$

The formula $T(S)$ for any construct S is obtained by tracing the shortest and longest paths through S through a *static* analysis of the program text. A fundamental part of the approach is to include control times and control atomic blocks in the schema. The pure model assumes no interferences from other software that may be running concurrently or from hardware such as interrupts.

The next section shows how schema can be defined for common program elements. We then discuss implementation methods that take the underlying compiler and machine architecture into account. An extension of the technique that also involves dynamic paths and includes run-time context is also outlined.

7.3.2 Basic Blocks, Statements, and Control

One choice for atomic blocks is the set of lexical objects of the programming language. Such atomic blocks are at a very fine granularity with respect to time and the language components. With this choice, we first consider schema for assignment statements and procedure/function calls of the form

$v := $ Exp and PF_name(E_1, . . . , E_n), respectively,

where v is a variable name, *Exp* is an expression, *PF_name* is a procedure or function name, and the E_i are the actual parameters of the procedure call. Each E_i can be an expression.

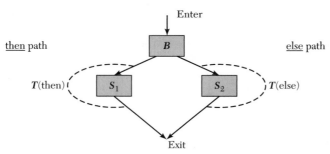

Figure 7.2   if/then/else paths.

For simplicity, assume that expressions have the syntax

```
Exp ::= v | c | PF_name(E₁, . . . , Eₙ) | ( Exp₁ ø Exp₂ ),
```

where c is a constant, $ø$ is a binary arithmetic operator, and the Exp_i are also expressions of type *Exp*. The addition of other expression types, such as those with unary operators, is straightforward.

The atomic blocks and their execution times may be obtained from a separate analysis of the compiler and target machine. A typical set for the above language fragment follows.

- $T(x)$: *Retrieve the value of a constant or variable x.*
  This may equal the time to load a register or it could be zero if the retrieval time is included as part of a binary operation.

- $T(.v)$: *Obtain the address of a variable v.*
  When an address is known at compile time, $T(.v) = [0, 0]$ for that variable.

- $T(:=)$: *Do an assignment.*
  Often, this is just the store time of the target machine.

- $T(ø)$: *Perform the binary operation ø.*
  For example, T could be the cost of doing a register-to-register operation.

- $T(c/r)$: *Call and return from a function or procedure.*

- $T(par)$: *Pass a parameter to a function or procedure.*
  Several variations may exist, such as $T(call\_by\_reference)$ and $T(call\_by\_value)$, describing different parameter passing methods.

A reasonable timing schema for the assignment statement is

$$T(v := Exp) = T(.v) + T(:=) + T(Exp).$$

Similarly, an expression might have the following schema, which depends on its form:

$$T(Exp) = \text{if } Exp=v \text{ then } T(v) \text{ -- atomic}$$
$$\text{else if } Exp=c \text{ then } T(c) \text{ -- atomic}$$
$$\text{else if } Exp=(Exp_1 \text{ ø } Exp_2) \text{ then } T(Exp_1)+T(ø)+T(Exp_2)$$
$$\text{else -- } Exp=PF\_name(E_1, \ldots, E_n) \ldots \text{ See below.}$$

A procedure or function call may have the behavior

$$T(PF\_name(E_1, \ldots, E_n)) = T(c/r) + n \times T(par) + T(PF\_body)$$
$$+ T(E_1) + \ldots + T(E_n),$$

where *PF_body* is the code body for the procedure. $T(E_i)$ may be zero if the parameter is a simple variable or constant; otherwise, it is equal to the cost of evaluating the expression.

▶ Examples: Assignment and Procedure Call

1. $T(\text{ a } := \text{ b } + \text{ c }) = T(.a) + T(:=) + T(b) + T(+) + T(c).$
2. Let $median(x, y, z)$ be a function with three parameters.

$T(\text{median(a+1, b/c, d)}) = T(c/r) + 3T(par) + T(median\_body) + T(a) +$
$\qquad T(+) + T(1) + T(b) + T(/) + T(c) + T(d).$

median_body is the code for the function *median*.

3. Consider the compilation of the statement in the first example. For one architecture, a compiler might produce this target code:

```
load b in R1
load c in R2
add R2 to R1
load address of a in R2
store R1 in R2 indirect.
```

This corresponds in a straightforward way to each atomic block; for example, $T(.a) = T(\text{load address of a in R2})$. A compiler for a different machine could produce this code:

```
load b in R1
add c to R1
store R1 in a.
```

Here $T(.a) = T(c) = [0, 0]$. ◆

Timing schema for conditional statements, such as *if/then/else* or *case*, are derived from abstractions of standard realizations. As an example, we use a general *if/then/else*:

```
if B₁ then S₁ elsif B₂ then S₂ elsif . . . elsif Bₙ then Sₙ end if;
```

The meaning can be expressed in terms of more primitive objects:

```
              < B₁ >
        Transfer on false to 2
              < S₁ >
        Transfer to next
   2 :        < B₂ >
        Transfer on false to 3
              < S₂ >
        Transfer to next
   3 :          .

                .

                .
   n :        < Bₙ >
        Transfer on false to next
              < Sₙ >
   next : ...
```

The primitive objects for a construct X are denoted by $< X >$ in the above.

The transfer instructions *Transfer on false to x* and *Transfer to x* are the control flow objects for the *if/then/else* statement. Assume for simplicity that conditional and unconditional transfers take the same time, denoted by $T(if)$. Then, the bounds for the statement are the best and worst case paths, which may be computed as follows. First, we give an expression for the time bounds when any S_k is selected and executed.

Let $[t_{kb}, t_{kw}]$ be the time bounds for executing an arbitrary S_k, which includes the time to pass through the preceding Booleans. Then,

$$[t_{kb}, t_{kw}] = T(S_k) + \min(k+1, n) \times T(\mathit{if}) + \sum_{i=1}^{k} T(B_i), \text{ for } k = 1, \ldots, n.$$

By convention, when a scalar s is used in an interval expression, it is interpreted as a pair $[s, s]$. In the above, $\min(k+1, n)$ evaluates to a scalar. Then,

$$T(\mathit{if}\ B_1\ \mathit{then}\ S_1\ \mathit{elsif} \ldots \mathit{elsif}\ B_n\ \mathit{then}\ S_n\ \mathit{end\ if}) = [t_b, t_w],$$

with $t_b = \min\limits_{k \le n}\left(\min(t_{bk}), n \times t_{\min}(\mathit{if}) + \sum_{i=1}^{n} t_{\min}(B_i)\right)$ and $t_w = \max(t_{kw})$ over all k.

Manual computation of these times is clearly a lengthy and error-prone task.

Loops are less tedious but more interesting. Some analysis is necessary in order to bound the number of iterations through a loop. To illustrate the ideas, consider the classical *while* statement

```
while B loop S end loop;
```

A natural implementation is

```
start:    < B >
          Transfer on false to next
              < S >
          Transfer to start
next:  ...
```

Assume again for simplicity that

$$T(\mathit{Transfer\_on\_false\_to\_x}) = T(\mathit{Transfer\_to\_x}),$$

and denote this control cost by $T(\mathit{while})$. Then if the loop is executed n times, $n \ge 0$, the cost is

$$T(\mathit{while}\ B\ \mathit{loop}\ S\ \mathit{end\ loop}) = (n+1) \times T(B) + n \times T(S) + (2n+1) \times T(\mathit{while}).$$

To obtain this result, imagine an auxiliary local counting variable n that is maintained (fictitiously) in every loop:

```
n := 0 ; while B loop n := n+1 ; S end loop; (*)
```

The statements involving n take zero time to execute.

The exact value of n will rarely be known in advance. However, best and worst case bounds on the number of iterations can usually be obtained. (Otherwise, there is no hope for timing predictability!) Let these bounds be denoted by $N = [n_{\min}, n_{\max}]$. The timing schema then becomes

$$T(\mathit{while}\ B\ \mathit{loop}\ S\ \mathit{end\ loop}) = (N+1) \times T(B) + N \times T(S) + (2N+1) \times T(\mathit{while}).$$

How can these iteration bounds be determined? The same program proving techniques that are used to show that loops terminate can also be employed to find tight and safe values for N; the form with the auxiliary counting variable, (*) above, is most convenient for this purpose. Generally, the approach is to obtain an appropriate loop invariant, say I, from which the bounds can be derived. I is an assertion that is true before entering the loop, before the first statement is executed on every iteration, and upon exiting the loop. It is the responsibility of the analyst to prove that a candidate invariant I satisfies these conditions.

▶ **Example: Timing a Program**

The program fragment below, taken from [Haase81], computes

$$x = \max(1, a, b)$$

in a nonobvious, roundabout fashion.

```
x := a;
if x < 1 then x := 1; end if;
while x < b loop x := x + 1; end loop;
```

Including a loop count variable n, the while statement has the invariant

$$(x \geq 1) \wedge (n < x) \wedge ((b > 1) \Rightarrow (n \leq b - 1))$$
$$\wedge ((b \leq 1) \Rightarrow (n = 0)).$$

This invariant provides upper and lower bounds on n as a function of b, giving the loop bounds $N = [0, \max(0, b-1)]$.[2] Suppose that $b \leq b_{max}$ and $b_{max} > 1$, so that $N = [0, b_{max}-1]$; and let $T(x := a) = 2$, $T(x < 1) = 2$, $T(if) = 1$, $T(x := 1) = 1$, $T(x < b) = 2$, $T(while) = 1$, and $T(x := x+1) = 3$. Then the program fragment would have execution times in this interval:

$$[2 + (2 + 1) + (2 + 1), 2 + (2 + 1 + 1) +$$
$$(2b_{max} + 3(b_{max} - 1) + (2(b_{max} - 1) + 1))]$$
$$= [8, 7b_{max} + 2]. \blacklozenge$$

Similar methods can be employed to produce schema for other common sequential programming forms. Examples include different types of *case* statements, *for* and *repeat until* loops, and various guarded command constructs. The schema approach is also useful for specifying and analyzing the timing behavior of statements and functions that deal explicitly with time, such as *Clock* and *delay* functions. In these operations, it is also of great interest to have an error bound on the value of time that they compute, use, or return.

▶ **Example: *Clock* Function**

Consider a function named *Clock* that returns the current value of real time, for example, as defined and used in Section 7.2. Generally, *Clock* will access or compute some approximation ct to real-time rt satisfying the relation

$$ct = rt \pm \varepsilon,$$

where the error bound ε may depend on such things as the tick interval and accuracy of a computer clock chip. Expressing this with intervals, we have

$$CT = RT + E,$$

[2]Note that this particular invariant does not lead to a proof that $x = \max(1, a, b)$.

where ct is in CT and $E = [-\varepsilon, \varepsilon]$. The value of ct is obtained at a point in real time somewhere between the start and end events surrounding the execution of the *Clock* function.

Suppose that $T(Clock)$ has been determined. Let RT_{end} be the real-time bounds at the time that the end event for *Clock* occurs and RT_{start} be the corresponding real-time bounds at the start event for the same *Clock* call:

$$RT_{end} = [rt_{emin}, rt_{emax}]$$
$$RT_{start} = [rt_{smin}, rt_{smax}].$$

It would be desirable to know the range of possible values ct returned by *Clock* as a function of either RT_{end} or RT_{start}. We derive an expression for the former.

Because ct is obtained between the start and end events of the *Clock* call, we have

$$CT = RT + E = [rt_{smin}, rt_{emax}] + E. \text{ (*)}$$

But

$$rt_{smin} = rt_{emin} - t_{\min}(Clock).$$

Substituting for rt_{smin} in (*) above, we get

$$CT = [rt_{emin} - t_{\min}(Clock), rt_{emax}] + E.$$

Rearranging terms, we get the desired expression below. The value of ct returned at RT_{end} is in the interval

$$CT = RT_{end} + [-t_{\min}(Clock), 0] + E. \blacklozenge$$

Execution time bounds for concurrent programs have also been studied with the schema approach. A system S of n parallel noninteracting programs $S_1, \ldots, S_n$, with $n > 1$, is represented by the notation

$$S = S_1 \| S_2 \| \ldots \| S_n.$$

One proposed schema assumes a maximal parallelism implementation, that is, a separate processor for each program. In this case, we have

$$T(S) = T(\|_n) + \max_i (T(S_i)),$$

where $T(\|_n)$ is the cost associated with initializing and, subsequently, synchronizing the termination of the programs, and

$$\max_i (T(S_i)) = [\max_i (t_{\min}(S_i)), \max_i (t_{\max}(S_i))].$$

The concurrency cost $T(\|_n)$ might reflect, for example, an initiation of the programs through an n-way broadcast or through a sequence of binary forks.

It is also feasible to devise schema for common synchronization primitives. These include mechanisms for shared variable interactions, such as locks and semaphores, and message passing primitives for distributed environments. The schema contain terms for waiting times for the blocking primitives, such as the semaphore P or *signal* operation. To obtain bounds on these, some knowledge of the arrival times or rates of the unblocking primitives must be assumed.

The basic schema idea provides a manageable and useful model for predicting execution times that are safe, particularly for worst case estimates. However, there is a host of practical issues that must be addressed in order to adapt the model so that predictions are also tight.

7.3.3 Schema Practice

One decision affecting the predictability and the practical convenience of the timing schema approach is the choice of granularity or "size" for an atomic block. In the last section, the atomic blocks were selected at the level of the terminal or lexical objects of the programming language. This choice works well if the code generated by a compiler for each program corresponds in a straightforward way to the parsing structure of the program. For many compilers, the correspondence holds for control constructs but may not be satisfied when producing target code for expressions, assignments, and statement sequences.

Compilers may use the information of related atomic blocks to generate the code for one atomic block. They sometimes consolidate several atomic blocks into one. Other optimizations, such as removing code from loops, are commonly done. The net effect of these optimizations is to produce both loose and unsafe timing estimates: Actual best and worst cases may be much less than predicted, so that the best case is unsafe while the worst case is too loose. (An "unsafe" best case is usually a much less serious concern than an unsafe worst case.) As an aside, it should be noted that some well-known designers recommend a simpler and less-optimized compilation approach for clarity and maintainability (e.g., [Wirth86]).

► Example: Compiler Optimization

In one experiment with the schema, the statement sequence

$$S = S_1; S_2$$
$$= a := b + c; x := x + a$$

compiled into the following code for the GNU C compiler on the Motorola MC68010 computer:

```
a := b + c  ⇒       mov  @b, d0
                    add  @c, d0
                    mov  d0, @a
x := x + a  ⇒       add  d0, @x.
```

Here, @a means the memory address of variable a and d0 denotes data register 0. The first statement is compiled without any optimizations, producing essentially the same code as in Example 3 at the beginning of the previous section (Section 7.3.2). However, the second statement, which is structurally identical to the first, is optimized to generate only one machine language instruction, taking advantage of the knowledge that a is already in the register d0 and x is both an operand and an assignee. ◆

An approach to solving these problems is simply to increase the granularity of the lowest level atomic blocks. Natural choices for larger units are the assignment statement and straight-line sequences of assignment statements; these are simply the basic blocks as defined in program control flow graphs. Statements with conditional and loop control would still be decomposed into multiple blocks, with the control flow treated as separate blocks as before. Thus, for example, suppose that S_i, $i = 1, \ldots, 6$, are assignment statements in the following program:

```
if B₁ then S₁;
S₂ ; S₃ ; S₄ ;
while B₂ do begin S₅ ; S₆ end.
```

These larger atomic blocks would be $<B_1>$, $<S_1>$, $<S_2; S_3; S_4>$, $<B_2>$, and $<S_5; S_6>$. The control objects associated with the *if/then* and the *while* statements are defined as before.

Yet another useful and complementary technique is to *paramaterize* the schema. Contextual information on particular uses or instances of constructs is passed through the parameters. With this method, an assignment statement

```
v := Exp
```

may have the schema

$$T(v := Exp) = T(v, v\_type) + T(:=, v\_type, Exp\_type) + T(Exp, Exp\_type).$$

The time bound here has the general form $T(construct, parameter\_list)$, where *construct* is the timed program construct and *parameter_list* provides data about the particular instances of the construct.

Parameterized schema are also convenient when several reasonable formula might exist for the same construct, depending on the compiler and family of target architectures. A good example is the *while* statement. Instead of the realization presented in the last section, a different compiler for the same target machine group might implement it more efficiently as:

```
start:   < B >
         Transfer on false to next.
again:   < S >
            < B >
         Transfer on true to again.
next :   ...
```

The timing behavior has the schema

$$T(while\ B\ loop\ S\ end\ loop) = (N+1) \times T(B) + N \times T(S) + (N+1) \times T(while).$$

To handle both versions, the control part for all iterations of the loop can be paramaterized to $T(while, N)$, giving

$$T(while\ B\ loop\ S\ end\ loop) = (N+1) \times T(B) + N \times T(S) + T(while, N),$$

where $T(while, N) = (2N+1) \times T(while)$ in our original version and $T(while, N) = (N+1) \times T(while)$ for the above faster implementation.

The parameterized method is also useful when different times exist for the branch instructions on the target computer. In our experiments, the compiler produced code according to the simple realization given in Section 7.3.2, but the underlying architecture had different branching times. The *while* control schema was

$$T(while, N) = N \times T(JRF_{fail}) + T(JRF_{succ}) + N \times T(JRA),$$

where JRF_{fail} is a conditional jump whose branch is not taken, JRF_{succ} is one whose branch is taken, and JRA is an unconditional jump. Each branch consumes a different amount of time. Going further, these jumps may also be parameterized as $T(JR, type)$, with

$$T(JR, succ) = T(JR_{succ}),$$
$$T(JR, fail) = T(JR_{fail}), \text{ and}$$
$$T(JR, uncond) = T(JRA).$$

The schema are all based primarily on a *static* analysis of the program text. An exception is the count on loop bounds; to obtain these, the run-time values of data and control must be taken into account. This pure static method with loop counts produces very satisfactory results in some cases, but in general can yield loose predictions because the paths traced through the program text include many *infeasible* ones. An infeasible path is an impossible execution sequence; it cannot occur because of the program logic. Infeasible best and worst case paths are the reasons for loose bounds, given that the underlying hardware has predictable timing behavior.

A typical case is where a short (long) execution path through one part of a program implies a long (short) path through a subsequent portion. Static analysis pairs the two short (long) paths together, even though it is semantically impossible for them to be part of the same execution sequence. Another common example occurs in nested loops. The number of iterations of an inner loop is often dependent on the particular iteration of the outer loop.

► **Examples: Infeasible Paths**

1. Scheduler   One multiprocessor scheduler algorithm [Bic&Shaw88] has this outline:

```
mp_scheduler::
      loop
            Search_Process_List ;      --P1
            if ready_process then Allocate_Idle ; end if; --P2
            if ready_process and no_idle_processor then Preempt ; end if;
            exit when no_ready_process or not_preemptible ;
      end loop;
```

The worst case of phase *P1* is when there are no ready processes on the process list, resulting in *ready_ process = false*. The second phase *P2* then has its shortest execution time because it immediately exits the loop. Static analysis includes the impossible sequences of the best path of *P1* with the best path of *P2*, and the worst path of *P1* with the worst path of *P2*. Consequently, the schema predictions are loose. The program also contains a doubly nested loop (not shown) where the time of the inner loop changes on every iteration of the outer loop.

2. Insertion Sort   Consider the following standard implementation of an insertion sort of an array of n elements $A(0 .. n-1)$.

```
for i in 1 .. n–1 loop
        j := i ; x := A(i) ;
        while ( j ≥ 1 and A(j–1) > x ) loop
                A(j) := A(j–1) ; j := j–1 ;
        end loop ;
        A(j) := x ;
end loop ;
```

The inner *while* loop executes i times on the ith iteration of the outer loop in the worst case, giving a total of

$$1 + 2 + \ldots + (n-1) = n \, (n-1)/2$$

executions of the inner loop. A straightforward static analysis assumes the global worst case of $n-1$ executions of the inner loop for each execution of the outer loop, giving a much larger count of $(n-1)^2$.

3. Image Processing [Puschner&Koza89]   The image of an object and its background is represented by an $n \times n$ array of pixels. It is desired to find the "center" of the object. To do this, the two-dimensional image array is scanned using a nested loop. Most of the pixels have background intensities and are ignored. For each pixel that is part of the object a fairly lengthy computation involving its neighbors is performed in order to accumulate a weighted sum. Using our static path methods, a worst case of n^2 object pixels is assumed, whereas the object can cover no more than cn pixels where c is a small constant greater than one. ◆

One technique that eliminates many infeasible program paths is based on a more *dynamic* analysis that incorporates additional context and language semantics. Paths through a program are described and restricted using the language of regular expressions (Section 5.1), extended with intersection, negation, and "wild" cards. For example, one can state that whenever one part of (or partial path through) a program is taken or executed, another part is not taken. Each such path description covers or includes *all* feasible paths through the program. The correctness of a path specification is established by a simple application of program proving methods.

▶ **Example: Program Path Specifications**

Frequently, such as in the *Scheduler* example, when one part A of a program S is executed, another part B is always also executed, where A and B are not contiguous. This restriction can be specified by the path expression

$$E_1 = ((\text{- } A \text{ -}) \cap (\text{- } B \text{ -})) \cup ((\neg \, (\text{- } A \text{ -}) \cap \neg \, (\text{- } B \text{ -})).$$

The notation "-" means any string of statements. The expression E_1 states that all paths through S contain either paths through both A and B or paths through neither A or B. ◆

Suppose that the expression E_0 denotes the set of paths through a program S that is obtained by a straightforward static analysis. E_0 contains all feasible paths, denoted by F, and also generally many impossible or infeasible paths. The timing bounds $T(S)$ that we have used in the last subsection give the best and worst case paths from E_0. Let the expressions $E_1, \ldots, E_k$ each represent a set of paths that also cover F. Each set specifies different constraints on the paths. Then the intersection

$$E = E_0 \cap E_1 \ldots \cap E_k$$

still covers F; that is, $F \subseteq E$.

The expression for E is manipulated to eliminate the intersections and to produce an equivalent union of expressions:

$$E = X_1 \cup X_2 \cup \ldots \cup X_n \, ,$$

where each X_i is a regular expression representing program paths. The time bounds for each expression

$$T(X_i) = [\, t_{min}(X_i),\, t_{max}(X_i)\,]$$

can be computed essentially using the standard schema approach. The final result for $T(S)$ is now

$$T(S) = T(X) = [\min_i\, (t_{min}(X_i)),\, \max_i\, (t_{max}(X_i))].$$

The result is much tighter, but still safe, bounds. However, the computations can be quite complex and time consuming, mainly because of the difficulties in handling negation and intersection in regular expressions. Various heuristics and some approximations are used to simplify the process.

The schema model has been implemented and tested for many small programs. Variations included systems with both small and large atomic blocks and with both static and dynamic path analyses. Prediction adjustments for hardware interferences, particularly interrupts and memory refresh (Section 7.5), were incorporated. The experiments were done using a subset of the C language, the GNU C compiler, and a Motorola MC68000 target machine.

One set of results for large atomic blocks is presented in Figure 7.3. Comparisons with carefully measured times show that the predictions are always safe, are often surprisingly tight when only static analysis is used, and are very tight in most cases with dynamic analysis. The bounds obtained with static paths for the *mp_scheduler*, *insertion_sort*, and image processing (*calc_center*) programs are all quite loose, and confirm the above informal analysis. These are the programs described in Examples 1, 2, and 3 of the last section (Section 7.3.3).

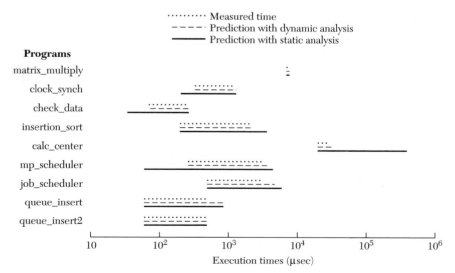

Figure 7.3 Schema timing experiments.

EXERCISES 7.3

1. Consider the conditional statement

```
if B₁ then S₁ elsif B₂ then S₂ elsif ...
elsif Bₙ then Sₙ else Sₙ₊₁ end if;
```

This has the same form as the one treated in Section 7.3.2, except for the addition of the last term. Derive a timing schema for this statement.

2. Devise a timing formula or schema for this *repeat/until* statement:

```
repeat S until B,
```

where S is an arbitrary statement and B is a Boolean expression. State your assumptions about the underlying realization of the statement.

3. Below is a program fragment that computes an integer approximation to sqrt(n) for n a non-negative integer.

```
a := 0 ;
while (a+1)² ≤ n loop a := a+1 ; end loop;
```

Suppose that the first assignment takes one time unit, the second (incrementing a by 1) takes two time units, evaluating the Boolean expression takes three time units, and $T(while) = 1$. Assuming the *while* schema of Section 7.3.2, give best and worst case bounds for the execution of the program when n is in the range $6 < n < 17$.

4. For the *Clock* function example described in Section 7.3.2 derive an expression relating CT to RT_{start}, assuming that $T(Clock)$ is available.

5. Following is a simple variant of the Nuclear Power Plant Monitor described in Section 2.3. (The application is not relevant to the exercise.)

```
loop
    TS ; FH ; SR ;
    delay_by(50);
end loop
```

TS, FH, and *SR* are codes that handle time, faults, and sensors, respectively, and *delay_by* is a relative delay function that blocks or delays the caller by 50 time units. Let RT_{start} denote the real-time bounds at the start of the loop part of the program, that is, $RT = RT_{start}$ the first time through the loop at the start event of *TS*.

(a) Derive an invariant assertion relating RT to RT_{start} that is true at the start event of *TS* every time through the loop. Let $T(loop)$ be the control cost for looping and n be the loop count.

(b) Let $T(delay\_by(t)) = t + [1, 2], t>1, T(loop) = 1$, and $T(TS) + T(FH) + T(SR) = [x, y]$.

What constraints exist on the values of x and y in order that each cycle (loop) be completed within 100 time units?

▶ 7.4 PREDICTION BY OPTIMIZATION

This approach also works at the source program level. Instead of directly tracing paths as in the timing schema method, it analyzes flows in the control flow graph of a program, and treats execution time prediction as an optimization problem. Best and worst case predictions are derived from optimal solutions to integer linear programming (ILP) problems. Our presentation follows the model developed in [Li&Malik95; Li_et_al95]. A similar model and set of techniques were also developed and used in [Puschner93;Puschner&Schedl97].

A program S can be represented as a *control flow graph* (CFG) with basic blocks as nodes and control flows between blocks as directed edges. A basic block B is a maximal sequence of code where control enters at the first instruction of B, and exits only after its last instruction. The large atomic blocks described in Section 7.3.2 are essentially basic blocks.

Figure 7.2 shows a CFG for a standard conditional *if/then/else* statement

```
if B then S₁ else S₂ end if;
```

where B is a basic block, and the boxes labelled S_1 and S_2 could each be a basic block or a CFG. A looping *while* statement

```
while B loop S end loop;
```

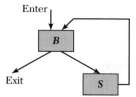

Figure 7.4 CFG for a *while* statement.

has the CFG sketched in Figure 7.4; B is a basic block and the S box is either a basic block or a more complicated CFG.

The worst case execution time of S is expressed as a linear function of the execution times of each basic block as follows:

$$t_{max}(S) = \Sigma_i \, c_i \, x_i.$$

The summation is over all basic blocks B_i. The variable x_i is the number of times that the ith block is executed in the worst case. c_i is the worst case execution time of B_i; control times are included as part of the execution time of a block. The best case $t_{min}(S)$ can be written as as a similar linear expression. The problem is to find all of the x_i counts for each of the worst and best cases.

► **CFG Example**

Figure 7.5 contains the CFG for the program fragment analyzed in Section 7.3.2 that computes $x = max(1, a, b)$. The worst case execution time is

$$t_{max}() = c_1x_1 + c_2x_2 + c_3x_3 + c_4x_4 + c_5x_5 \, ,$$

where the c_i and x_i are defined as above. ◆

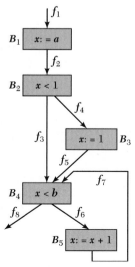

Figure 7.5 Control flow graph example.

The CFG can be used directly to provide some constraints on the values of the block execution counts x_i. The idea is that flows through each block are conserved: each block count x_i equals the sum of the flows through all the input edges to the block, which also equals the sum of the flows through the output edges of the block. These flow constraints are called *structural* constraints.

▶ Example: Structural Constraints

In Figure 7.5, the flows are labelled by f_i, $i = 1, \ldots, 8$. The flow f_i denotes the number of times that control passes through the edge during execution. The structural constraints are given by the following set of flow equations that must be simultaneously satisfied:

$$\{x_1 = 1, x_1 = f_1 = f_2, x_2 = f_2 = f_4 + f_3, x_3 = f_4 = f_5,$$
$$x_4 = f_3 + f_5 + f_7 = f_6 + f_8, x_5 = f_6 = f_7, f_8 = 1\}. \blacklozenge$$

Other constraints, such as loop counts and path restrictions, are semantic in nature; these are called *functional* constraints. Many such constraints can be expressed as linear inequalities, or as disjuncts of conjuncts of linear inequalities, involving the block counts x_i.

▶ Examples of Functional Constraints

1. Suppose that the loop count in the example above (Figure 7.5) is known or proven to be [2, 14]. Then, the block counts must satisfy the following inequalities:

$$2x_1 \leq x_5 \leq 14x_1.$$

2. Suppose that only one of the two basic blocks A and B are executed in a program; that is, in any run, either A is executed and B is not or vice versa. Then, the block counts satisfy the following disjunct of conjuncts:

$$((x_A \geq 1) \wedge (x_B = 0)) \vee ((x_A = 0) \wedge (x_B \geq 1)). \blacklozenge$$

The computation of $t_{\max}(S)$ can then be formulated as a set of optimization problems, each of which is an integer linear programming (ILP) problem. Each ILP problem is of this form:

Find the nonnegative integers x_i that maximizes the function

$$t(S) = \Sigma_i\, x_i c_i$$

subject to equality and inequality constraints given by the structural and functional constraint equations.

There is always a set SC of equations representing the structural constraints of a program and obtained from the CFG. Typically, there will also be another set FC of equations (inequalities and equalities) for functional constraints that must be satisfied such as those derived from loop bounds. The SC and FC equations can be viewed as conjunctive constraints—all must be satisfied. In addition, there will usually be some functional constraints that can be expressed in disjunctive form. This is the case in the second example above which has the form $(a \lor b)$, where a and b are conjuncts of equations:

> Either SC, FC, and a must be simultaneously satisfied or SC, FC, and b must be satisfied.

Each combined set that denotes conjuncts of constraints gives rise to a separate ILP problem, producing different values for $t(S)$ and the x_i counts. In general, there will be many such sets of constraints. For example, if we have $(a \text{ or } b)$ and $(c \text{ or } d)$ and $(e \text{ or } f)$, then 2^3 ILP problems will result, one each from $<SC, FC, a, c, e>$, $<SC, FC, b, c, e>$, ..., and $<SC, FC, b, d, f>$. The desired worst case $t_{max}(S)$ is the maximum over all the $t(S)$ answers. A similar formulation is possible for the best case running time $t_{min}(S)$.

Experiments with the ILP approach yield the same kinds of results and accuracy as the timing schema methods and path extensions described in the last section (7.3). (In fact, the authors claim that all of the path restrictions described by regular expressions and used in the schema model can also be described within the ILP framework [Li_et_al95]). For each program tested, the number of ILP problems that had to be solved due to disjunctive constraints was manageable, even though the general case generates an exponential number.

The same types of architectural and interference analyses must be made for the underlying hardware platform as were required in the schema model. Some of these hardware and software interference issues are discussed in the next section.

In summary, the two analysis approaches, timing schema and ILP model, appear equivalent in power and promising. The principal differences lay in the notations for expressing path or functional constraints—extended regular expressions or equations and inequalities—and in the processing algorithms—manipulating regular expressions or solving ILP problems. The ILP technology and tools are well-developed, while a similar infrastructure for schema does not exist. On the other hand, the timing schema produces cumulative bounds and lends itself more easily to program reasoning.

▶ EXERCISE 7.4

Consider the following program fragment:

```
morecheck := true; i := 0; correct := true;
while morecheck loop
    if data[i]<0 then
        correct := false; morecheck :=
        false;
    elsif i≥DataSize then
        morecheck := false;
    else i := i+1;
    end if;
end loop;
return correct;
```

(a) Draw the CFG for this fragment.

(b) Give the set of structural constraint equations for your CFG.

(c) Specify as many functional constraints that you can find that can be expressed as conjuncts of disjuncts of linear equalities and inequalities, involving the block counts. Assume that $DataSize = 15$.

▶ 7.5 SYSTEM INTERFERENCES AND ARCHITECTURAL COMPLEXITIES

Timing analysis in practice must also incorporate the effects of a variety of hardware and software interferences. These effects can be estimated provided that they have known and determinate behavior. One major class of such interferences is caused by *interrupts*, for example, from timers and IO devices such as sensors. These interrupts preempt the running program and transfer control to some operating system software that "handles" the interrupt. When bounds on interrupt handling times and on interrupt frequencies are available, execution times can be adjusted to include the processor sharing between a program and the interleaved interrupt handling that occurs during its execution.

Assume that there is only one kind of interrupt and an associated interrupt handler *IH*. Consider first a particular execution of a program S. Let $t(S)$ be the execution time of S without the interrupt, $t'(S)$ be the execution time of S in the presence of the interrupt, $t(IH)$ be the interrupt handling time, and f be the interrupt frequency (number of interrupts per unit time). $t(IH)$ should also include the times to save the context of the running program, switch to *IH*, and later resume the interrupted program. Then

$$t'(S) = t(S) + t'(S) \times f \times t(IH).$$

Rearranging terms, we obtain

$$t'(S) = t(S)/(1 - f \times t(IH)).$$

We can now extend this result to intervals. Let $T(IH)$ be the execution time bounds for the interrupt handler and $F = [f_{\min}, f_{\max}]$ be the interrupt frequency bounds. The execution time interval $T'(S)$ for S including processor sharing with this single interrupt class is then

$$T'(S) = T(S) / (1 - F \times T(IH)).$$

Note that the analysis assumes that $f \times t(IH) < 1$, that is, that the handler does not consume the machine. A more subtle point is the possibility of "fractional" interrupts in the above equations; but the best and worst case bounds in $T'(S)$ must assume only an integer number of interrupts. Consequently, the results must be adjusted upward, if necessary, to ensure that

$$t'_{\max}(S) = t_{\max}(S) + k \times t_{\max}(IH)$$

for some integer k, in order to eliminate partial handling of the last interrupt. A similar downward adjustment must also possibly be made to $t'_{\min}(S)$.

The effects of more than one handler can be included in a straightforward way to obtain

$$T'(S) = T(S) / (1 - \Sigma_i (F_i \times T(IH_i))),$$

where F_i and IH_i refer to the ith interrupt class, and the summation is over all interrupts i.

Several other architectural interferences and features must be taken into account. Included are refresh for dynamic random access memories (DRAMs), pipelining of instruction executions, and cache memories [Patterson&Hennessey98]. To obtain timing data for these hardware elements, some combination of measurement, simulation, and analysis is generally required. This can be done at the level of atomic or basic blocks, or at a larger granularity such as a program or function.

DRAM storage devices are restored or refreshed periodically by hardware in order to maintain their content. Typically, the refresh process has higher priority than the CPU for accessing memory, and thus causes increases in execution times of normal programs. This increase is usually a small percentage, but can vary widely. For example, on an older machine, the Motorola MC68010, the measured interference varied between 0% and 7%, with both extremes unlikely [Park92]. However, any DRAM interferences are dominated, and more than offset, by the unpredictability of cache behaviors.

Two approaches are possible for including the effects of instruction and data caches. One could just turn the cache(s) off, and pay the price of decreased performance. An alternative set of strategies is to pre-allocate all or part of the cache(s) to real-time tasks, assuming that there is enough cache space [Kirk89]. In most cases, neither of these approaches is practical, and more elaborate measurement and analysis techniques are needed.

Both the schema and the ILP methods have also been adapted to predict the timing behavior of these complicated architectural features of computers. For example, some useful results have been obtained for cache memories and RISC processors (e.g., [Lim_et_al95]). At the level of machine instructions and sequences of machine instructions, the effects of pipelining and caching can be included in timing predictions using "micro-analysis" techniques that examine micro-instruction implementations of an architecture [Harmon,Baker&Whalley94].

At this point, finding safe and tight execution bounds for nontrivial programs is still a research problem. The deterministic timing behavior of computer hardware is unpredictable in general, even though the average behavior is spectacular. Fortunately, for some applications, it is possible to ignore processing time, essentially assuming an infinitely fast machine; and for many others, it is feasible to ignore some of the above architectural interferences. Many of the delays that do occur and affect deadlines are due to the interaction and communication between machines and between processes.

▶ EXERCISE 7.5

Assume that in the absence of any architectural interferences a program S is predicted to execute in times bounded by $T(S) = [10^6, 10^7]$, where the times are in microseconds.

(a) Suppose that interrupts from a single source enter at a frequency $F = [5, 10]$, where the numbers denote interrupts per second, and that the interrupt handling time $IH = [1000, 1500]$. What are the predicted execution bounds for S in the presence of these interrupts; that is, what are the bounds $T'(S)$?

(b) Suppose that DRAM refresh consumes between 0% and 1% of the time that would normally be taken by the CPU. How would this affect the best and worst case times for the execution of S?

8

Keeping Time on Computers

Computer clocks and time servers are critical parts of real-time control and monitoring software. In this chapter, we first survey briefly the many different ways in which clocks and time are used in computer systems. Section 8.2 then describes desirable and required properties of computer clocks—properties that are generally assumed to hold, but often do not. Following this, logical and physical clock servers are discussed. The final section presents some of the basic ideas in centralized and distributed clock synchronization. The subject of time keeping—computer time and other kinds—is surprisingly complex and still receiving much attention.

▶ 8.1 TIMER APPLICATIONS

Clocks and time are used in computers, and elsewhere, for a surprising variety of purposes. A basic application is to measure or specify the occurrence time of an event, either as an absolute clock value, which is "wall" or calendar clock time, or as a duration relative to some preceding event. We have done this extensively throughout the book, for example, when defining deadlines, periods, faults, and the duration of computations. The relevant event is often declared as a *timeout* event.

A second use of time is to indicate potential *causality* among events: if one event logically follows or precedes another, then its time of occurrence should be greater than or less than its logical predecessor or successor, respectively. Thus, the relative values of time stamps on events can denote possible causality. Common applications here include times for file or program version updates, for message sends and receives, and for activity starts and stops. Note that time stamps impose a total order on events. However, the time order between two events does not necessarily imply a causality relation between them; causality imposes only a partial order on events.

When it is impossible, difficult, or inefficient for processes to communicate, clocks provide a means for synchronizing activities and for validating messages. For example, military, space, and air traffic systems employ time for synchronizing among distributed entities. A sequence of traffic lights along a road may be synchronized using time: One set of lights may be set to turn green, say, at a fixed time interval Δt after its predecessor turns green; Δt is selected so that an automobile can smoothly traverse the distance between the two lights. Message encryption with time stamps is also one way to ensure reliable and secure communications and to authenticate users [Denning82].

Yet another application of time is as a generator of unique identifiers for objects, assuming that each call of a clock returns a different value. The clock acts as a strictly increasing monotonic function here, always returning a value greater than that returned by it's previous call—and, therefore, a unique value.

As clocks have become more accurate, time has become the standard means for precisely measuring distance and position. Perhaps the most spectacular example of this application is the Global Positioning System (GPS). It was developed in the 1970s by the U.S. Department of Defense as a navigational aid for military systems. GPS signals, in deliberately degraded form, were made available for civilian use and are now an essential part of our infrastructure.

The basis, in highly simplified form, is as follows [Ashby94]. Let c = 299,792,458 meters per second, the speed of light in free space. The time t_{pq} for a light signal to propagate from a process p to a process q separated by a distance L is

$$t_{pq} = t_q - t_p = L/c,$$

where t_p is the time that the signal originates at p and t_q is the time that it arrives at q. Assume that four satellite transmitters at known positions $r_i = (x_i, y_i, z_i)$ and times t_i, $i = 1, \ldots, 4$, send their positions and times to a receiver at unknown position $r = (x, y, z)$ and unknown time t. The receiver's position and time can then be found by solving the four equations

$$| \, r - r_i \, | = c \, (t - t_i), \, i = 1, \ldots, 4,$$

for the unknown variables r and t. Much additional complexity arises in practice when relativistic and other effects are included.

GPS is implemented with a large number of orbiting satellites that cover the earth and continuously broadcast time and position signals [Dana97]. GPS receivers read these signals and correct for various errors to provide precise time and position information. In particular, a GPS receiver can be used as a basis for computer time.

► 8.2 PROPERTIES OF REAL AND IDEAL CLOCKS

Historically, time has been computed from astronomical observations of the stars and rotations of the earth with respect to the sun. Since 1967, much more accurate atomic clocks have been used. They are based on the frequency of vibration of the cesium(Cs) 133 atom: One second is defined as 9,192,631,770 periods of Cs133. This time measurement is so accurate that time (and the speed of light) is also used for defining standard length or distance (the meter), replacing the physical meter stick maintained for many years in France. The GPS system described in the last section has about 24 satellites orbiting the earth, each containing an atomic clock.

International Atomic Time (TAI) is maintained in Paris by averaging a number of atomic clocks from laboratories around the world. However, TAI is too accurate in some respects for our physical universe. In particular, the earth's rotation is slowing down by several ms per day, causing the natural solar day to get longer and longer as measured by TAI. The world time standard, named Universal Coordinated Time (UTC), keeps the accuracy of TAI and a long-term synchronization with the solar day by adding corrective "leap seconds" to the TAI-based clock approximately once a year.

UTC signals are available through GPS receivers and through specialized radio stations. For example, the National Institute of Standards and Technology (NIST) broadcasts a signal over its short wave WWV radio station at the beginning of each UTC second. These signals can be read by radio receivers attached to computers. UTC signals can also be accessed directly through some electric utility power lines.

It is convenient to define a clock *CLOCK* as a mapping from real time to clock time:

$$CLOCK: \textit{Real-Time} \rightarrow \textit{Clock-Time}.$$

If $CLOCK(t) = t$, then *CLOCK* is a perfect or ideal clock. The clocks closest to perfection that exist are TAI and UTC timers. We will call these *standard* clocks and denote one by C_s; that is, $C_s(t) = t$ is assumed.

Computer times, on the other hand, are computed from quartz crystal "tickers" with occasional synchronizations with standard clocks or other computer clocks. They can deviate considerably from standard clock times. The reasons are many. Quartz crystals do not oscillate as precisely and uniformly as Cs 133; the time between ticks may be too large; computer clocks may not be synchronized carefully or correctly; the time computation, done in software, may have errors or unaccounted overheads; or there may be malfunctions or failures somewhere in the system, for example, in the clock circuits, power supplies, or the communications link between a standard clock and the machine. Computer clocks can be packaged as separate multi-functional chips that offer calendar time, periodic counters, and delay interrupts, or more simply as unadorned sources of periodic interrupts.

A computer clock C should maintain at least the following four desirable properties [Marzullo84].

1. **Correctness** The clock should contain a reasonable approximation to the correct time. More precisely, at any time t, its value should be within some bound ε of a standard clock C_s. We can express this property as

$$| C(t) - C_s(t) | \leq \varepsilon.$$

   For clocks that are not broken, for example, clocks that are not stopped or producing random values for time, and for clocks that have sufficiently small tick granularity, the main source of inaccuracy is *drift*.

2. **Bounded Drift** Drift is the rate of change of the clock value and is given by the first derivative $d(C\,t)/dt$.[1] A perfect clock has unit drift, since $C_s(t)=t$. To

---

[1] Computer clocks are discrete rather than continuous and differentiable, so we should really be using an expression such as $(C(t+\Delta t) - C(t))/\Delta t$ instead of the derivative. However, assuming the tick interval or granularity is small enough, the clock C can be closely approximated by a differentiable function.

maintain the accuracy of a working clock, it is important that the drift error not exceed some given bound ρ, that is,

$$\left| dC(t)/dt - 1 \right| \leq \rho.$$

A convenient way to interpret this property is as follows. For real times t_1 and t_2, $t_2 > t_1$, we have

$$(t_2 - t_1)(1 - \rho) \leq C(t_2) - C(t_1) \leq (t_2 - t_1)(1 + \rho) .$$

Typically, crystal-controlled clocks in computers have drift errors ρ less than 10^{-5}. This translates to a maximum loss or gain of 10 μsec every second or roughly 1 sec/day.

3. **Monotonicity** We normally expect clocks to be monotonic increasing in value. That is,

$$\text{for all } t_1 \text{ and } t_2, \text{ such that } t_1 > t_2, C(t_1) \geq C(t_2).$$

This property is especially important if we are using time to represent possible causality among events. Monotonicity is violated whenever we correct a fast clock by resetting its value backwards. It also violated every autumn when local clocks are switched from daylight savings to standard time. A serious set of monotonicity problems is exemplified by the infamous Y2K problem: "incrementing" an abbreviated year from 99 to 00, as a way to represent the change from the year 1999 to the year 2000. Whenever clocks "roll over," monotonicity is violated.

A stricter form of monotonicity is often required—each successive clock reading should be strictly greater than the the previous one. To obtain this property, the time between any two successive clock accesses must be greater than the clock's tick and update interval.

4. **Chronoscopicity** [Kopetz&Ochsenreiter87] At any time, it should be possible to measure a time interval with a clock reasonably accurately. This means that sudden large changes in value should not occur, even when correcting a clock. Thus, for equal real-time intervals $t_2 - t_1 = t_4 - t_3$, $t_2 > t_1$ and $t_4 > t_3$, it should be the case that the clock interval $C(t_2) - C(t_1)$ is approximately equal to $C(t_4) - C(t_3)$. In the limit, there exists some bound γ on the second derivative of the clock function:

$$\left| d^2C(t)/dt^2 \right| \leq \gamma.$$

Violations of this property can cause undetected missed deadlines and falsely detected missed deadlines, depending on whether negative or positive changes are made to a clock.

▶ 8.3 CLOCK SERVERS

A timer service usually offers at least two operations to clients, a function to retrieve the current timer value and a procedure to change or set the time. Each has an absolute or calendar time version, and also one that deals with durations or time intervals, such as a given number of clock ticks. We use the term *clock server* to describe this service utility.

One common set of definitions for the operations is the following:

`Get_Time :`	Returns the absolute clock time.
`Get_Duration :`	Returns the number of ticks or time units t since the timer was last set (or, if it was last reset to some value v, return $v + t$).
`Set_Time(t) :`	Changes the real-time clock to t. (Alternatively, t could be an increment or decrement value, so that the clock is changed *by* t.)
`Set_Duration(t) :`	Sets the interval timer to t. This is frequently a reset operation, where $t = 0$.(Alternatively, change the value by t, where t is an increment or decrement.)

A more complex utility might also have facilities for dynamically creating and destroying different types of timers. Examples are

```
clock1 := Create_Calendar_Clock
clock2 := Create_Duration_Clock
```

Identifiers for the clocks are returned by the *Create* functions, and stored in the variables *clock1* and *clock2*. Such abstract timers can be realized on one or more hardware clocks by software sharing.

At a higher level, a server may also provide *delay* functions that block a process until some interval has expired or some absolute time has been reached. As above, absolute and relative time versions may be available:

`delay_by(Δt) :`	Block the calling process for Δt units of time.
`delay_until(t) :`	Block the calling process until time t has been reached.

A related service offers asynchronous alarm clock mechanisms. These allow a user to specify the generation of an asynchronous timeout event at some future absolute or relative time. Here, the calling process is not blocked; it just sets the alarm clock and continues. These kinds of clocks are also known as "one-shot" timers. An example is

`Set_Alarm(Δt) :` Generate a timeout event at the current time + Δt.

Of course, there must be some means to catch the alarm event that occurs when the timer expires.

A hardware count-down timer is convenient for implementing delay and alarm functions. At each clock tick, its value is decremented by one; when the value reaches zero, an interrupt occurs. The timer value can be changed (set) by program during execution. Unlike the basic clock server operations described above, the delay and alarm functions assume a fairly complex operating system infrastructure that supports processes and events, for example, operations and data structures for blocking, waking up, and scheduling processes and for generating and catching events.

8.3.1 Lamport's Logical Clocks

In a seminal paper on clocks and time, Lamport presented a solution to the causality application when events are distributed over any type of communicating network of processes [Lamport78]. Each process p has a *logical* clock server that updates and returns values from a *logical clock* L_p. The relative values of the logical clocks indicate potential causality among events. Let $L_p(e)$ be the value of L_p at the occurrence of event e. If an event e_1 at process p precedes event e_2 at process q, where p and q may be the same or different processes, it is necessary that $L_p(e_1) < L_q(e_2)$. The following simple but elegant algorithm ensures that this relation holds.

After an event internal to p occurs, L_p is incremented by one; a more accurate way of saying this is that L_p is incremented *between* any two internal event occurrences. Thus, the values of L_p at the occurrence of internal events in p indicate potential causality, as required: if event e_1 precedes event e_2, then $L_p(e_1) < L_p(e_2)$.

Suppose now that we have two processes p and q, where p sends a message m to q; sending and receiving messages are considered the only external events. The problem is to ensure that q's clock value after receipt of m is larger than p's clock value when it transmits m, since the send event, say e_1, logically precedes the receive event e_2. At the same time, the monotonicity of the clocks must be maintained.

To solve this problem, we first time stamp m with L_p, that is, send both m and $L_p(e_1)$ when sending a message. Then, on receipt at q, reset L_q to a large enough value, for example, any value satisfying

$$L_q(e_2) > \max(L_p(e_1), L'_q(e_2)),$$

where L'_q is the value of the clock at e_2 before the reset. This also ensures that the clock value of e_2 is greater than that of any event on q that precedes e_2. An obvious choice for the new L_q is

$$L_q(e_2) = \max(L_p(e_1), L'_q(e_2)) + 1.$$

Note also that L_p must be incremented after each send event on p so that any succeeding event on p will have a larger clock value.

► Example of Logical Clocks

Figure 8.1 has three processes, p, q, and r, each with their own logical clock, and each handling internal events, denoted by dots (.), and external message events, represented by the ends of arrows between the communicating processes. The clocks are all initialized to zero. The computed logical times appear at or directly after the events. The first message receipt by q from p occurs when q's clock is at time 2 and p's clock is at 3. L_q is then reset to 4, since this is equal to $\max(3, 2) + 1$. Similarly, q sends a message at its time 5 to r; at the receive at r's time 9, r resets its clock to $10 = \max(5, 9) + 1$.

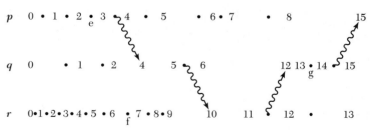

Figure 8.1 Operation of logical clocks.

Note that the algorithm ensures that if event e_1 on process p precedes e_2 on q, then $L_p(e_1) < L_q(e_2)$. However, the converse is not necessarily true. If $L_p(e_1) < L_q(e_2)$, then it is not necessarily the case that event e_1 on process p precedes e_2 on q. There may not be any causal relation between the two events. ◆

▶ Example of No Causality Between Events

Consider the system of processes, events, and logical clock values in Figure 8.1 again. The event e precedes the event g, and the clock values have the relations $L_p(e) < L_q(g)$ as required. However, we also have the clock relation $L_p(e) < L_r(f)$, and yet there is no causal relation between the events e and f. ◆

An extension of Lamport clocks to a more complicated mechanism called *vector clocks* was invented to solve this problem [Fidge91]. By looking at the vector clock times of two events, one can tell whether there exists a causal relation between them.

Lamport's logical clock scheme also provides an approximate form of synchronization: when the processes communicate often, their clocks converge to roughly the same values and proceed at about the same rates. The clocks are also monotonic, an important property achieved only with some difficulty by real clocks.

8.3.2 Monotonic Clock Service

A monotonic and (approximately) chronoscopic server for a real computer clock can be realized by using some care whenever it becomes necessary to adjust time forward or backward. We assume that the clock is not broken but must be corrected occasionally due to drift errors. The general idea is to have the server return values at a slower or faster rate than its normal real-time rate until a negative or positive change, respectively, is made.[2] The clock is chronoscopic and has bounded drift over the make-up period and outside of it.

One straightforward technique adjusts the clock rate up or down by a factor of two. Thus, if our clock runs fast during some period and has to be set back by an interval Δt, the server can simulate a slower running monotonic and chronoscopic clock until Δt simulated time units have passed; this occurs if the server ticks uniformly at $1/2$ the rate of real time. If the clock has to be set forward by some Δt, then ticking uniformly at twice the rate of real time will make up the difference in $2\Delta t$ of simulated time. We derive these results below.

Let ct be the time reported by the clock server and rt be the corresponding correct real time at some point where a positive correction of Δt is to be made; that is, $rt = ct + \Delta t$, and the clock is to be set forward by Δt time units. Suppose that the clock server now ticks at twice the real time rate for an interval Δt. Then at real-time $rt' = rt + \Delta t$, the computer time ct' will equal

$$ct' = ct + 2\Delta t = rt - \Delta t + 2\Delta t = rt + \Delta t.$$

That is, both the current time and real time are identical at ct'.

---

[2]If the goal was only monotonicity and a positive change was required, the change could be implemented instantaneously; no adjustment of the clock rate is needed.

Suppose that the clock is to be set backwards, that is, $rt = ct - \Delta t$ at the correction time. Then, by a similar argument, running the computer clock at half its speed for $2\Delta t$ of real time will result in a time

$$ct' = ct + \Delta t = rt + 2\Delta t$$

at real time $rt' = rt + 2\Delta t$. In this case, the change is made up in $2\Delta t$ time units. These clock arguments can be confusing, so we give an example with real numbers.

▶ Example: Smooth Forward and Backward Adjustments

Suppose that clock time is 10:00 and real time is 11:00. The clock should be adjusted one hour forward. We can accomplish this adjustment by running the clock at double the real-time rate for two hours as measured by the modified clock. The clock will then read 12:00 and real time will be 12:00. The normal real time rate of the clock is then resumed.

Let the clock read 10:00 as before, but suppose now that real time is 9:00. The clock should be set back one hour. To do this in a monotonic and partially chronoscopic manner, we run it at one half the real-time rate until it reads 11:00; this takes two hours of real time, so real time is also at 11:00 at this point. At 11:00, the normal clock rate, approximately equal to the real-time rate, is resumed. ◆

The above technique generalizes to other changes of the clock rate, besides one-half or two. For example, suppose that a clock rate of 3/4 the real-time rate is selected in order to make up negative corrections. Then, a correction of Δt will be made up in $4\Delta t$ of real time.

These kinds of smooth adjustments can be implemented either directly by interpreting clock interrupts appropriately or indirectly by modifying the value returned by a hardware clock. In the former case, if a factor of two is being used, we simply interpret each tick as either half or double the actual tick time. A software implementation that modifies the values read from a computer clock is discussed next.

8.3.3 A Software Clock Server

As an example of a software clock server, we will follow the same organization as given in [Marzullo84] for his monotonic version. Imagine a software timer connected to external clients that may wish to read or update the clock; that is, the timer is a software module implementing the service. Internally, this timer accesses a clock that is run from a hardware chip. Figure 8.2 illustrates the idea.

The server interface to the external world consists of two operations, similar to those presented at the beginning of the section:

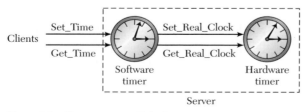

Figure 8.2 Organization of clock server.

Set_Time(amount): Set the clock forward (*amount*>0) or backward (*amount*<0) by the value *amount*. This operation is typically used by a clock synchronization routine.

Get_Time: Return a monotonic and chronoscopic approximation to the clock time.

Internally, the server can call two routines that access the real hardware clock:

Set_Real_Clock(amount): Reset the hardware clock forward or backward by *amount*.

Get_Real_Clock: Return the current value of the hardware clock.

Under normal operation, there is no time to be made up, and *Get_Time* will return the hardware clock time obtained from *Get_Real_Clock*; that is, the software and hardware timers are identical. A *Set_Time* call causes the software clock to deliver smaller or larger times than the hardware clock, depending on the sign of the *amount* parameter. When the clock is "running" faster or slower as a result of a *Set_Time* call at time t, the server uses t, the value of the amount to be changed, and the time of the *Get_Time* call to compute the time value to return. The hardware clock is reset by *amount*, using *Set_Real_Clock*, after the change is made up. If *Set_Time* calls can occur in bursts more quickly than the corrections can be made up, then some type of queueing mechanism must be added.

▶ 8.4 CLOCK SYNCHRONIZATION

The usual way to keep a computer clock correct is to synchronize it sufficiently often with one or more other clocks. Typically, this can be accomplished by comparing it with some centralized standard clock and making the appropriate positive or negative correction. Such a synchronization with real time (standard clocks) is termed *external* clock synchronization. Typically, GPS or NIST receivers can be used to obtain standard clock UTC signals (Section 8.2).

When a centralized standard clock is not available or easily accessed, for example, in some space, military, and transportation systems, another approach is to compare the clock with several standard clocks or with clocks from other computers over some kind of network. In some distributed systems where standard clocks are not reliably available, correctness may be sacrificed for or approximated by synchronization; that is, the goal is to maintain all clocks in the network at the same value, even if the value is not correct. This is called *internal* clock synchronization. Both centralized and distributed clock synchronization are examined in the next two subsections, starting with the former.

8.4.1 Centralized Synchronization

We follow approximately the model developed in [Marzullo84]. Suppose that a clock $C(t)$ in a computer is to be synchronized with a standard clock $C_s(t)$. For example, the computer could be a workstation and $C_s(t)$ obtained through a satellite or a network (Figure 8.3). Let $C(t)$ have bounded drift ρ, that is,

$$| \, dC(t)/dt \, - 1 | \leq \rho.$$

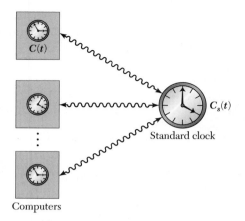

Figure 8.3 Centralized synchronization.

Assume also that the system maintains an error bound $E(t)$, which gives the maximum error of $C(t)$ at time t; real time is thus in the interval

$$[C(t) - E(t), C(t) + E(t)].$$

The error bound $E(t)$ could be stored in a "synchronization server" that computes clock corrections and sends corresponding *Set_Time* commands to the clock server. Alternatively, the bound could be stored in the clock server itself and, perhaps, returned with $C(t)$ on a *Get_Time* call.

Suppose that the clock was set to r at its last correction or reset, and let ε be the clock error at the correction time r. ε could be the result of the error in $C_s(t)$, errors in transmitting $C_s(t)$ to the computer, or the time uncertainty and overhead in actually performing the reset. Thus, when the clock is reset, real time is in the interval $[r - \varepsilon, r + \varepsilon]$. At any time t after the reset, we have

$$E(t) = \varepsilon + drift\_since\_r,$$

where *drift_since_r* is the clock drift since the reset time. The maximum drift error is obtained directly from the definition of drift ρ given in Section 8.2:

$$drift\_since\_r = \rho(C(t) - r).$$

The clock should be reset frequently enough so that $E(t)$ is always less or equal to some given bound, say *EPS*. At reset time, the standard clock value $C_s(t)$ is obtained and assigned to both r and $C(t)$, that is, $r \leftarrow C(t) \leftarrow C_s(t)$. The reset error ε may be a constant, or it may vary from call to call; in the latter case, it could be recomputed at each communication with the standard clock.

How often should the clock be reset to maintain the *EPS* bound? From the above, we want

$$E(t) = \rho(C(t) - r) + \varepsilon \leq EPS.$$

Consequently, the synchronization interval must satisfy

$$C(t) - r \leq (EPS - \varepsilon)/\rho.$$

Since everything on the right-hand side of the inequality is known, the desired interval can be determined. Our analysis assumes only drift error. If more serious failures or errors can occur, then other means of detection, analysis, and recovery are needed. Note also that the synchronization interval is the time as measured by the computer clock, not a time interval on the standard clock.

▶ **Example: Computing the Synchronization Interval**

Suppose that a clock must be accurate to within one second ($EPS = 1$). Let $\varepsilon = 0.5$ seconds and $\rho = 6 \times 10^{-6}$. Then, using the above results, we get

$$C(t) - r(t) \le (1 - 0.5)/0.000006 = 83,333 \text{ seconds,}$$

which is approximately one day. Thus a clock error bound of one second will be maintained by synchronizing at least once a day, as measured by the computer clock. ◆

8.4.2 Distributed Synchronization

Distributed synchronization involves a set of machines and servers connected in a network. Assume $n > 1$ computers, identified by the numbers $1, 2, \ldots, n$; each computer i has a clock $C_i(t)$. Some of these clocks, say $m < n$ of them, may be arbitrarily faulty. The goal is to synchronize the clocks with each other, rather than with a centralized comparison clock, so that the "good" ones all have approximately the same values.

In order to accomplish this, it is necessary that the computers transmit their clock values to each other. The problem is that the "bad" clocks could be very bad indeed. For example, a clock could be stopped,[3] could have an erratic drift rate, or could lose or gain bits while computing or transmitting time. One effect may be that the defective clock is two- or multifaced—it sends completely different values to different machines at roughly the same time. The bad values may be transmitted for some time before the error is detected and fixed. The following example, taken essentially from [Lamport&Melliar-Smith85], illustrates the possible effects of a bad clock in a distributed system.

▶ **Example: Three Computers: One Bad Clock, Two Good Clocks**

Suppose that a system contains three computers, called X, Y, and Z, each with its own clock, C_X, C_Y, and C_Z, respectively. C_Y and C_Z are good clocks, containing and transmitting times of 3 P.M. and 4 P.M., respectively. However, C_X is a bad two-faced clock, transmitting 2 P.M. to C_Y and 5 P.M. to C_Z. Figure 8.4 shows this scenario.

Computer Y thus sees clock values 2 and 4 from its neighbors, as well as is own value of 3. Computer Z, on the other hand, sees values 3, 4, and 5. There is no reason for either of the good machines to change their clocks to the same value, such as 3:30 P.M. The good clocks cannot be synchronized in this case. However, if less than one third of the clocks are bad—for example, no more than one out of four—then we can achieve such desirable fault-tolerant behavior as described next. ◆

---

[3]Note that a stopped clock is not accurate for very long, but is both monotonic and chronoscopic!

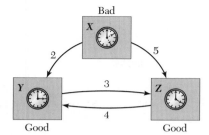

Bad

X

2   5

Y   3   Z

4

Good   Good

Figure 8.4   Intolerance of a bad clock.

There are many methods that have been implemented or proposed to handle these situations. One of the most popular and useful fault-tolerant algorithms is based on averaging. The general idea is for each machine to replace its clock value by the average of all the clock values in the system, after discarding any obviously faulty values. We present the variation called CNV ("interactive convergence algorithm") described in [Lamport&Melliar-Smith85].

An important requirement for the algorithm is that the frequency of synchronization be restricted: The clocks are synchronized often enough so that any two good clocks, C_i and C_j, maintain a given bound

$$| C_i(t) - C_j(t) | \leq \varepsilon.$$

A clock C_j is defined as bad relative to C_i if the ε bound is exceeded. Assume also that the number m of faulty clocks satisfies the relation

$$n \geq 3m + 1, \qquad (*)$$

that is, less than one third of the clocks can be bad.

At synchronization time, each machine i reads all its neighbors' clocks and resets its clock C_i to the average

$$\sum_{j=1}^{n} C'_j/n,$$

where $C'_j = C_j$ if $| C_i - C_j | \leq \varepsilon$ and $C'_j = C_i$ otherwise (C_j is bad). Then all of the good clocks C_i and C_j will be set so that

$$| C_i - C_j | \leq (3m/n)\varepsilon. \blacklozenge$$

The relation (*) above is important since $n > 3m$, the expression $(3m/n)$ is less than one. Thus, if the good clocks are within or equal to the ε bound, they will be reset so that their difference is less than the bound. Note also that a clock substitutes its own value for a potentially faulty value in the averaging computation; an alternative in this case might be to assume one less clock and thus not use any value at all.

We give an informal proof of this result. Let C_{ik} and C_{jk} be the value of k's clock that is used by the good clocks of i and j, respectively, when computing their new average. If k has a nonfaulty (i.e., good) clock, then $C_{ik} = C_{jk}$. If k's clock is faulty (bad), then

$$| C_{ik} - C_{jk} | \leq 3\varepsilon.$$

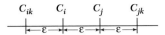

Figure 8.5 A worst case for faulty C_k.

This relation holds because the algorithm ensures that both $\mid C_{ik} - C_i \mid \le \varepsilon$ and $\mid C_{jk} - C_j \mid \le \varepsilon$, and also assumes that the relation $\mid C_i - C_j \mid \le \varepsilon$ is maintained for good clocks. Figure 8.5 shows one worst case situation where the bound is achieved. Thus we have a difference of at most 3ε for at most m clocks. Consequently, the average for a clock C_i will differ by at most $3\varepsilon m/n$ from that of any other good clock C_j. This establishes the desired result.

We have not included either the effects of network transmission times and errors in reading other values, or the overheads in performing the averaging. In practice, it is not the clock values themselves, but the differences between clock values, that are averaged. That is, the new clock value at machine i is computed as

$$C_i + \sum_{j=1}^{n} \Delta_{ji}/n,$$

where Δ_{ji} is C_j - C_i if $\mid C_j$ - $C_i \mid \le \varepsilon$ and 0 otherwise.

This policy reduces any errors related to the fact that the clocks participating in the averaging calculation cannot be read at exactly the same time. For example, if each clock is read instantaneously but at different times during a small synchronization interval, then the differences $C_j(t) - C_i(t)$ for t in that interval should not change appreciably for good clocks j. Errors in reading a neighbor's clock, particularly those due to transmission delays, can be incorporated by adding a corresponding error factor, say γ, to ε in the averaging algorithm; i.e., Δ_{ji} is $C_j - C_i$ if $\mid C_j - C_i \mid \le \varepsilon + \gamma$.

How often should the clocks be synchronized? The synchronization period should be the amount of time that it takes for any two good clocks to drift from $(3\varepsilon m/n)$ to ε apart from each other. (Assume that the clock values are initially within the bound $(3\varepsilon m/n)$ of each other.) If all the good clocks have a drift bounded by ρ, then the maximum drift between two clocks during a time interval Δt is

$$\Delta t\,(1 + \rho\,) - \Delta t\,(1 - \rho) = 2\Delta t\,\rho.$$

Setting this equal to $\varepsilon - (3\varepsilon m/n)$, we get the desired result for the required time interval:

$$\Delta t = (\varepsilon - 3\varepsilon m/n)/(2\rho).$$

A more complex synchronization procedure is necessary if we don't insist that the good clocks maintain the ε bound with respect to each other and we require that good clocks use (approximately) the same values from other clocks, even faulty ones. The last assumption says that even if a bad clock is multifaced, that is, presents differing values to different clocks at the same time, all the good clocks will agree on the same value for a bad clock. This assures that all good clocks will generate the same value at synchronization time. Algorithms for this variation use the *median* of a set of clock values, rather than the average. Two algorithms are presented in [Lamport&Melliar-Smith85], both based on solutions to the "Byzantine Generals" problem and both requiring many rounds of message passing among the participants. As in CNV, less than one third of the clocks can be faulty.

The median methods are not normally used in practice because of their high communication costs. A different approach that has seen extensive use is the probabilistic method developed in [Cristian89]. Compared with the median algorithm, it requires far fewer message exchanges.

► EXERCISES 8

1. Give an example in which a violation of the chronoscopic property can cause an undetected missed deadline.

2. Give an example illustrating how the use of a clock that is chronoscopic but has a large drift can result in an undetected missed deadline.

3. (a) Suppose that a clock rate of 3/4 the real-time rate is used to make up negative corrections on a monotonic clock. Show that a correction of Δt will be made up in $4\Delta t$ of real time.

(b) Let a positive clock correction be made up by speeding up the clock rate by 4/3 the real-time rate. How long will it take to make up the correction? Prove your answer.

4. Sketch the algorithms for the *Set_Time* and *Get_Time* operations of the Clock Server (Figure 8.2). Use pseudocode in some programming language, such as C, Java, or Ada.

5. Compare the CNV algorithm with a similar averaging algorithm that *throws away*, that is, ignores, clock values that differ by more than ε instead of replacing them by one's own value. What are the bounds on the difference between any two good clocks? Assume, as in the CNV case, that $n \geq 3m + 1$ for the modified algorithm.

CHAPTER 9

Programming Languages

Many programming languages have been especially designed or modified to handle the unique requirements of real-time problems, for example, [Halang&Stoyenko90]. In Section 9.1, we discuss some of the most important features that must appear in a real-time language. A detailed examination of how these features are realized in several interesting programming languages then follows in subsequent sections. A separate section on language and programming ideas for software fault tolerance is also included.

The chosen languages are Ada [Ada95], Java with real-time extensions [Naughton&Schild97;RTJEG00], CSP and its Occam implementations [Hoare78, 84;Inmos84,88], Esterel [Berry&Gonthier92], and Real-Time Euclid [Kligerman& Stoyenko86]. Ada is presented and emphasized because it is an international standard, because it is very influential, and because it has a large and rich set of facilities—some might say excessively so. Java is probably the most popular general purpose and object-oriented programming language of the late twentieth and early twenty-first centuries, and is being adapted for real-time use. CSP and Occam, also influential and used for both practical and theoretical work, is notable for its small and elegant features.

Esterel provides a novel event-oriented language for programming the "reactive" part of an application, that is based on an appealing model of computation with some similarities to statecharts (Section 4.2). The last selection, Real-Time Euclid, is a research language with an accompanying system that was designed for predictability; it also nicely illustrates the integration and interactions among different systems components. Popular languages such as C, C++, or even Fortran are not covered because they lack many required features, and must be adapted extensively or restricted severely in order to meet real-time software needs.

▶ 9.1 REAL-TIME LANGUAGE FEATURES

Real-time applications require the same general-purpose language constructs as do most other domains. However, they also need some additional features which are often either not available or sufficiently developed. Many of these are closely connected to the underlying operating system. The most important can be grouped into one of the following areas: *time access and control, concurrency control, exception handling,* and *predictability.*

In order to control and monitor the timing behavior of a program, there must be mechanisms or primitives for dealing with both absolute and relative time. Basic operations are those typically implemented by a clock server (Section 8.3) to *set* a clock or timer, and to *read* the value of the timer object. Higher level instructions to *delay* a task or put it to sleep for some time, and those that generate *timeout* signals are also important. These may be part of more abstract control constructs, such as one that specifies a periodic activity with a start time, period, deadline, and a body of code to be executed. At the lowest level, access to a periodic *tick* event or interrupt may suffice as a basis for programming the other operations. The essential timing behaviors of the clock server should be clearly defined, for example, the overheads and the clock properties related to accuracy, drift, monotonicity, and chronoscopicity (Section 8.1).

Concurrency is an inherent part of the real-time world. Software constructs should exist for defining, synchronizing, communicating among, and scheduling the execution of parallel activities. In addition to conventional higher level facilities for parallel programming, there is a need for mechanisms that allow a finer degree of hardware control and a closer coupling with timing. For example, a real-time language may provide declarations or statements that deal directly with interrupts, IO, storage allocation, and task scheduling.

Unusual behaviors and faults, both in hardware and software, must be detected and handled gracefully. It should also be easy to distinguish unusual behaviors from normal ones. Language structures that define, test for, and assist in recovery from exceptions are extremely useful for most applications. Without the assistance and discipline that exception handling features can offer, it is too easy to write programs that are incorrect, unreliable, fault intolerant, hard to understand, and difficult to maintain.

Programs must be both functionally predictable and timing predictable. The latter, of course, is the single most distinguishing requirement for real-time programs. Timing predictability implies that constructs have well-defined timing characteristics that are readily apparent or derivable from the program text. Some engineers equate predictability with a requirement for deterministic language constructs, but these are really two different dimensions: one can write predictable or unpredictable programs with or without these constructs, and nondeterminism is sometimes extremely convenient.

Languages that are overloaded with facilities and special cases are usually too complex to satisfy predictability requirements. It is also the case that the use of certain language features, such as recursion and dynamic data structures, can easily result in unpredictable timing behaviors even though they can produce concise and elegant programs. For example, dynamic storage management and the associated garbage collection mechanisms as defined in Java systems can interrupt application computations and take an indeterminate amount of time to execute [Uckun&Gasperoni98].

▶ 9.2 ADA

The Department of Defense (DoD) in the United States sponsored an international competition in the mid-1970s for the design of a common programming language to be used for all DoD applications. A particular emphasis was placed on real-time needs.

The winner was a French design produced by J. Ichbiah's team at CII Honeywell Bull. The language was named *Ada* to commemorate Ada Lovelace who is considered the world's first programmer. She earned this distinction by developing some programming ideas and code around 1840 for Charles Babbage's original computer design. Ada was accepted as a standard in 1987 and has been widely used throughout the world in the military, industry, and academia, as well as the DoD.

Unfortunately, it did not prove entirely suitable for one of its main intended applications—real-time computing. One problem was the inherent unpredictability of some of its tasking and timing features, for example, see [Baker&Shaw89]. To correct these and other perceived problems, a committee proposed a number of changes and additions which culminated in the Ada 95 standard [Ada95]. This is the version discussed here.

Ada is a very large language containing many interesting, influential, and innovative features for both general purpose programming and more specialized applications. The features most relevant for real-time systems can be divided into four classes.

One class is concerned with programming-in-the-large, reusability, and other software engineering topics. The language provides an advanced elaboration of a variety of concepts related to modules and objects. The main type of program unit or module in Ada is the *package*. A module requires separate specification and implementation parts, where the specification defines the interface of the unit. The interface of a package describes the procedures, types, and data that the package exports (makes available to other modules) and the external packages that it imports (uses in its implementation). Object-oriented features that allow type extensions, such as classes, inheritance, and polymorphism are included. Hierarchical program libraries are also defined as a required part of any implemented Ada system.

A second major class is the *tasking* features for concurrent programming. Ada has constructs for defining tasks, scheduling and controlling their execution, synchronizing them through either the rendezvous or a monitor-like scheme (protected types), and handling interrupts (events). A high-level *exception* mechanism is the third innovation. Programs can declare, raise, and handle exceptions, all in a structured fashion. The final, and extremely important, area is *timing*. Ada offers two timing packages, one of which provides a comprehensive set of real-time facilities. Tasking, exceptions, and timing are discussed in more detail in subsequent sections.

Ada has a *core* component and six *annexes*. The core is the general purpose language that is implemented in any Ada system. The annexes define specialized additions for particular application areas. The six annexes are: systems programming, real-time systems, distributed systems, numerics, information systems, and safety and security. We will cover some of the most relevant and unusual parts of the core, as well as selected features in the systems programming, distributed systems, real time, and safety and security annexes since many of these are particularly convenient for real-time programs or are intended specifically for real-time use.

9.2.1 Core Language

The core features of principal interest are those related to concurrency, synchronization, time, and exception handling.

Tasks and Time

The main active program object is the *task*, which corresponds closely to the operating systems notion of a process or a thread. Tasks can access and program with time, and also control their own timing behavior to some extent, through a standard *Calendar* package and two *delay* functions. The *Calendar* package provides a time-of-day clock function, named *Clock* that returns a value of type *time*, and operations to construct *time* from and split *time* into its components: year, month, day, and seconds (*duration*).

A task can be suspended for a time duration or until a given value of calendar time is attained, through the *delay* and *delay_until* statements, respectively. Below is a program outline in Ada for a periodic process named *P* that uses some of these features.[1] Comment lines are preceded by two dashes (--). (In Section 2.2.1, we used similar code to illustrate a cyclic executive.)

```
-- Body for a periodic process P
task body P is
     period : duration;
     next : time := Clock + period; -- initialize "next"
     -- other declarations
begin
     -- initializations
     loop
          delay_until next;
          -- The code for P is inserted here.
          next := next + period;
     end loop;
end P;
```

Protected Types

Controlled access to shared data can be programmed with *protected types*. These are data objects and associated access procedures that are executed in a mutually exclusive fashion after a *barrier* or Boolean entry condition is satisfied. The protected type is a combination of facilities defined in monitors and conditional critical regions ([Bic&Shaw88]).

Consider once again a bounded buffer used by a producer and a consumer task, as developed in Section 4.1.1. The same general organization is used except that the buffer is a data object rather than a process or task. *Buffer* is a shared data type as illustrated in Figure 9.1. It is written as a protected object to ensure the mutually exclusive and conditional access required by this resource.

The *Buffer* type defines two access procedures, *Deposit* and *Remove*, for inserting and removing messages, respectively, from the type; these procedures are termed *entries*. Ada program skeletons for the *Producer* and *Consumer* tasks are given next. An entry into an object is invoked by first naming the object, then adding the entry name and parameters, using a standard dot notation. For example, *Buffer.Remove(m)* calls the *Remove* entry of *Buffer* with parameter *m*.

---

[1]This "naive" application of the Ada core timing features should not be used for precise or critical timing situations. (See Section 9.2.2.)

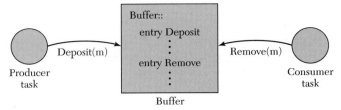

Figure 9.1 Bounded buffer as a protected type.

```
-- Producer and Consumer tasks

task body Producer is
        m : data; -- data is some user-defined type.
begin
        loop
                -- Generate the next data object m.
                Buffer.Deposit(m); -- Deposit m in the buffer.
        end loop;
end Producer;

task body Consumer is
        m : data;
begin
        loop
                Buffer.Remove(m); -- Remove the next item from the Buffer.
                -- Use and consume m.
        end loop;
end Consumer;
```

The *Buffer* object definition has both a specification part and an implementation part. The specification lists the two entry procedures of the type, and declares the data structures that are private (internal) to it and not available to external users. The implementation part is called the *body*, similar to the task case. Each entry has a Boolean guard or barrier that must be satisfied before the call can be executed. The complete definition follows, with the specification first.

```
-- Specification of Buffer
protected Buffer is
        entry Deposit(m : in data);
        entry Remove(m : out data);
private
        buf : data(0 . . 99);
        inb, outb, full : Natural := 0;
end Buffer;

-- Implementation of Buffer
protected body Buffer is

        entry Deposit(m : in data)
                when full < buf'Length is
        begin
                buf(inb) := m;
                inb := (inb + 1) mod buf'Length;
                full := full + 1;
        end Deposit;
```

```
        entry Remove(m : out data)
                when full > 0 is
        begin
          m := buf(outb);
          outb:= (outb +1) mod buf'Length;
        full := full - 1;
        end Remove;


    end Buffer;
```

The barrier to each entry is preceded by the keyword *when*. For example, there must be elements in the buffer (*full* > 0) before a *Remove* can be entered; similarly, there must be some available buffer slots (*full* < *buf'Length*) before the body of *Deposit* is executed.[2]

It is useful to imagine that a unique critical section lock, say L_P, is associated with each protected type *P*; L_P is locked on each successful entry call and unlocked when the call terminates, thus ensuring mutual exclusion. Tasks may be queued on this lock awaiting routine entry with barrier testing. The barrier is re-evaluated for queued tasks only when an entry routine exits.

Functions, which have a type and return a value, have interesting semantics when they are defined in protected types. They are required to have *read* access only to the private data of the type. Consequently, any Ada implementation can permit parallel function executions. Procedures, on the other hand, are also allowed to update the private data. Standard readers–writers constraints are thus specified for protected functions and procedures: procedures are executed in mutual exclusion with respect to other procedures and functions of the type, whereas functions can be executed concurrently.

An entry call can be made conditionally, subject to its being executed immediately, through the use of a *select/else* sequence. A standard example is a busy wait loop on an entry call:

```
loop
    select
            Server.Resource_Request(pars);
            exit;
    else
    -- The Server.Resource_Request call is not accepted immediately.
            null;
    end select;
end loop;
```

If the entry call after the *select* (*Server.Resource_Request(pars)*) is not taken immediately, the statements in the *else* clause (in this case, only *null*) are executed. The loop causes the conditional call to be tested continuously until it is executed. Instead of the *null* statement, a more interesting computation could be specified, in which case we no longer have a "busy wait."

---

[2]*Length* is an array "attribute." For any one-dimensional array *A*, the expression *A'Length* gives the number of index values in *A*.

Another *select* feature, called a *timed_entry_call*, employs the *delay* or *delay_until* function to specify a timeout on an entry call. If a call is not taken within a given time, an alternative sequence of statements is executed. The alternative is separated from the entry call portion by the keyword *or*, and consists of a delay statement followed by an arbitrary sequence of statements, as illustrated by this example:

```
select
      Radar.Turn;
or
      delay 15.0;
      -- The call hasn't been selected in 15 seconds.
      -- Do something else.
end select;
```

Task Communications: Rendezvous

Tasks can synchronize indirectly through entries on protected objects as illustrated in the bounded buffer example. They can also do so *directly* through entries on *accept* statements in other tasks. In its simplest form, a client task *C* might invoke a server *S* with the entry call

```
S.entry_name(pars)
```

where *entry_name* is the name of the entry call and *pars* are its parameters. The server task *S* receives the call with this *accept* statement:

```
accept entry_name(pars) do
      statement_list
end;
```

Communications between the two tasks are synchronous: *C* blocks on the entry call until *S* accepts it and completes the execution of the *statement_list*; *S* blocks on the *accept* until *C* or some other client issues the entry call. This interaction is called a *rendezvous*, a term that is now an accepted part of computer jargon. Both tasks, *S* and *C*, continue execution in parallel after the rendezvous.

Tasks may define a selective list of accepts on their entry calls, that depend on given conditions or time. The alternatives are coded in a *select* statement, with *or* as a separator. In addition, Boolean guards, similar to barriers, can define conditions for selection of an entry. Below is a *Buffer* task that implements the same functions as the protected type presented earlier in this section. Figure 9.2 shows the interactions

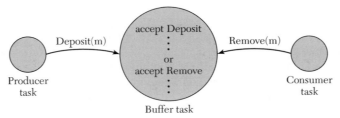

Figure 9.2 Bounded buffer as a separate task.

among the *Buffer*, *Producer*, and *Consumer* tasks. This model, in which the *Buffer* is a separate task, is analogous to the CRSM model presented earlier in Section 4.1.

```
-- Buffer Task
task body Buffer is
      buf : data(0 . . 99);
      inb, outb, full : Natural := 0;
begin
      loop
          select
              when full < buf'Length =>
                  accept Deposit(m : in data) do
                      buf(inb) := m;
                      inb := (inb + 1) mod buf'Length;
                      full := full + 1;
                  end;
          or
              when full > 0 =>
                  accept Remove(m : out data) do
                      m := buf(outb);
                      outb := (outb + 1) mod buf'Length;
                      full := full - 1;
                  end;
          or
              terminate;
          end select;
      end loop;
end Buffer;
```

If several alternatives are possible at the same time, one is selected nondeterministically. The *terminate* alternative is selected if there are no active tasks that could call *Buffer*; this terminates the *Buffer* task. As an aside, a protected type can be implemented more efficiently than a task that performs the same function; an Ada task is a larger "heavyweight" object. Given the choice, small resource managers, such as *Buffer*, should be coded as protected types.

An *else* clause may also be used in a selective *accept* list. If none of the accepts can be taken immediately, the statements associated with the *else* are executed. Timeouts, using the *delay* and *delay_until* statements, can be programmed in a manner similar to entry calls on protected objects. If a rendezvous is not made by the designated time, control is transferred to the statements following the *delay* or *delay_until* statement.

Exceptions

Ada has a particularly clean scheme for declaring, raising, and handling exceptions. An exception is an unusual situation that occurs during execution and that requires special processing. The term usually refers to errors, faults, and abnormal or exceptional behaviors; however, they can be defined for arbitrary purposes by the applications programmer. Exceptions are a built-in type of the language. Thus, for example, one could write

```
missed_deadline, overload, bad_temperature : exception;
```

which declares the three variables, *missed_deadline*, *overload*, and *bad_temperature*, to be of type *exception*.

If the condition corresponding to the intent of an exception variable occurs, the exception can be signalled with the *raise* operation. A typical example is

```
if elapsed_time > deadline then raise missed_deadline; end if;
```

A signalled or "raised" exception causes a forced transfer of control to a handler. Handlers for one or more exceptions are placed in an *exception* block and distinguished by *when* clauses, as illustrated by the following program segment.

```
begin
      -- This is the normal code block. It can conditionally raise 3
      -- exceptions,
      -- depending upon the program execution state.
         . . .
      if elapsed_time>deadline then raise missed_deadline; end if;
         . . .
      if overload_condition then raise overload; end if;
         . . .
      if temperature_is_bad then raise bad_temperature; end if;
         . . . .
exception
      -- This is the exception block.
      when overload =>
          -- overload exception handling code
      when missed_deadline =>
          Log_Fault;
          if threshhold_exceeded then Call_Operator; end if;
      when bad_temperature =>
          -- bad_temperature handler
end;
```

Whenever the code "*raise missed_deadline*" is executed, there is a direct and immediate transfer to the corresponding handler in the *exception* block. If a handler for an exception doesn't appear in the local context where it is raised, the exception is propagated to a dynamically enclosing context. Common exceptions are built in to the language along with default handlers. Examples include *Constraint_Error*, such as divide by zero or array index not within bounds, *Program_Error* such as object not accessible, and *Storage_Error* such as space exceeded.

9.2.2 Annex Mechanisms for Real-Time Programming

The *Systems Programming* annex of Ada offers some useful facilities for handling interrupts, shared variables, and tasks. A *Task_Identification* package specifies operations that access the identity of a current or a calling task; and a *Task_Attributes* package permits the association of user-defined properties to tasks. These packages allow users to write their own task schedulers and resource servers. For example, the function *Current_Task* returns the identity of its caller; and the expression *Resource_Request'Caller* yields the caller of *Resource_Request*, more precisely, the identity of the task being serviced within the entry name *Resource_Request* in an *accept* or a protected procedure call. An implementation must also support interfaces to machine code through a *Machine_Code* package; this allows the insertion of machine language code, including IO and other privileged instructions when appropriate.

There are two attractive and higher-level program models for interrupts, both of which are supported in Ada. Both models view the hardware that generates an interrupt as a task or process that calls a software handler with an interrupt message. In Ada, an interrupt is equivalent to an entry call by the hardware. The interrupt-handling software is treated either as a task that accepts the interrupt or as an entry in a protected object (Figure 9.3).

In the task approach, the software handler has the general form

```
accept interrupt _name(pars) do
        -- Handle interrupt.
end;
```

where *interrupt_name* identifies the interrupt and *pars* are any data associated with it. Entry calls can be directly mapped into physical memory addresses that correspond to the interrupt locations in the target computer; this is accomplished with an Ada *pragma*, which is a declarative note to the compiler, usually concerning optimization, listing control, or error checking.

► Examples of Interrupt Handling

1. At the termination of an IO operation, the interrupt could be sent to the task *IO_Handler* with the entry call

```
IO_Handler.end_of_io(status).
```

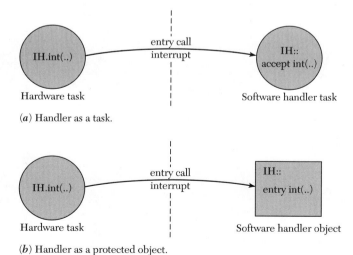

(*a*) Handler as a task.

(*b*) Handler as a protected object.

Figure 9.3 Interrupt models in Ada.

The handler task *IO_Handler* would include the statement

```
accept end_of_io(m).
```

2. A hardware clock that emits periodic "tick" interrupts may be connected to a *Timer* task that counts ticks and to user tasks that read or reset the counter. The interrupt is modelled by the entry call *Timer.tick*; user calls are *Timer.read_counter(v)* and *Timer.reset*. This organization is sketched in Figure 9.4(*a*).

The *Timer* task has the outline

```
task body Timer is
     ...
begin
     ...
     select
          accept tick do
               c := c+ 1;
          end;
     or
          accept read_counter(v) do
               v := c;
          end;
     or
          accept reset do
               c := 0;
          end;
     end select;
     ...
end Timer; ♦
```

The above tasking alternative is considered obsolete in Ada 95, mainly because of the execution overhead incurred by tasking. Instead, the model of protected types is recommended and supported more extensively. Thus, redoing Example 2 above, the *Timer* task would be replaced by a protected type, as in Figure 9.4(*b*). The handler for the *tick* interrupt would be this entry in the protected type *Timer*:

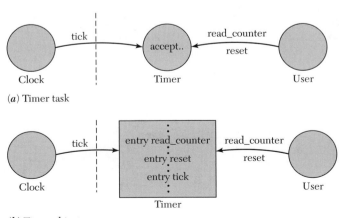

(*a*) Timer task

(*b*) Timer object

Figure 9.4 Clock, timer, and user interactions.

```
. . .
entry tick is
begin
        c := c + 1;
end tick;
. . .
```

A package named *Interrupts* is available for attaching, connecting machine storage addresses to, and naming interrupts and handlers.

The *Distributed Systems* annex is an ambitious attempt to provide some support for implementing distributed applications, certainly including real-time ones. In particular, there are facilities for defining partitions of a program and for communicating among partitions. One or more partitions may reside in each node of a distributed system. Partitions are classified as either *passive* or *active*. Passive partitions have no threads of control; they correspond to storage areas containing data or code that may be used or shared by active partitions. Active partitions communicate with one another through remote procedure calls.

Some specific support for real-time programming is provided in the *Real-Time* annex, especially in the areas of priority and scheduling control, timing, asynchronous task control, and tasking restrictions. Through appropriate pragmas, tasks may be assigned priorities and scheduled preemptively on a priority basis. Similarly, priorities can be associated with protected interrupt-handler objects.

Priorities may change dynamically when accessing protected objects; a priority ceiling policy (Section 6.4) is used unless specified otherwise.[3] Inheritance also occurs during a rendezvous—an accepting task inherits the priority of the caller. Different policies for servicing entry calls can be chosen. First-in-first-out and priority queuing are both available within the language, and either can be selected with pragmas.

A timing package, called *Real_Time*, offers a better mechanism for accessing, controlling, and manipulating time than does the core *Calendar* package. In particular, the *Clock* function is guaranteed to return monotonic time, and time has a higher resolution. Clock "ticks" must be separated by no more than 1 ms, and functions exist to convert time data to nanoseconds, microseconds, and milliseconds. An implementation is required to document, through an Ada *metric*, important upper bound information such as the size of a forward clock jump, the execution time of a *Clock* function call, and the delay in responding to expired *delay* and *delay_until* statements. The periodic task *P* coded at the beginning of Section 9.2.1 would perform as desired using the *Real_Time* package and appropriate priorities.

Tasks can be suspended and resumed by other tasks using functions defined in the *Asynchronous_Task_Control* package. While not recommended in general because of its interactions with other features of the language, particularly blocking primitives and priority scheduling, this package is useful for constructing small applications on top of simple run-time systems where little is hidden under the Ada code. Many reductions on the complexity of tasking can be declared with a *Restrictions* pragma. For example, no dynamic priorities or no use of *terminate* within a selective *accept* might be specified. Compilers can use this information to generate more efficient run-time systems.

---

[3]Many of the priority ceiling and inversion results discussed in Section 6.4 were produced in the context of attempting to deal with problems of the earlier Ada 83.

Finally, a *Safety and Security* annex is concerned with programming for safety-critical systems and others, such as systems for electronic funds transfer. These systems need extraordinary assurances of correctness. Included are pragmas and documentation requirements to ensure, for example, that uninitialized variables are set to predictable values; that the object-level code corresponding to Ada source language constructs can be reviewed; that implementation decisions, such as parameter passing conventions or run-time storage management methods, are known; and that run-time values of designated objects are available for debugging and analysis at programmer-specified declaration or statement points.

In summary, the Ada designers have produced a thoughtful, complete, and concept-rich language that goes far beyond any of its predecessors or competitors. The principal criticism is that the language contains perhaps *too* much. A thoughtful analysis prepared for the U.S. Department of Defense concludes that Ada is superior for real-time warfighting applications when compared with other language alternatives [Ada&Beyond97].

▶ 9.3 ADA AND SOFTWARE FAULT TOLERANCE

Failures can occur during the execution of computer systems due to hardware or software *faults*, where a fault is some defect in the system. Software faults are most often caused by errors in specification and design, and, less frequently, by coding mistakes. *Fault tolerance* refers to the ability of a computer system to continue to meet its service requirements in the presence of faults. Originating with the first computers, a considerable technology has evolved for modelling and treating hardware faults [Avizienis, Kopetz&Laprie87]. The field of software fault tolerance, however, is still in its infancy.

The first subsection defines the types of faults that may occur in a system, and then gives an overview of methods for preventing, detecting, and recovering from failures. Section 9.3.2 describes two approaches to design diversity, recovery blocks and *n*-version programming; examples of Ada implementations are discussed.

9.3.1 Software Failures: Prevention, Detection, and Recovery

A useful and interesting classification of software (and hardware) faults in distributed systems is given in [Cristian91]. The unit of possible software failure is a *server*. This is a generic object that responds to a given set of input operations or messages; operations can be requested or messages sent, either directly by clients of the service or implicitly by the passage of time. Also specified are the responses, either output or state changes, that are made to each input. Examples of such servers are: a radar subsystem that receives signal inputs and user commands, and responds appropriately; a process scheduler that is invoked explicitly by a controlling process or implicitly at the end of a time frame; or a clock server that responds to read requests, update operations, and synchronization messages.

A software server is working correctly if it is responding with the right outputs or state changes, and within specified time intervals, to its inputs; otherwise a failure or fault occurs. Servers may fail in several different ways. An *omissions* failure is one where the server does not respond to an invocation or input. This might occur in a buffering system that drops inputs whenever the buffers are all full, without notifying the producer; or in one that doesn't respond to output requests from a consumer whenever the buffers are empty.

A *crash* is defined when a server has an omissions failure followed by no response to all subsequent inputs, until possibly a restart. *Amnesia* and *pause* crashes are those that can be restarted, without any or some state restoration, respectively; a *halt* crash never restarts. An example of a pause crash would be a server that is deadlocked; for restart and recovery, it may be possible to set the state of the server and other involved objects back to a previous check-pointed value.

Perhaps less dramatic, but equally important, are *response* failures. These occur whenever input to a server produces an incorrect output or state transition. Response failures are associated with conventional errors in requirements, design, or programming. Finally, *performance* or *timing* failures are defined when a server does not respond within its specified time interval—the response is either too early or too late.

The major problems in fault tolerance are fault *prevention* or *avoidance*, fault *detection* and *assessment*, and fault *recovery* and *correction*. Prevention is, of course, the best solution wherever it is feasible. The recommended way to avoid most software failures is to produce correct requirements and design specifications, ideally using formal methods such as those presented in Chapters 3 through 5. Typically, specifications are inconsistent, ambiguous, incomplete, or don't describe accurately the intent of the client. For example, the extended finite state machine for the controller of the train crossing gate given in Section 3.4 and Figure 3.12 is incomplete because it doesn't include timing constraints. Many specification errors that would result in faults can be discovered through intensive analysis and simulation.

Given a correct specification, faults can still occur because of implementation mistakes. Such program errors are found by conventional debugging and, where possible, through program proving. However, the above techniques are rarely, if ever, sufficient to produce a fault-free system. Algorithms may be incorrect, the different possible types of failures that a component can experience may not be known, and the interactions between the software and its environment are almost never predictable in total.

In the train crossing gate application, for example, the sensors that indicate train entry or exit from the crossing area may fail in a variety of ways: they may generate extraneous signals, they may neglect to generate a signal, or they may not be able to handle overload conditions when multiple trains enter quickly. These types of hardware errors must, of course, be expected. An associated software mistake might be not to anticipate and test for the kinds of incorrect and untimely data caused by the sensor errors; for example, a simple consistency requirement is that the number of trains entering the crossing must always be greater or equal to the number that have left the area. In summary, the design engineer must expect faults and provide appropriate handling and identification mechanisms.

Formally, a run-time fault is defined when some assertion on the system state is violated. Detection thus involves evaluating some Boolean condition at an appropriate time or place. Ideally, the damage associated with a fault can then be determined from the values of the state variables at the time of detection. Performing these two functions in a practical setting is much more complex. Unfortunately, a failure is often detected some time after it initially occurred and after it has produced additional damage that masks out the original cause.

Recovery and correction involve somehow putting the system in a consistent state, correcting or isolating the error if possible so that the fault does not immediately recur, and continuing or repeating execution. Two standard approaches to fault recovery are *forward* recovery and *backward* recovery. The backward method is similar to the one adopted in most conventional operating systems and database systems: System states are stored or "checkpointed" at frequent intervals; on an error or abort, the state is "rolled back" to the most recent checkpoint and the computation is repeated. This is a very attractive technique, but not always possible to use in a real-time application. The state may be unrecoverable, especially if an operation has affected the physical environment. Consider a robot performing some manufacturing operation, say cutting a metal part. If some fault occurs during the operation when half the part has been cut, it may not be possible to undo the partial execution, that is, "sew" the part back together again, and repeat with a corrected or backup robot. Backward recovery may also require too much time.

For forward recovery, a consistent future state is determined, the system is forced or placed into that state, and execution is resumed from that point. As an example, a pressure or location sensor that is periodically sampled might occasionally produce an erroneous data fault because of some intermittent external disturbance. A forward recovery solution is to discard the bad data and use an extrapolation of previous samples as part of the next future state. In the robot example above, a consistent future state might be obtained by discarding the partially manufactured part and starting on a new part. Typically, forward recovery time is more predictable and faster than the time for rollback. In both approaches to recovery, some noncomputer intervention may be necessary in order to isolate, repair, or determine the cause of the fault or to recover. For example, an air traffic control system or an on-board flight control system might switch from automatic to manual mode when certain faults are detected.

Exception handling facilities such as those in Ada are programming language mechanisms for implementing fault tolerant software. Assertions on states can be checked within blocks, exceptions raised and propagated on violations, and exception handlers called to perform the assessment and recovery procedures.

Several models and approaches to the software fault tolerance problem have been developed. One set of techniques employs the *transaction processing* ideas developed for database systems, such as concurrency control, atomicity, serializability, and consistency. An example is the *time-sensitive object* paradigm [Callison95], which defines a data-centered view of real-time systems as an alternative to the popular process or task-based one. The *imprecise computation* method [Liu_et_al94] has also been proposed for avoiding and handling timing faults. Here, a task may be decomposed into two parts, a mandatory part and an optional part that may be skipped if there is not enough time to complete it. In another variation of the imprecise computation technique, a task may have several versions, each executing for different lengths of time and producing results of different precisions; the version selected for execution depends on the time available. This last alternative is an example of *design diversity*. We discuss its two most popular realizations in the next section and present some realizations using Ada constructs.

9.3.2 Approaches to Design Diversity

The accepted way to achieve reliability and fault tolerance in hardware devices is through redundancy. Several identical copies of a component are maintained. In one approach, only a single copy is used at any time; if it fails, the copy is replaced by a non-faulty clone. Alternatively, a number of copies can be in execution simultaneously and the results of each are compared; some decision procedure, such as majority voting, is used to arrive at an acceptable result. There is a serious problem with directly using these methods for software. If one copy has an error, then *all* copies will have that same error![4] Therefore repeating a computation with a clone or comparing results from several copies produces the same error. (Some timing errors are exceptions to this latter statement, since repeating, by definition, means that the component(s) will be executed at a later time.)

Recovery Blocks

One well-known mechanism that uses design diversity for software fault tolerance is *recovery blocks* (RB), originally developed in the 1970s at the University of Newcastle Upon Tyne [Randall75]. Several different versions of a program are collected together and run in sequence until some version passes an acceptance test. This test is a program-testable assertion or Boolean expression that is checked after the execution of each version. If all versions fail, then an external recovery must be initiated. Generally, the versions are written by the same person or team, and differ in their algorithms or in the environmental variables that they access. For example, several sensors of differing precision or complexity may be used for the same input, such as location, presence, temperature, or pressure; or the versions could correspond to different signal processing algorithms.

▶ ### RB Example: Clock Synchronization

Suppose that a workstation periodically keeps its clock synchronized with a centralized server. The server of first choice is one available on the local area network, designated LAN; if that fails, a wide area network time server, denoted WAN, can be used; if the WAN server has a fault, a satellite SAT is used. In the worst case, that is, SAT failure, the workstation doesn't reset its clock.

The workstation time is kept as a pair *<My_Clock, My_Error>*, as in Section 8.4.1; each server responds with a *<Clock, Error>* pair. A server is considered faulty if any of three conditions hold: it doesn't respond within a given time *dt*; its clock value differs from *My_Clock* by more than *eps*; or its error differs from *My_Error* by more than *delta*. The algorithm for retrieving and computing the *<Clock, Error>* pair is assumed different for each server. Below is a program fragment for doing this in recovery block form, using Ada-like constructs:

```
V := 0 ; -- Initialize the version number V.
loop
        V := V + 1 ; response := true ; -- Prepare to run the next version.
        if (V>3) then -- All versions have been tried: unrecoverable error.
                raise Timer_Error;
        end if ;
        select
                when (V=1) => accept LAN.Time(C, E) ;
        or
                when (V=2) => accept WAN.Time(C, E) ;
```

---

[4]This problem does not normally occur in hardware, unless there are logical errors in its design. The efficacy of the redundancy approach is based on the physics of the components and their probability of failure.

```
        or
                when (V=3) => accept SAT.Time(C, E) ;
        or
                delay dt ; response := false ;
        end select;
        -- Test the acceptance assertion and exit the loop if it evaluates to
        --      true.
        if response then
                exit when (abs(My_Clock- C) ≤ eps) and ((My_Error - E) ≤
                        delta) ;
        end if ;
    end loop;
    MY_Clock := C ; My_Error := E ;♦
```

The method is an example of backward recovery since the state is restored on a failure of the acceptance test and the next version is tried.[5] The worst case timing is the sum of the times of all versions plus the *Timer_Error* exception part; this may be excessive. One suggested technique to improve upon the timing is to have all versions execute in parallel on different processors, so that if one version fails, its successor has already completed part or all of its computation. Note also that the RB technique may not work if the acceptance assertion involves time, such as a deadline. For example, let the acceptance test be

```
elapsed_time < deadline
```

in which *elapsed_time* is the time starting from first entry to the block. Then if the assertion fails the first time through, it will always fail!

N-Version Programming
In this scheme, developed at UCLA (e.g., [Avizienis89]), *n* different versions of a program are also produced, but *independently* by different teams. The same specification is used by each team. All versions are executed in parallel, and a decision or voting procedure determines the accepted result of a computation. The idea underlying the *n*-version programming (NVS) method is that independently written programs are unlikely to have the same errors.

▶ NVS Example: Clock Synchronization

We use the same example as in the RB discussion above, except that an attempt is made to access all three timers, LAN, WAN, and SAT, in order to make a decision. In this NVS variation, *n* = 3 and each server is assumed to be written independently. A clock is deemed acceptable if it responds within a given time interval *dt* and passes a *Range_Check,* which is essentially the acceptance assertion used in the RB example. The resulting clock time is the average of the acceptable clocks, provided that at least two timers have values within range; the error is computed as the maximum error of the acceptable clocks. We use *accepts* in the workstation code, assuming that the servers interact only with our workstation through entry calls.

---

[5]Time continues to march forward, so the state cannot be entirely restored in general.

```
n := 0 ; V1 := V2 := V3 := false ; C := E := 0 ;
loop
      select
            when ¬V1 => accept LAN.Time(C1, E1) do
                  V1 := true ;
                  if Range_Check(C1, E1) then
                        n := n+1 ; C := C+C1 ; E := max(E, E1) ; end if ;
                  end ;
      or
            when ¬V2 => accept WAN.Time(C2, E2) do
                  V2 := true ;
                  if Range_Check(C2, V2) then
                        n := n+1 ; C := C+C2 ; E := max(E, E2) ; end if ;
                  end ;
      or
            when ¬V3 => accept SAT.Time(C3, E3) do
                  V3 := true ;
                  if Range_Check(C3, E3) then
                        n := n+1 ; C := C+C3 ; E := max(E, E3) ; end if ;
                  end;
      or
            delay dt ; exit ; -- No response from timers. Leave loop.
      end select ;
      exit when ( V1 ∧ V2 ∧ V3 ) ; -- Leave loop if all timers have
      --      responded.
end loop ;
-- Choose result.
if n > 1 then My_Clock := C/n ; My_Error := E ;
else raise Timer_Error; end if; ◆
```

Despite the obvious appeal of NVS, it has some limitations and has been the subject of much controversy. It is not evident that different teams writing program versions from the *same* specification will make independent errors. In fact, the experimental evidence seems to be the opposite—programs have similar errors and fail in similar ways [Leveson95]. In principle, the timing behavior of NVS is superior to that of RB because all results are computed in parallel; however, the decision-making procedure can be quite complex and the parallel computations must be synchronized. Error recovery is somewhat ad hoc. Faulty versions could be eliminated or some form of "community" recovery can be adopted [Avizienis89]. In community recovery, a faulty program is reset with the agreed-upon results and the internal state of the nonfaulty versions. In the synchronization example, $3 - n$ faulty timers would be set to C/n and E, provided that $n > 1$.[6]

Several applications have used a combination of the RB and NVS approaches, especially in safety-critical systems such as those for aircraft control. For example, the flight control software for both the Boeing 737/300 and Airbus A-320 has multiple version components. Each component is self-checking; this is accomplished either through an RB-like acceptance test or by comparing results from different algorithms.

---

[6]This particular example is especially simple, since there can be at most one faulty timer.

Components are executed sequentially (if necessary) in RB fashion; if a component fails, the system switches to another one of independent design.

► 9.4 JAVA AND REAL-TIME EXTENSIONS

Java was originally designed in the early 1990s for programming embedded controllers for consumer products, such as microwave ovens. Instead, it has become the most popular *general purpose* language of the day. It was strongly influenced by C++ and its object orientation, and by modern notions of concurrency, especially threads and monitors. In addition to these features, perhaps the main reasons for Java's widespread adoption are its portability ("write once run anywhere") and its ease of use over the Internet via *applets*. We introduce some of the basic concurrency mechanisms in the language, then discuss the problems in using Java for real-time applications, and finally present some interesting extensions proposed by the Real-Time for Java Expert Group [Naughton&Schild97; Lea97; RTJEG00].

Java is fundamentally object-oriented (OO), and the OO framework is also employed to define the active objects of concurrency. These are the Java threads. The *Thread* class is the basis or ancestor class for all threads. Particular threads may be specified by subclassing the *Thread* class (with the *extends* keyword), and programming a *run* method[7] for the new object; the *run* method contains the thread's executable code.[8]

A thread instance is activated by calling the *start* method. This call invokes the *run* method of the thread. For example, the call

```
Producer.start();
```

would make the thread named *Producer* ready for execution. *Producer*'s code, its *run* method, might do some computing and then insert some data m into a buffer by calling the *Deposit* method of a *Buffer* object, say with

```
Buffer.Deposit(m);
```

The *Buffer* object might be an instance of a general class for bounded buffers, say *BB*, and declared with the code

```
BB Buffer = new BB();
```

Other methods available from the *Thread* class for managing threads include *join*, which causes a caller to wait until a thread completes before continuing execution. Consider a *Process_Data* thread which must wait until a *Get_Data* thread terminates before it can continue. To do this, *Process_Data* would call

```
Get_Data.join();
```

---

[7]The term "method" refers to a named function, procedure, or operation defined in a Java class.
[8]A second standard, but more complicated, way to declare a new thread is by creating a class that implements the *Runnable* interface.

The *join* routine will also take a parameter that defines a time limit for waiting for the target thread to terminate, that is, a timeout on the *join*. The *Thread* class also supports a *sleep* method that delays or blocks the calling thread for a given time.

Somewhat like Ada, control of shared data within objects is achieved through a form of monitors. The keyword *synchronized* associated with methods in an object declares that the methods must be implemented to guarantee mutually exclusive access by threads; only one thread at a time can be executing a synchronized method of a given object. This mutual exclusion is identical to that obtained in Ada with protected types (Section 9.2.1). However, Java has more conventional synchronization primitives that can be used within a synchronized method.

In particular, there are *wait*, *notify*, and *notifyAll* methods. A *wait* will always block the calling thread and release control, that is, the lock, of the monitor object. *notify* will wake up, that is, unblock, one waiting thread provided that there is at least one waiter; otherwise, it has no effect. All waiters are awakened by a *notifyAll*. A timeout parameter can also be specified with a *wait*; the thread unblocks on a timeout if it hasn't been notified earlier.

▶ Bounded Buffer Example

Here is a Java class named *BB* that implements a bounded buffer. In the example given above, a *Producer* thread invokes the *Deposit* method on an instance of *BB* named *Buffer*.

```
class BB {
        private int inb = 0, outb = 0, full = 0;
        private buf = new Object[99];

        synchronized void Deposit(Object x) {
                while (full == 100)
                        try{ wait(); } catch(InterruptedException e) {};
                buf[inb] = x;
                inb = (inb + 1) % 100 ; // '%' is the modulus operator.
                full = full + 1;
                notify();
        }

        synchronized void Remove(Object x) {
                while (full == 0)
                        try{ wait(); } catch(InterruptedException e) {};
                x = buf[outb];
                outb = (outb + 1) % 100 ;
                full = full - 1;
                notify();
        }
}
```

The first two statements of both routines perform almost the same functions as do the entry barriers to the analogous Ada routines in Section 9.2.1. In *Deposit*, for example, whenever *full* = 0, the calling thread will block on the *wait*; a subsequent *notify* by another thread executing a *BB* method will wake up a blocked thread. The *try* and *catch* clauses are part of the Java exception handling scheme. In *BB*, they allow for some interrupt, an *InterruptedException*, to also undo the *wait*. The curly brackets following *catch* enclose the exception handling routine that would be invoked when the *InterruptedException* is raised or *thrown*. ♦

The major problems with using conventional Java for real-time applications are that it is unpredictable and it doesn't permit user control of system resources, such as main memory. Priorities can be attached to threads, but there is no obligation that a system schedules exactly or fairly according to priority. Priority inversions can easily occur when using synchronized methods in monitors. As mentioned earlier, essential run-time utilities, particularly the garbage collector that scans and reclaims the heap storage for objects that are no longer needed, can asynchronously interrupt computations and run for unbounded amounts of time.

While Java has an elaborate and complete *Date* class that provides access to absolute time and the date as well as operations on them, the granularity of the clock is coarse, in the order of milliseconds. Time is also treated loosely in methods that permit a timeout or delay, such as *wait*, *sleep*, and *join* (but these do allow nanosecond level specifications). The semantics only specify that a time expiration occurs at some time greater or equal to the specified parameter, but how much greater is not known. Also, like most object-oriented systems, it is subject to inheritance anomalies.

A comprehensive and voluminous proposal to extend Java and rectify these problems appears in [RTJEG00]. The real-time extensions are quite interesting also because they incorporate many of the important technical ideas presented earlier in the book. The principal new features relate to thread and memory management.

Two new thread classes, subclasses of *Thread*, are defined: *RealtimeThread* and *NoHeapRealtimeThread*. Fixed priority preemptive scheduling is the required default implementation policy, including the priority inheritance protocol for avoiding priority inversion in monitors. The priority ceiling protocol is an additional option; other options are possible but they must prevent unbounded priority inversions. The real-time threads have a large number of new methods, as well as a variety of parameters, that can be used to characterize the threads and control scheduling. Essentially, they allow the specification of periodic, sporadic, and aperiodic processes. Instances of *NoHeapRealtimeThread* cannot reference objects from the Java heap, cannot interact with the system's garbage collector, and are run with a higher set of priorities than the garbage collector; thus, these threads can safely and predictably interrupt the garbage collector.

Control of memory, excluding the garbage-collected heap, is also supported. Objects may be allocated to *scoped*, *physical*, or *immortal* (long-lived) storage. Scopes are blocks of code in which memory for a set of objects is allocated and deallocated. They can be entered and exited, in a nested fashion; storage for objects instantiated in a given scope is deallocated on leaving the scope. Objects that reside in immortal memory are shared among all threads, and remain accessible until an application terminates. The physical memory facilities allow object allocation to explicit physical (hardware) regions.

The proposed timing mechanisms are high-resolution versions of both absolute and relative time; time objects have nanosecond precision. There is also an interesting extension of relative time called *RationalTime* that deals in frequencies, such as the number of cycles per second. In addition, one can create any number of either periodic or one-shot timers that will generate an event at the end of a given period or at the expiration of a given time, respectively. Reaction to these and other events can be programmed using either asynchronous event handlers or mechanisms for the asynchronous transfer of control. The proposal also contains a requirement that there be a mapping, that is, a binding, between POSIX signals and equivalent Java asynchronous events whenever the underlying operating system supports POSIX signals. (POSIX is discussed in the next chapter.)

There is little doubt that one or more forms of real-time Java will become more widely available and used. What still remains to be tested and confirmed is whether software that satisfies many of the deterministic constraints appearing in real-time applications can be generated. Java, and especially including the proposed real-time extensions, appears to suffer from the same problems as Ada, only more so: it is too large a language.

▶ 9.5 CSP AND OCCAM

In the late 1970s, Hoare proposed some programming constructs for distributed computing in the form of a small language called communicating sequential processes (CSP) [Hoare78]. The concepts were later refined and developed into a theory [Hoare85]. CSP has been influential in both the theory and practice of programming. As one example, the Ada *select* statement borrowed ideas from CSP. Many CSP notions were commercialized in a complete language, named Occam, and an associated multicomputer system, the Transputer, that was marketed for real-time applications (e.g., [Inmos84,88]). We present the major ideas in CSP/Occam, omitting many of the details.

The principal innovations in CSP are its IO and use of nondeterministic guarded commands. IO between processes is defined as synchronous message passing over named, typed, one-to-one, unbuffered, and unidirectional channels. The IO operations for communicating real-time state machines (CRSMs), described in Section 4.1, is modelled directly after CSP. Nondeterministic guarded commands were originally defined by Dijkstra [Dijkstra75]. Hoare embedded IO within guarded commands in a clever way; this combination provides the basis for process synchronization in CSP.

Dijktra's guarded commands take the form $G_i \rightarrow C_i$ and appear in a list of nondeterministic possibilities. In the syntax given below, they are separated by *or*s. The general form of a command list is

```
G₁ → C₁ or G₂ → C₂ or . . . or Gₙ → Cₙ
```

where the guards G_i are Boolean expressions and the commands C_i are statement sequences. The interpretation is that only the commands corresponding to *true* guards are eligible for execution at any time, and that only one of the eligible ones is actually selected; the choice is made nondeterministically.

The command lists are embedded within control structures that define either a conditional list of alternatives or a looping version as follows:

```
conditional:    if command_list fi
looping:        do command_list od
```

If a guarded command list is surrounded by an *if/fi* pair, then an alternative is indicated; the list is exited after the execution of the selected alternative. A loop is indicated by a *do/od* pair surrounding the guarded command list; execution of the list is repeated until all of the guards are *false*. The next two examples demonstrate in particularly simple settings the ideas and rationale underlying guarded commands.

▶ **Examples of Guarded Commands [Dijkstra75]**

1. The program

```
if x ≥ y → m := x or y ≥ x → m := y fi
```

computes the maximum of x and y. If $x = y$, then one of the two commands, m := x or m := y, is selected nondeterministically. The programmer need not select which choice should be made when $x = y$; either choice produces a correct answer. Using a conventional *if/then/else*, the programmer is forced to choose the execution path.

2. The following code computes the greatest common divisor of two positive integers X and Y, which we denote as $\gcd(X, Y)$. The basis for the program are these results:

$$(1)\ \gcd(x, y) = \gcd(y, x \bmod y) \text{ when } x \neq y \text{ and}$$
$$(2)\ \gcd(x, y) = \begin{cases} \gcd(x - y, y) \text{ if } x > y \\ \gcd(x, y - x) \text{ if } y > x \\ x \text{ if } x = y. \end{cases}$$

Program:

```
x := X; y := Y;
do
        x > y → x := x - y
             or
        y > x → y := y - x
od
```

The loop body keeps repeating as long as either $x > y$ or $y > x$. (Note that a compiler or run-time system can choose the order of testing for these conditions.) When the loop finally exits, $x = y = \gcd(X, Y)$. ◆

A process P wishing to send a message m to another process Q on a channel ch connecting P and Q issues the output command

```
ch(m)!
```

Q receives the message with the input command

```
ch(x)?
```

P blocks until Q is ready for the IO or Q blocks until P is ready. If both are ready and the IO is selected, it occurs instantaneously; both processes then continue onto their next statements. At the receiving side (Q), the effect of the IO is identical to the assignment statement x := m. For the sender P, the effect is equivalent to a *null* statement.

In CSP and Occam, an input command may also appear at the end of a guard, using the general form:

```
Boolean_expression & channel_name(target_variable)?
```

If the *Boolean_expression* evaluates to *true*, then the input may occur as part of the guard. In this form, the expression ressembles an Ada *select*, where the *Boolean_expression* appears in the Ada *when* clause and the input is analogous to an *accept*.

An output command, however, cannot appear in a guard. This choice was made mainly because an implementation becomes more complex when both input and output are permitted in guards. This restriction has been controversial because of the resulting asymmetry between input and output, as the next example illustrates.

Next is an outline for our standard *Buffer* process that defines a bounded buffer (e.g., Section 9.2.1), written in the style of CSP/Occam. *Buffer* is connected to a producer process by a *Deposit* channel and to a consumer process by a *Remove* channel. Also, because only an input command can occur in a guard, the removal activity requires an additional channel, which we call *Request_Remove*, to notify *Buffer* that a *Remove* is forthcoming.

```
Buffer :: ...
            in := out := full := 0;
            do
                ( full<n & Deposit(Buf(in))? ) →
                        begin
                                in := ( in + 1 ) mod n;
                                full := full + 1
                        end
                            or
                ( full>0 & Request_Remove()? ) →
                        begin
                                Remove(Buf(out))! ;
                                out := ( out + 1 ) mod n ;
                                full := full −1
                        end
        od
```

The producer process will insert an element *m* into the buffer by sending a single *Deposit* message to the *Buffer*:

```
Deposit(m)!
```

However, the consumer process must execute two IO instructions in sequence in order to obtain an element from the buffer:

```
Request_Remove()! ; Remove(m)?
```

Note that this kind of "handshake" is not required for the task version of *Buffer* in Ada because the rendezvous also includes the execution of a statement list, associated with the *accept*, that can contain output for the entry call. Essentially, CSP programs communicate through message passing, while Ada provides a synchronous procedure call. The CSP/Occam constructs are at a lower level, but admit to more efficient implementations.

Also available in Occam are low-level delay and clock access functions. These have a superficial similarity to the CRSM timing operations (Section 4.1.2), but are quite different in detail. A local clock can be declared as a channel-like entity with a *TIMER* declaration. For example,

```
TIMER: Clock1;
```

declares that *Clock*1 is a local clock. To access this timer, an input command such as

```
Clock1? now
```

is employed. This returns a time or ticker value of *integer* type in the variable *now*, relative to some arbitrary and implementation-dependent time "origin."

A delay is obtained with a *TIMER* by using the keyword *AFTER*. For example,

```
Clock1? AFTER now PLUS 10
```

will cause the invoking process to wait until the *Clock*1 timer attains the value of *now PLUS* 10. Note that the expression after *AFTER* is interpreted as a timer value, not as a time relative to the call.[9]

Occam processes are scheduled according to statically-assigned priorities. The system also provides for user pre-allocation of hardware resources: processes can be allocated to machines and Occam channels can be identified with physical Transputer channels.

Occam has been used successfully for building relatively small embedded controllers, and as a research and teaching language, particularly for Transputer multicomputer environments. It is a much smaller language than either Ada or Java. On the other hand, Occam lacks many features of these larger languages, for example, module structures for programming-in-the-large.

▶ 9.6 ESTEREL CONCEPTS

Almost all real-time programming languages, including Ada, CSP, and Real-Time Euclid, are complete general purpose languages with additional constructs for concurrency and for controlling and accessing time. Esterel is a thought-provoking exception that has some similarities with statecharts (Section 4.2). It was invented by researchers in southern France in the early 1980s and has undergone a number of changes since then. Our presentation is based primarily on their 1992 definitions [Berry&Gonthier 92].

The purpose of Esterel is to provide a deterministic language for programming the *reactive* part of an application—the part that interacts with, accepts, monitors, and controls the signals and events of the environment. It is intended to be used in conjunction with a general purpose host language that is responsible for the more conventional data handling and computational aspects of an application. Like statecharts, it assumes an underlying machine that is infinitely fast: the system reacts *instantaneously* to input events.[10]

It is convenient to view the execution of an Esterel program as a state machine. The system is in a given state until one or more events occur. These events cause the system to undergo a "reaction" and enter a new state. The reaction may consist of generating events (output), accepting events that were generated during the reaction, and performing arbitrary but terminating computations. The elements of the state transition

---

[9]The equivalent delay in the CRSM notation (Section 4.1.2) is expressed by *Clock*?[10].
Similarly, the effect of the Occam
```
Clock1? AFTER x
```
is the same as the CRSM sequence
    Clock(*now*)?; *Clock*? [*x* - *now*].
[10]This assumption is called the *synchrony hypothesis* in the Esterel literature.

reaction occur in zero time, but are order preserving if in sequence. A reaction terminates at the "fixed point" defined when there are no more actions that may be executed.

The reactive interface consists of *signals* and *sensors*. Both have a name and a type,
where the type gives the data type of a message or value associated with the signal or
sensor. For example, a temperature sensor may have the declaration

```
Temperature(degrees).
```

Signals correspond to events in the system that occur instantaneously. The last value of
a signal S can be read at any time with the operation

```
?S.
```

When signals occur, they are broadcast instantaneously.

There is no event associated with a sensor. It just has a value that can be accessed
in the same way as a signal with the "?" operator. Thus, a sensor can be viewed as a data
interface whose current value is always available through polling. In order to deal with
time, explicit time signals or sensors need to be defined; for example, a signal may correspond to a tick interrupt or a sensor could be connected to a clock.

Signals can be produced externally from the environment or internally during a reaction. Such signals are *broadcast* throughout the system. A signal S with value v is generated with the command

```
emit S(v).
```

Signals with the same name *collide* if they are generated (and thus broadcast) at the
same time; for example, several parallel components could emit the same signal during
a reaction. As part of the signal declaration, the programmer specifies how signal values
are combined when a collision occurs. This collision handling is defined in a *combination function*.

▶ Signal Collision Example

Let *beep*(v: *integer*) be an output signal on a digital watch giving the number v of beeps
to be emitted by the watch's audio beeper. Suppose that the watch beeps once every
hour, via the command *emit beep*(1), and that an alarm component beeps twice every
second [*emit beep*(2)] when the alarm time expires. If the alarm time expires on an
exact hour, both types of beeps occur simultaneously. When *beep* is declared, the programmer can include a combination function, say, that adds the values of the signal.
Thus, if the alarm goes off at an exact hour, the collision would generate the signal command *emit beep*(3). ◆

The language has some standard statement constructs, such as assignment, conditional, loop, procedure call, parallel execution, null, and halt. All except halt execute infinitely fast, that is, in zero time. The *halt* statement is the only one that takes "time"; it
never terminates. *Halt* essentially puts the underlying machine in a wait state.

Other than the somewhat strange timing behavior of *halt*, the statement semantics
of the standard statements are the normal ones. Variables in parallel statements cannot
be shared. Only signals and sensors are shared.

The most basic and useful signal handling form is the *watching* statement

```
do statement_list watching signal_event
```

which provides a generalized timeout on the event *signal_event*. If *statement_list* terminates before the event occurs, then the watching statement terminates; otherwise, the watching statement terminates as soon as *signal_event* occurs. It is used most often in conjunction with *halt* to specify a wait for an event to occur. For example,

```
do halt watching S
```

executes the nonterminating *halt* until the signal S occurs. This particular form is given the more recognizable syntax

```
await S.
```

A second signal handling statement is

```
present signal_event then statement1 else statement2 end.
```

This tests for the presence of the event *signal_event* in the current reaction, and takes one of the two branches depending on the result.

The last interesting basic feature is a trap mechanism that is used for exiting loops and raising exceptions. The command

```
exit T
```

appearing in the *statement_list* part of the construct

```
trap T in statement_list end
```

forces an immediate exit from the *trap* statement. The trap *exit* is equivalent to the *raise* exception in Ada.

Higher level constructs can be formed from the basic Esterel statements. One useful example is a general *await* or *watching* on multiple occurrences of a given signal. It can be used in statements such as

```
await 1000 meter
```

where *meter* is a signal; the meaning is to delay until the next 1000 occurrences of *meter* have been received. In general, the occurrence count can be an integer expression.

The basic loop is an infinite loop. Loops that exit after a given count or when a given condition becomes true can be implemented using the trap mechanism.

Several other useful loop forms are also defined. An *upto* statement

```
do statement_list upto 10 S
```

terminates after exactly 10 instances of the signal S have occurred, regardless of whether or not *statement_list* has finished executing. Its meaning is given by the basic statements

```
do statement_list; halt; watching 10 S.
```

The *halt* ensures that the *upto* lasts until the signal occurrence count has been reached.

Another convenient loop type executes its body every time a signal occurs. It has the form

```
every S do statement_list end
```

The meaning is

```
await S ;
loop
        do statement_list upto S
end
```

A handler may be associated with a signal "timeout" with this syntax:

```
do statement1 watching S
   timeout statement2
end
```

If the signal *S* occurs during the execution of *statement1*, control is transferred immediately to *statement2*; otherwise (*S* does not occur), control completely bypasses *statement2*. In terms of more primitive statements, this construct can be expressed as

```
trap T in
        do statement1 ; exit T ; watching S ;
        statement2
end
```

▶ **Examples of Esterel Code**

1. Gate controller This is the controller for the railway crossing gate, which was defined and presented in detail in Sections 3.3 and 3.4. The events, *Train_Entering, Train_Leaving, Open_Gate,* and *Close_Gate,* are signals here.

```
count:=0;
loop
        await
            case Train_Entering do
                        count := count + 1 ;
                        if count=1 then emit Close_Gate
            case Train_Leaving do
                        count := count - 1 ;
                        if count=0 then emit Open_Gate
        end
end
```

We have used two other higher level, but simple and convenient, constructs in the code: a *case* within the *await,* and the form

```
await signal do statement_list
```

as a substitute for the two-statement sequence

```
await signal; statement list.
```

Note that there is no nondeterminism in the code (or in Esterel). The tests for the two signals are done sequentially in the order shown.

2. Mouse clicker Input from a mouse device is classified into single clicks (*SC*), double clicks (*DC*), or selections (*SS* for selection start and *SE* for selection end), depending on the time interval between a button push (*D*) and a button release (*U*). The reader should review the clicker example in Section 4.1.3 where this application was defined and developed for CRSMs. For the Esterel solution, assume a *tick* signal emitted by an external clock. Let s ticks be the maximum interval between D and U that determines a single click and d ticks be the threshold time between a U and a following D for a double click; these times were given earlier as t_{SC} and t_{DC}, respectively. The following Esterel code receives a sequence of input button events and emits appropriate *SC*, *DC*, *SS*, and *SE* signals depending on the times between input signals.

```
. . .
loop
   await D ;
      trap T in
            do await U ; watching s tick
               timeout -- Selection has been recognized.
                  emit SS ; await U ; emit SE ; exit T
            end ;
            -- Single click constraints are satisfied.
            do await D ; watching d tick
               timeout -- Single click has been recognized.
                  emit SC ; exit T
            end ;
            -- Either (a) a single click followed by a selection
            -- or (b) a double click is being recognized.
            do await U ; watching s tick
               timeout -- case (a)
                  emit SC ; emit SS ; await U ; emit SE ; exit T
            end ;
            -- case (b)
            emit DC
      end
end
```

The textual program is somewhat awkward for this problem compared with the graphical CRSM solution or a statechart, mainly because of the four levels of nesting (*every*, *trap*, and *do* with *timeout*). An equivalent program in Ada would have a structure similar to the Esterel code. ◆

The designers have devised a clever compilation method that generates an efficient sequential state machine (automaton) from an input program. All internal signals are eliminated during the compilation process; parallel statements are replaced by interleaved sequential transitions while maintaining determinacy. The underlying assumption of an infinitely fast machine means in practice that the target system must react sufficiently quickly to input signals so that the indicated processing and state changes can be performed before other inputs occur. [Berry&Gunthier92] assert that these reaction times can in fact be measured, allowing users to verify that speed requirements are met.

▶ 9.7 THE REAL-TIME EUCLID SYSTEM

The Real-Time Euclid project was an interesting and pioneering academic effort to develop a language and system that permitted a priori guarantees that programs would meet their timing constraints during execution [Kligerman&Stoyenko86;Stoyenko87]. The language is a real-time extension of the parallel programming language Concurrent

Euclid [Cordy&Holt81] designed at the University of Toronto by R. Holt and his students; it has also been influenced by a successor, Turing Plus [Holt&Cordy85]. Only a brief description is presented here.

Processes, as usual, are the active objects of concurrency. They can synchronize and share resources through *monitors*, similar to the protected types of Ada and synchronized methods of Java, but with (almost) standard *wait* and *signal* primitives on *condition variables*. A *wait* on a condition variable causes the invoking process to block on the variable. A *signal* on a condition variable will wake up a blocked process; if there are no processes blocked on the condition variable, a signal operation is ignored.

Processes in Real-Time Euclid may also communicate outside of monitors through similar wait and signal primitives, and a *broadcast*. Timing determinism is achieved by restrictions on the language and by adding timing information to some key constructs. Processes and data structures are statically defined, and cannot be dynamically created or modified.

A wait on a condition variable has an associated timeout. For example, the *wait* call

```
wait cv noLongerThan 15 : cv_expired
```

causes the caller to block on the condition variable *cv*. It also indicates that the exception *cv_expired* is raised if the calling (and waiting) process has not been awakened within 15 time units. Assuming that this is the only process waiting on *cv*, the wakeup occurs if and when another process issues a signal operation on *cv*:

```
signal cv.
```

Loops are bounded by specifying a maximum number of iterations using a range expression, *exp1* .. *exp2*, where the two expressions, *exp1* and *exp2*, evaluate to integers at compile time and $|exp1 - exp2| + 1$ is the upper bound on the iteration count. For example, the code

```
for i: 15 .. n
        statement_list
end for
```

would loop through *statement_list* no more than $(n - 15) + 1$ times, where n is known at compile time. (Early exits can be taken from a loop with an *exit* statement.)

Processes may be periodic or sporadic. A time frame associated with each process defines either its period and deadline (periodic process), or its minimal separation time and deadline (sporadic process). Pre- and post-conditions that must be satisfied on each activation may be specified. Exceptions are raised and handled through one of three different methods: (1) a *kill* statement causes the target process to terminate after raising the exception; (2) a *deactivate* statement terminates the current frame of the process; and (3) an *except* statement saves the state of the process, invokes an exception handler, and resumes the execution of the excepting process. In each case, the target of the exception could be the process itself or some other process.

Real-Time Euclid programs are analyzed for schedulability through a complex and exhaustive process that essentially simulates all possible paths and resource contentions. Starting at the machine instruction level, time bounds for noninteracting segments of compiled programs are estimated. Hardware nondeterminacies, such as those caused by caches and DMA operations, are ignored and assumed to have no effect on the results. Delays and contentions are then bounded in a second phase. The underlying scheduling mechanism is earliest deadline first (EDF); queuing on monitor locks and condition variables is first-in, first-out.

The system was implemented on a 3-node, distributed microprocessor system (NS 320000s connected by a multibus), with one node allocated solely to timekeeping. Experiments to validate the ideas were done with two simulated applications—a control system for a power station and a communications protocol.

The project illustrates the need for a close coupling among the various software elements of a real-time system. This includes the application programming language, the compiler, the run-time system, and the controlling operating system.

▶ EXERCISES 9

1. Implement in Ada a general semaphore initialized to zero. Recall that a semaphore has two operations, a P and a V, that operate on a nonnegative integer. The V operation increments the integer by one. The P operation decrements the integer by one *if possible*; otherwise, it waits (until a V operation makes it possible). Give two different designs for the semaphore object, one as a *protected type* and the second as a *task*.

2. Program an Ada task for the absolute time alarm clock defined in Question 3 of the exercises of Section 4.1. Let the clients and controller of the alarm clock use entry calls corresponding to the *start*, *stop*, *Wake_Me*, *Wakeup*, and *Reset* channels.

3. Consider the definition of a bounded *Buffer* as a protected object given in Section 9.2.1. Describe in detail the modifications you would make so that the following constraints are also satisfied:

> Every *Remove* must be directly preceded by at least one *Deposit*, and there must be a time delay of at least dt time units between servicing of successive operations.

4. Suppose that an object in space is tracked with a computer by obtaining its location approximately periodically through some communications mechanism. The velocity is defined as

$$v_{new} = (pos_{new} - pos_{old})/(t_{new} - t_{old}),$$

where pos_{new} is the current position obtained at time t_{new}, and pos_{old} and t_{old} are the corresponding position and time, respectively, obtained during the previous cycle. There are three different ways to receive the location, given by the routines Get_Pos_R, Get_Pos_C, and Get_Pos_S;

these represent, for example, position sensing by radar, digital communications, and indirect satellite.

The velocity is considered erroneous if

$$| v_{new} - v_{old} | > velocity\_bound,$$

where v_{old} is the velocity computed during the previous cycle and *velocity_bound* is a given bound on the possible change. A sensor is also defined as erroneous if Get_Pos doesn't return a reading within some given time dt after its call.

(a) Write a recovery block solution to the velocity computation problem, assuming that the sensors (Get_Pos) are tried in the above order.

(b) Give a three-version programming solution. Assume that the velocity is computed as an average of the good (nonerroneous) velocities, provided that at least two are acceptable. Use an Ada-like notation as in the text examples.

5. Consider the mouse clicker recognizer described in Esterel in Section 9.5. Express the recognizer in (a) Ada and (b) CSP/Occam, and compare these with each other and with the Esterel version. Comment on the relative advantages and disadvantages of each notation for solving this problem.

6. Suppose that a vending machine dispenses champagne and fois gras, costing 25 euros and 50 euros, respectively. The machine accepts 10 and 25 euro bills as input, and returns change in units of 1, 5, 10, and 25 euro bills. Write an Esterel program segment that controls the behavior of this vending machine. Input signals are *ten-in*, *twenty-five-in*, *champagne-request*, *fois-gras-request*, and *cancel*. Outputs (emitted) are *champagne*, *fois-gras*, *one-euro*, *five-euro*, *ten-euro*, *twenty-five-euro*, and *beep*. A beep is an indicator that more money must be inserted for the particular selection made.

CHAPTER 10

Operating Systems

The principal functions of operating systems (OS) are to manage the hardware and software resources of the computer and to provide services to users [Bic&Shaw88]. Real-time systems also require such OS functions and services. In a stand-alone, single-language system, for example, in Real-Time Euclid or in some Ada implementations (Chapter 9), these functions are coded in the run-time support of the programming language. This is also the case for smaller embedded systems that are often produced on a larger development environment and then downloaded to the target.

The alternative is a separate real-time operating system, as described in Section 2.4. For both approaches, that is, the operating system as an independent entity or as the run-time support for a programming language, the OS acts as the interface between the hardware below it and the application programs—typically a set of periodic and sporadic processes—above it in the software functional hierarchy (see Figure 2.6). In this chapter, we return to and continue the early discussions in Chapter 2 where software architectures were introduced; here, as the last part of the book, we outline the OS mechanisms and support used to construct application architectures.

While real-time OSs must perform many of the same general functions and offer the same general services as conventional OSs, they have different detailed requirements that follow directly from the nature of the area. *Predictibility* is undoubtedly the most important requirement. This property applies most critically with respect to time—all services must be executed *within* bounded and known times, and *at* times that are controlled and known. It also applies to the usage of other resources of the system, such as storage, IO devices, and files. It is equally important that functionality and fault management, that is, fault detection and handling, be predictable. Usually, this means that the behavior in each of these domains is also deterministic.

A second requirement is *visibility* and *control* for all system components. In a conventional OS, much of the hardware and system is deliberately hidden and abstracted from the user or applications designer. The user of a real-time OS, however, must be able to access and control the behavior of its components in order to guarantee predictability. The trick, of course, is to do this while, at the same time, providing useful and convenient abstractions for the user.

A real-time OS should be an *open* system—one that defines an appropriate and flexible set of mechanisms, but does not force particular policies on users. It should be possible to define a wide range of policies, for example, different policies for task scheduling, depending on the application. Otherwise, it is much more difficult to build one-of-a-kind and stand-alone systems that satisfy given particular constraints.

The next section describes the most important real-time OS services and functions in centralized and distributed systems. The architectures of several sample commercial and research OSs are discussed briefly in Section 10.2, including a separate section on POSIX. The next two sections then cover some issues in task management and hardware interface control in more detail. Many of the methods and techniques used at the OS level have been presented in other parts of the book, and will only be cited where necessary; for this reason also, this chapter is relatively short.

▶ 10.1 REAL-TIME FUNCTIONS AND SERVICES

Almost all of the services presented here are variations of those available in standard OSs for uniprocessor, multiprocessor, and distributed hardware architectures, but adapted to provide predictability, visibility, control, and openness. Many of these are similar to analogous functions needed in real-time programming languages (Section 9.1), and often are the same functions; that is, the programming language calls an OS routine to perform the function.

Functions that access and control both absolute and relative *time* are one obvious necessity; examples are operations for reading and setting clocks, or for delaying for a given time. It is important that clocks maintain the basic properties of time (Section 8.2), since the integrity of a real-time system depends to a large extent on the integrity of the clock functions. Consequently, many of the clock-related operations execute at the highest priority levels of a system, and are not interruptable. Timer(s) at the OS level should also return values of a fine granularity, in order to satisfy user needs for a variety of granularities and tick sizes.

A second major set of services is *process and thread management*. Included in this category are operations to create and initialize, activate, and terminate real-time tasks. There may also be direct support for periodic and sporadic processes. Facilities for task scheduling need to be accessible, so that an application writer can dictate when a scheduler is to be called and what scheduling policy is to be used. Certainly, preemptive versions of both deadline and priority-based schemes, as well as priority inheritance policies, should be easy options for a developer. Primitives for synchronizing and communicating among processes must also be defined and available to the applications writer.

Related to these services are operations for generating and handling software interrupts or events, and for doing context switches. Interrupt and event facilities may also be employed to implement *exception handling* services. These provide software methods for creating or designating exceptions, saving state and transferring control on exception occurrences, and defining appropriate handlers.

Utilities for *device management* are normally not accessible at the applications-OS interface. However, these utilities *are* needed for real-time systems in order to control and access sensors, controllers, timers, and conventional IO devices. Some of the required functions are those for initiating an IO operation, for reading the state of a device, and for defining and connecting interrupt handlers. There should also be utilities that allow new real-time devices to be attached easily.

An important class of IO devices consists of communications devices and network controllers, which provide the interfaces and conduits through which messages may be transmitted among the nodes of a distributed system. Real-time *network* services are the software that implement this communications. The communications protocols and mechanisms have more stringent reliability and predictability constraints than those for more conventional general purpose systems—messages need to be delivered on time almost all of the time, in spite of hardware faults. Many multimedia systems, such as those that deliver TV images and sound in non-safety-critical consumer applications, have somewhat softer constraints even though they have deterministic real-time requirements.

Administration and allocation methods for *main storage* must also be adapted to a real-time context. Users cannot pass responsibility to the OS to perform this management transparently, but must instead do it themselves, thereby maintaining control; suitable primitives should be provided by the OS for managing the memory resource. Regardless of whether or not a virtual memory architecture is employed, allocation is normally restricted to parts of the real physical memory space so that unpredictable faults and accesses to secondary storage are avoided. Because of these latter problems, allocation of main memory is often done statically and permanently when a process is first created.

Filing services are also offered by some real-time OSs. Occasionally, real-time files can be stored entirely in main memory, thus avoiding the faulting and access problems noted above. More commonly, secondary storage, that is, disk memory, is required; and care must be taken to allocate, deallocate, and access these devices predictably and efficiently when performing file operations. This frequently means that file storage is pre-allocated at creation time and that a file is mapped to contiguous regions of secondary storage.

Detailed specifications of a real-time OS service need to be available to the applications developer. They should include the resource needs of the service, as well as its functional behavior. How long does each service call or invocation take under various circumstances—expressed as best and worst case bounds? How much storage does the service require? This kind of data must be advertised for lower level functions, such as blocking, context-switching, and interrupt handling, and for more abstract and higher level services such as filing.

▶ 10.2 OS ARCHITECTURES

In the following two subsections, we present a representative selection of some interesting architectural features from commercial and research OSs. Two early systems, the RC4000 and Thoth, are first mentioned because of their influence on many subsequent developments.

The RC4000 system, designed by Per Brinch Hansen in the late 1960s (Chapter 8 in [BrinchHansen73]), was both a general purpose and a real-time OS, noted particularly for its conceptual elegance. It was one of the first systems to use the process model for a real-time OS—or for a general purpose OS—extending the abstraction to describe hardware IO interfaces as well as the internal software. The system was also justifiably famous for its very clean set of four message passing primitives for process synchronization and comunication—*send_message, wait_message, send_answer,* and *wait_answer.*

The Thoth real-time system was developed in the mid-1970s, as a university research project [Cheriton79]. Its main goals were portability and providing support for processes in a real-time setting. Emphasis was placed on performance and predictabilty. Especially interesting were Thoth's message passing operatons, very fast and simple versions of *send/receive/reply* primitives, and its attention to timer services connected to a real-time clock.

10.2.1 Real-Time UNIX and POSIX

Starting from the late 1980s, many commercial real-time operating systems were instances of "real-time UNIX"; examples are LynxOS [Lynx93] and Real/IX [Furht_et_al91]. These were obtained by extensive modification and redesign of the basic UNIX kernel. Today, most implementations of real-time UNIX conform to the IEEE POSIX standard and its real-time extensions [Gallmeister95; POSIX93; POSIX98].[1] Commercial examples of such POSIX compliant systems include RTMX O/S [RTMX00], LynxOS [Lynx00], and VxWorks [WindRiver00]. As well as C language bindings, the functions supported by POSIX also interface in a straightforward way to modern real-time programming languages, particularly Ada and real-time versions of Java.

The active objects in a POSIX system are called *pthreads*, and are the POSIX version of threads [Nichols_et_al96]. Pthreads are used to represent the periodic or sporadic tasks of an application. Generally, a POSIX compliant system contains one or more UNIX processes, each consisting of multiple pthreads of execution. Threads are created through a *pthread_create* function, or indirectly through a *fork* or *exec* call.

A typical implementation will maintain a small data structure for each thread, containing its current state (register values, program counter, stack pointer, . . .), status (ready, blocked, running, . . .), scheduling information such as priority and policy, timing data, and perhaps other information. The thread data structure and associated POSIX functions could be part of the OS kernel or it may be implemented almost entirely in user space; some combination of these two extremes, a so-called two-level scheduler, is an attractive alternative that offers the benefits of both. A major goal is to permit and facilitate the control of scheduling and resource allocation by an application.

Integer priorities are assigned to threads at the time of creation, and can be changed dynamically during execution. Scheduling is basically preemptive priority scheduling, with two possibilities for equal priorities. One is simple first-come, first-served—the FIFO highest priority thread will execute until it blocks, terminates, or is preempted by a higher priority thread; in the first case, it is placed at the end of the FIFO ready queue for its priority. The second method is round-robin for each priority—the thread at the front of the highest priority ready queue will execute for at most a

---

[1]POSIX is an acronym for Portable Operating Systems Interface. We will use the term to refer to both POSIX and its real-time extensions.

fixed quantum or slice of time; if it is still executing when its time slice expires, it is placed at the end of its ready queue. (Section 6.1 describes the pure forms of these algorithms). There is also a "hook" for users to insert their own scheduling methods, for example, EDF.

Traditional UNIX processes have separate address spaces. In contrast, the pthreads comprising an application often reside in a single process and consequently share the same address space; that is, one process with multiple threads. Most OSs will dynamically swap all or part of memory onto disk during execution, typically in units of pages when this type of virtual memory is supported by the underlying architecture. For real-time applications, the use of this swapping feature may completely destroy timing predictability. One solution, available in POSIX, permits a thread to permanently lock designated parts or all of its address space in main memory; the routines *mlock*, *mlock-all*, *munlock*, and *munlockall* perform memory locking and unlocking functions.

Threads may be synchronized with semaphores, mutex locks, and condition variables. Semaphores are standard counting semaphores, while mutex locks are essentially binary semaphores intended to be used around critical sections to assure mutual exclusion. POSIX defines the two standard mechanisms to avoid priority inversion that can result with mutex locks during execution: both the priority inheritance and priority ceiling protocols (Section 6.4) are supported.

Condition variables with associated *wait*, *signal*, and *broadcast* operations permit thread blocking and wakeup within the context of a mutex lock. For example, the operation

```
pthread_cond_wait(not_busy, mxlk)
```

will cause the calling thread, say *P*, to block on the condition variable *not_busy* and release its mutex lock *mxlk*. A subsequent

```
pthread_cond_signal(not_busy)
```

by another thread will wakeup *P* and put it on a queue for the mutex lock. Threads are serviced in priority order on both the condition variable and mutex queues. The combination of mutex locks and condition variables allows a straightforward implementation of monitors, such as those defined with synchronized methods in Java or in Real-Time Euclid monitors.

Processes and threads can communicate through standard Unix pipes or FIFOs, or through explicit message passing. Messages are prioritized by senders, and queued in priority order for receivers. This is the major difference between messages and pipes/FIFOs.

A new set of clock and timer facilities is also a part of real-time POSIX. It is possible to define multiple high-resolution clocks and timers, limited by the underlying implementation. Clocks have corresponding operations to set the time, return the current time, and return the resolution, where the resolution is the smallest distinguishable tick interval. At least one clock, named *CLOCK_REALTIME*, must be supported. Timers may be either one-shot or repeating (periodic). These timers can be set to "go off" or expire after a given interval and then generate an appropriate event or signal.

Signals are asynchronous software interrupts. They are supported in both UNIX and POSIX. Mechanisms exist to define signals, generate them, wait for them, and specify handler code to be executed when a signal occurs. Real-time POSIX adds a new kind of signal. In particular, the new signals can have associated data and priorities, and are queued when multiple signals of the same type are pending. Signal handlers receive queued signals in priority order.

For example, a signal named *fault* with data *info* can be sent to the process or thread P with the real-time POSIX function

```
sigqueue(P, fault, info).
```

A thread could wait for any of a set S of signals with a timeout *delta_t* by calling the function

```
sigtimedwait(S, info, delta_t).
```

Signals provide a convenient interface and implementation of the asynchronous facilities of languages such as Ada and real-time "Javas." They are used to specify exceptions, timeouts, message arrivals, and completions of input–output commands.

Input–output and filing have also been addressed in real-time POSIX. There is finer control of synchronized IO and methods for performing asynchronous IO. For example, a "hidden" disk cache or buffer is normally employed by UNIX for disk output. This feature can be bypassed when doing synchronous IO; applications can then be assured that IO is completed and the output data is on the disk when the operation returns. Disk allocations for files can also be controlled, both by preallocating or by specifying contiguous allocations, thereby giving the user a basis for predicting the timing behavior of filing operations.

10.2.2 Some Commercial and Research OSs

Most recently, real-time versions of the Linux and Windows NT operating systems are being developed and tested. Examples are RT-Linux [Humphrey_et_al99] and INtime [Obenland_et_al99]. Both of these examples have taken a similar approach that allows the non-real-time tasks to coexist with real-time ones. The general purpose OS (Linux or NT) is encapsulated as a single object and so is the real-time OS. In RT-Linux, all interrupts are intercepted by a real-time controller that then passes it on, either to the normal Linux kernel or the real-time OS. INtime captures the NT timer interrupt, which is the highest priority nonmaskable interrupt in NT.

Research OSs, as expected, are not so constrained and exhibit more diversity than the commercial ones. Among these are a number of "object-oriented" (OO) executives, each with differing views and definitions of the notion of an object. OO examples are the ARTS kernel [Tokuda&Mercer89], Maruti [Levi&Agrawala90; Saksena_et_al95], CHAOS [Gheith&Schwan93], and the P/ADT system [Callison&Shaw91]. Other interesting research systems include Spring [Stankovic&Ramamritham91], Mars [Kopetz_et_al89], RT-Mach [Tokuda,Nakajima&Rao90], Rialto [Jones&Rosu97], and Yartos [Jeffay,Stone&Poirier92].

Many general purpose operating systems are advertised or used also for real-time applications and for applications that also contain a significant non-real-time component. Such is the case for the older Dec VMS system and for some microprocessor OSs, for example, the V distributed system [Cheriton88]. The suitability of Windows NT as a real-time OS has been the subject of much study, for example, in [Baril99], [Obenland_et_al99], and [Jones&Regehr99]. While offering high-priority, real-time threads and fast bounded interrupt handlers, NT is missing several necessary features. These include priority inheritance, bounded times for many utilities, and imperfect timer services. (It is interesting that RT-Linux also experiences problems with their basic timer mechanisms [Humphrey_et_al99].)

Even though Windows NT is considered an "object-oriented" OS, it is still the case that OO operating systems are in their infancy, especially those designed for real-time use. Object-oriented systems generally have *active* and *passive* objects, as defined in Section 2.5. Active objects correspond to one or more execution threads, tasks, or processes; passive ones are associated with procedures, methods, or data types that may be invoked or accessed only by active objects. We give two examples of research OO systems that represent different ends of the object complexity spectrum.

► **Example 1: The P/ADT System [Callison&Shaw91]**

This OS is a particularly simple and basic use of the OO idea. Conventional processes and abstract data types (ADTs) are the active and passive objects, respectively. As illustrated in Figure 10.1, a process can call the procedures exported by an ADT, and ADTs can, in turn, call other ADTs.

An attractive feature of this scheme is that it is applicable to all levels of a system, including the hardware–software interface. Thus, for example, the behavior of the hardware that is directly controlled or connected to the software kernel can also be described in terms of processes and ADTs. Figure 10.2 shows a terminal keyboard interface implemented in this manner.

The *KB* ADT exports *getchar* and *putchar* operations that are called by a *user* process and the *keyboard_driver* process, respectively. The *keyboard* is represented by a hardware process; an interrupt is denoted by an *io_int* call by *keyboard* on the *IO* ADT, in a manner similar to the protected object programming model of Ada discussed in Section 9.2.1. In fact, the Ada tasking, protected object, and package facilities permit a straightforward implementation of the entire P/ADT scheme.

The architecture for P/ADT is sketched in Figure 10.3. The kernel runs on a uniprocessor and is layered in a conventional fashion. The system has statically defined processes with fixed priorities. Semaphores are used for synchronization. In the figure,

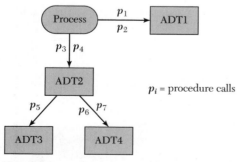

Figure 10.1 Processes and ADTs.

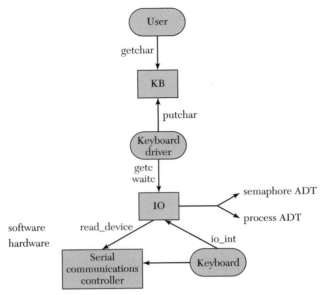

Figure 10.2 Keyboard interface.

common horizontal lines denote calling interfaces between services and the arrows indicate calls across the same level. Additional objects have also been added for network
communications. ◆

▶ Example 2: CHAOS [Gheith&Schwan93]

The CHAOS multiprocessor kernel is based on a more general and complex object
model. It has three layers of abstraction above the hardware, called CHAOS^{base},
CHAOS^{min}, and CHAOS^{arc}. The first, CHAOS^{base}, is the lowest level layer, sitting immediately above the machine architecture. The middle level, CHAOS^{min}, provides four
built-in primitive object classes: (1) a passive ADT, (2) an active ADT that executes an
ADT operation as a thread, (3) a passive monitor that implements a classic monitor with
waits and signals, and (4) a task with entries similar to an Ada task. Higher level objects
in CHAOS^{arc} are defined with these primitive objects and a policy object that acts as an
executive controller. A real-time application is constructed with CHAOS^{arc}.

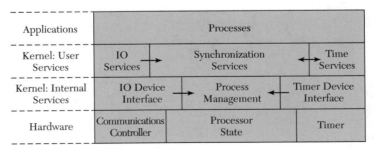

Figure 10.3 P/ADT layered architecture.

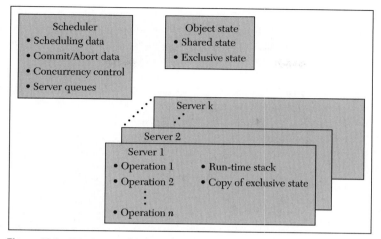

Figure 10.4 Structure of a CHAOS object.

An example of the structure of a CHAOS[arc] multithreaded object, taken from [Gheith&Schwan93], is outlined in Figure 10.4. Each *Server* is an active ADT and corresponds to a thread. Operation invocations all pass through the *Scheduler,* which is responsible for assigning them to threads; *Concurrency_Control* assures object consistency and atomicity of operations in conjunction with the *Commit/Abort_Data.*

The object state is divided into two parts: a *shared* part and an *exclusive* part. The shared component is accessible to all operation invocations of the object, whereas the exclusive part is copied on each invocation. This division is used in object concurrency control and error recovery. Backward recovery, which restores state to its pre-invocation value on a failure, employs the copied component; if an invocation terminates successfully and "commits," the copy is copied back atomically. CHAOS maintains a consistent view of the shared state throughout multiple parallel invocations; the shared part is also useful for forward error recovery, which sets the state to a consistent future value. ◆

► 10.3 ISSUES IN TASK MANAGEMENT

10.3.1 Processes and Threads

In almost all of the OSs listed in the preceding section, the objects corresponding to real-time tasks are implemented as *threads*. A thread is a "lightweight" process that shares resources, particularly address spaces and storage, with other thread objects; it is the basic unit of scheduling. Processes also typically exist also within an OS containing threads; in this organization, strongly influenced by UNIX extensions, a *process* is the entity that holds resources (except the CPU).

Even though it is desirable to design an application with static tasks in order to improve predictability, OSs typically provide operations to dynamically create and destroy threads, such as *fork* and *quit*, respectively. Consequently, users are able to define some mixture of static and dynamic tasks. One application is mode changes, where some threads from the old mode may be terminated while another set is created to handle the new mode. Operations for activating and suspending threads are also common. These are useful, for example, for periodic objects where a practical distinction can be made between blocking and resuming a task due to resource contentions, on the one hand, and activating and suspending a task at period boundaries and after execution, on the other.

Typically, user-specified priorities are associated with tasks. Examples are ARTS which provide static priorities and REAL/IX which has dynamic priority facilities in the form of a *set_priority* operation that can be called during execution by a subject process or its controller. Alternatively or in addition, real-time thread packages may allow the declaration of explicit timing constraints, similar to those provided by some programming languages. For example, the call to "fork" a new thread in CHAOS has the timing parameters: *start_time*, *run_time*, and *deadline* [Schwan,Gheith&Zhou90]; RT-Mach has a *rt_thread_create* primitive that creates a periodic or aperiodic thread with a comprehensive set of possible attributes including the above parameters and other timing data such as abort time and release time (periodic tasks).

10.3.2 Scheduling

CPU scheduling of processes or threads for most commercial systems is preemptive and priority based. Rate monotonic methods have received particular emphasis in recent times because of their predictability and constructive theoretical underpinnings. Many, if not most, OSs also include priority inheritance mechanisms for minimizing priority inversion. Some research OSs schedule tasks using the timing information directly, typically with an EDF policy. It is also possible to translate common timing constraints, such as deadlines, into equivalent priorities; most cases require dynamic priorities.

Two interesting scheduling approaches are taken by the Mars and Spring systems. In Mars, a feasible schedule for a set of tasks with well-defined timing and precedence constraints is produced "off-line," prior to execution, and stored in a table. During execution, a table-driven task dispatcher performs task allocation to processors efficiently and predictably. Spring distinguishes critical tasks from other real-time but noncritical ones. Critical tasks are scheduled statically and guaranteed a priori. The system also handles noncritical processes that may arrive dynamically. The OS attempts to build a new schedule including a newly arrived task in the current (guaranteed) schedule. If a feasible schedule is possible, the new task is then guaranteed by the system to meet its constraints.

A particularly interesting and creative version of CPU scheduling by guaranteed reservations appears in the Rialto system. Upon request, an object can receive a guaranteed allocation of x units of time every y units, where x and y are specified in the request, for example, 100 ms (x) out of every second (y). This is a continuous guarantee, meaning that at any future time t after a request of x out of y is granted, the object will receive at least x units of CPU time in the interval $[t, t + y]$. The application is for soft real-time systems, such as multimedia speech and video.

10.3.3 Synchronization and Communications

Operating system functions, especially at the lowest kernel level, often must execute either atomically or as locked critical sections. To achieve even logical indivisibility, it is still necessary that some parts of the system be executed in a physically indivisible manner as well, for example, in performing the operations that do locking. For uniprocessor environments, indivisibility can be ensured by disabling interrupts during the function execution. Spinning or busy-wait locks are the standard way to accomplish this in a multiprocessor architecture.

Conventional implementations of spinning locks use atomic instructions, such as *test_and_set*, to loop on a single shared memory cell [Bic&Shaw88]. They are often deficient for real-time OSs because they don't permit control over the order of service when several processors are competing for a lock and because they don't offer predictable and bounded spinning times. Spinning processors can also significantly slow other processors due to the increased load on the processor–memory interconnect.

Queuing spin locks, that is, [Anderson90], solve these problems in a non-real-time setting and have been adapted to real time by several groups [Molesky,Shen& Zlokapa90; Markatos92; Craig93]. The underlying idea is each waiting task spins on a separate "request" record or storage location; requests are queued by linking these locations. Real-time versions have been devised using *swap*, *compare_and_swap*, and *test_and_set* as atomic operations, for both coherent cache and nonuniform memory access (NUMA) machines, where applicable, and with both FIFO and priority granting order.

Variations of common higher level OS methods for synchronization and communications are also found in the real-time domain. Systems typically provide a broad range of synchronization objects with predictable timing behaviors, including mutual exclusion locks, semaphores, condition variables, events, signals, and messages. Locks and condition variables also permit a user to implement higher level monitors or conditional critical regions.

Timeouts are frequently associated explicitly with the operations that may cause the invoking task to block, such as *lock*, *P*, *wait*, and *receive*. As one example, RT-Mach, offers locks and condition variables, with operations *lock*, *unlock*, and *trylock* on locks and *wait* and *signal* on condition variables. *wait* and *lock* both have versions with a timeout parameter; for example,

```
mutex_lock(lock_name, to)
```

returns if the lock is not granted within *to* time units after the request. Another example is the timed condition variable wait defined in POSIX. The POSIX call

```
pthread_cond_timed_wait(cv,lock_name, abs_time)
```

will timeout and return if the condition variable *cv* is not signalled by *abs_time*.

Some care must be taken when implementing timeouts within these blocking primitives. The complexity arises because the waits on timeouts have to be coordinated with waits on the availability of the synchronization objects. Thus, conceptually, there may be two waiting queues—one for the object and an auxiliary one for time. An alarm clock utility, similar to those specified in Section 4.1.3, could be employed to define and generate timeout events. In turn, a synchronization object may be blocked, simultaneously waiting for such a timeout event and for a signal that the object is free.

An alternative is to keep timeouts as a separate function that a user can invoke optionally. Coding this option can be easily done using ideas from languages such as Ada. For example, suppose that a user wishes to perform a *P* operation on a binary semaphore named *BSEM*, and also generate a timeout if the call is not serviced within a time interval *to*. This can be accomplished with the following Ada fragment:

```
select
     BSEM.P ;
     -- a successful P within time to
or
     delay(to) ;
     -- timeout
end select ;
```

OSs are also beginning to include some support for distributed real-time communications over a network, usually in the form of message passing. Message *send* and *receive* primitives may be synchronous; that is, both sender and receiver are blocked until the communication occurs. This is the case for CSP IO, and for the Ada rendezvous at a higher level. Another common possibility is an asynchronous or nonblocking send coupled with a blocking receive; the sender continues executing immediately after issuing the send, while a receiver blocks until a message arrives. Messages may be buffered at the receiver end in an asynchronous send so as to minimize any loss of messages.

Primitive operations may support one-to-one communications, that is, a single sender to a single receiver, or a multicast or broadcast that is directed to a group of receivers. Multicast and broadcast are useful to send global state information to local nodes that need to maintain updated copies. Another application is sending control commands simultaneously to a group of recipients; for example, in an emergency situation, an ATC controller could multicast commands to all aircraft in a given space to enter a holding pattern.

The messages involved in all of the communications mentioned above have been termed *event messages* (e.g., [Kopetz97]). There is another class of messages, denoted *state messages*, that is particularly applicable to real-time data, such as sensor information. For these messages, the logical method of transmission is through an asynchronous send; each transmission atomically overwrites the previous data value at the receiver. The receiver will always read the latest version of the data. A message value is always returned immediately, so the receive is nonblocking. The semantics is thus similar to having a shared store between a sender (writer) and receiver (reader).

Timeouts at both the sender and receiver ends are especially convenient in a distributed environment. They can be used as indicators for possible transmission faults and delays, or for nonexistent receivers, as well as indicators that more conventional service and computational deadlines have been missed. As before, timeout facilities could be included as part of the OS-provided primitives, or they may be available in separate callable functions. Another important technique that also relies on good real-time clock services is message *timestamping*. The idea is that a message sender will also include the current time along a message. Timestamps not only give the receiver some idea of the age of the message data but also can be employed for causality purposes (Section 8.1).

► Communications Example: Systems V [Cheriton88]

The message passing scheme and implementation in V is a good example of software engineering that accommodates the often conflicting requirements of predictability, performance, and abstraction. The scheme is the only synchronization method in V.

Similar to its predecessor, the Thoth system, V has a synchronous send/receive/reply semantics with blocking at both the send and receive ends of a communication.

To transmit a message, a client process sends a message to a server and blocks on the *send* operation until a *reply* is received. A server process waits for a message with a *receive* operation, composes a response, and issues a *reply* to the sender. The same scheme is used for both local (intramachine) and distributed (intermachine) interprocess communications (IPC). Speed and determinism are assured by supporting small fixed-length messages[2] and by keeping a message packet template directly and permanently in the process descriptor, thereby avoiding several protocol layers. Other higher level IPC methods, such as remote procedure call, Ada rendezvous, and CSP IO, can be constructed relatively easily with the V primitives. Multicast communications are also supported. ♦

► 10.4 INTERRUPTS AND THE OS

This section is concerned with some low-level but important OS issues related to interrupt processing. Almost all systems are interrupt-driven in that many changes related to task wakeups, suspensions, and activations occur as a result of some hardware interrupt event. For example, most IO operations are generated through interrupts that denote IO arrivals or that signal the end of previously generated IO operations. Systems that are completely time-triggered can be driven by periodic timer interrupts connected to OS schedulers; and faults may be indicated through timeout exception interrupts. Timer interrupts are also used to signal the end of a delay function or an alarm clock wakeup event; they may also be the basis for computing real time in a clock service.

When an interrupt occurs, the CPU and OS go through a standard sequence of operations and routines, regardless of the application:

1. The state of the currently running task, say P, is saved, the interrupt is identified, and the associated interrupt handling routine is invoked.

2. The interrupt handler, sometimes called the interrupt service routine (ISR), is executed. Often, the ISR is not preemptible. In terms of the interrupt models presented for Ada in Section 9.2.2, the handler here can be interpreted most readily as an operation on a protected type.

3. In the simplest case, P's state is reloaded and P continues at the point where it was interrupted.
   or

3'. The interrupt handler has awakened a previously blocked task. This is the most common case. The task scheduler is invoked. It selects the next task, say P', for execution, and control is transferred to P'.

Interrupts generally have associated priorities or levels. If several interrupts are pending, the highest priority one is selected (by the computer hardware) for the sequence of steps above, and the lower priority ones are handled in order after step 2. (In some systems, ISRs can be preempted by higher priority interrupts, complicating the processing.)

---

[2]Large data segments are optional. The system is optimized for the more common short messages.

Step 1 is normally very fast and predictable. Step 2 is necessarily much longer, and designers of real-time OSs work hard on minimizing the time spent in an ISR. Typically, ISR times are measured carefully and publicized, both by software manufacturers and by users, for example, in LynxOS [Lynx93] and NT [Obenland_et_al99; Baril99].

As a final topic for this section, and book, we wish to further emphasize the crucial role played by the timer services and related interrupts. Underlying a complete real-time clock service are one or more physical clocks, and the software or hardware that maintains the required clock properties. The software, such as tick interrupt handlers, routines for maintaining time, and the routines for generating timeout and alarm clock wakeup events, must be among the highest priority and noninterruptable components of the OS. And because it is accessed so often and regularly, this software must also be very efficient. For example, if a clock ticked or was updated 1000 times per second (every millisecond) at a CPU cost of 100 microseconds per tick or update, then the CPU would be spending 10% of its time on this function. Real-time systems must pay attention to time!

▶ EXERCISES 10

1. Study a popular commercial *general purpose* operating system, and comment on the real-time implications of its policies and mechanisms in the following areas: process management, scheduling, synchronization, and communications; timer services; IO device management; main storage allocation; filing services; interrupt handling; and exception processing.

2. Repeat Question 1, only with a commercial *real-time* operating system.

Air Traffic Control System—Project Specifications

The project involves all or part of the design, implementation, testing, and analysis of a simplified air traffic monitoring and control system (ATC). The system is a variation of the simplified ATC example that is described briefly in Sections 1.1.2 and 2.2. A standard computer system, such as a PC or workstation, with a graphics display and accessible clock is assumed. The specifications are deliberately vague in some places, for example, in the formatting details of display output and command input. To a large extent, these depend on the particular computer employed and on the available software; we also wish to leave some scope for design creativity.

▶ A.1 PURPOSE

The purpose of the ATC is to assure the safety of aircraft traversing a given airspace and to assure their efficient traversal. To achieve these goals, the ATC must track or monitor each aircraft in the space and must be able to command an aircraft to change its path or its speed.

Safety means avoiding collisions. The safety constraint is defined in terms of minimum separation—at any time, no two aircraft may be closer than a given distance from each other, say 1000 feet in elevation and 3 miles in the horizontal plane. These numbers and units, and the others that are given below, should be treated as environment and design parameters that could be changed easily.[1] We will not be too concerned with efficiency, for example, trying to maximize aircraft throughput; however, the ATC should not degrade efficient operation except when the safety constraint may be otherwise violated. For the project, this means that unless two aircraft are, or are projected

---

[1]For example, we could specify 500 meters of elevation and 2 nautical miles in the horizontal plane.

to violate the minimum separation constraint, they will not be commanded to change their direction or speed.

▶ A.2 THE ENVIRONMENT

The *airspace* is a three-dimensional rectangle, say 100 × 100 miles in the horizontal plane and 25,000 feet high in elevation, bounded below by a horizontal plane at 15,000 feet, that is, above sea level (Figure A.1). An *aircraft* enters the space flying in a horizontal plane at a constant velocity. It maintains its altitude and speed unless directed by the ATC to change. Thus aircraft do not enter from above or below the space, and fly in a horizontal plane under normal conditions. An aircraft entering the space is "handed-off" to the ATC by its controlling neighbor site. When an aircraft leaves the space, it is handed off to a neighboring ATC.

All aircraft have radio communication that can be tuned to the ATC, allowing pilots and ATC controllers to speak directly to one another. We will not be concerned with the details of this voice communications part of the system. Almost all aircraft are equipped with "transponders" that return identification and location coordinates to radars, and with digital communications that allow sending and receiving of electronic messsages.

At the ATC site, there is a computer system with interfaces to a radar subsystem, digital communications subsystem, and display output and keyboard/mouse input for the human controller, as illustrated in Section 1.1.2. Figure A.2 illustrates the input and output interfaces provided by these subsystems.

There is also a radio communications system that is independent of the computer system. Among other uses, this voice system provides a back-up to the computer system in case there is a problem with computer communications, radar tracking, or other failures, or in case aircraft fail to correctly execute commands.

The radar subsystem scans the entire airspace every 15 seconds, returning a list of "hits" in a buffer that can be accessed by the computer. Hits are objects "seen" by the radar. The communications subsystem allows the ATC to send and receive digital messages.

The ATC controller, a human operator, interacts with the system and aircraft by inputting commands through the keyboard and through voice on the radio. The system communicates with the controller through the output display. The display shows various views of the state of the airspace, echoes operator input, and lists electronic messages that are received.

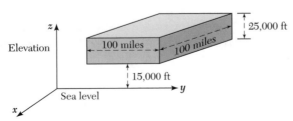

Figure A.1 The airspace.

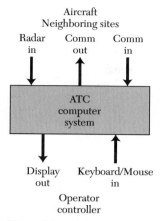

Aircraft
Neighboring sites

Figure A.2   Computer IO interfaces.

▶ A.3 INPUTS AND OUTPUTS

Inputs to the ATC computer system can arrive from the radar subsystem, from the digital communications interface, and from the operator keyboard and mouse. The system outputs consist of the operator display and the communications device.

A.3.1   ATC Inputs

The radar input is a hit list L with the following form and meaning:

$$L = size, Hit(1), Hit(2), \ldots, Hit(size).$$

Each hit element represents an object in the airspace. A hit $Hit(i)$ has the structure

$$Hit(i) = (aircraft\_id, (x, y, z)),$$

where *aircraft_id* identifies the aircraft hit or seen by the radar, and (x, y, z) gives the coordinates of the aircraft in the space. If an aircraft does not have a working transponder, the radar still returns a hit but with an *aircraft_id* field set to *"unknown."* The radar buffer is locked from computer access for a short time, say 1 millisecond, near the end of the 15-second period while the hit data is copied to it.

Input messages through the communications system are either messages from individual aircraft in the space or hand-off messages from a neighboring space. In the first case, the input is either a response to an operator command or it may be a request for permission to change elevation or velocity (e.g., because of unstable air in the aircraft's current flight path). A hand-off message contains an aircraft identity and projected airspace entry data, such as time, location, and velocity at entry.

Messages are received in a queue that can be read and emptied by the computer system. Each message in the queue is of the form

$$(sender\_id, message).$$

sender_id is the name of the message sender and *message* is the contents of the message.

Operator input consists of commands or information requests directed either toward individual airplanes or to all objects in the space, of requests for data in the ATC system, of corrections or changes to data maintained by the system, and of hand-off messages to be sent to a neighboring ATC site.

The operator can input any of the following commands to a designated aircraft:

- Change altitude by $\pm n \times 1000$ ft, where n is a positive integer.
- Increase or decrease its speed.
- Change direction in its horizontal plane.
- Enter or leave a *holding* pattern. A holding pattern is a closed flight path. One standard pattern is an oval or racetrack.
- Report its current position and velocity.

The operator can command *all* aircraft with either of the following:

- Enter or leave a holding pattern.
- Report aircraft identification, position, and velocity.

Operator requests to read or change internal systems data that represent the state of the airspace include:

- Add or delete an aircraft object.
- Change the position, elevation, or velocity of an aircraft.
- Display data record for a given aircraft.
- Project aircraft positions to *current_time* + n, where n is some integer number of seconds.

A.3.2 ATC Outputs

The system outputs are communications output and display output. To send a message m to a receiver R over the communications subsystem, the computer system emits the command

$$send(R, m).$$

The receiver R can be an aircraft or an ATC site. A message m can be broadcast to any listening receivers with the command

$$broadcast(m).$$

send and *broadcast* are both asynchronous (nonblocking)—the computer system proceeds immediately after executing the command.

Hand-off messages are sent to neighboring sites. Directed and broadcast messages can be transmitted to aircraft based on input commands from the operator. Messages are also generated internally based on systems state. In particular, a potential collision notification is sent if the system detects that aircraft are about to violate the minimum separation constraints. (This is considered a back-up in case the operator fails to command aircraft to take some safety action, or in case the aircraft fail to execute the operator commands—see below.)

In its normal mode, the display shows a plan (top) view of the airspace locating each aircraft in the space. Under operator control responding to command input, more complete data on each object are displayed. All electronic messages received from other aircraft and sites is also displayed. In addition, if the separation constraint is violated, or will be violated within 3 minutes, a pictorial alarm such as flashing or red icons is output, along with pointers to the offending objects. Pictorial alarms are also displayed whenever an unidentified object is detected by the radar or an identified aircraft is lost (no radar hit).

▶ A.4 SOFTWARE FUNCTIONS AND DATA, WITH TIMING CONSTRAINTS

The primary data structure in the ATC system is an airspace database containing a record of all aircraft in the space at the current time.[2] For each aircraft, there must be a structure including at least the following information:

$$aircraft\_id, current\_position, current\_velocity.$$

The software is responsible for performing the functions:

- Display a plan view of the space every 5 seconds, extrapolating if necessary to show the current position of each aircraft.

- Check all objects in the airspace for separation constraint violations at $current\_time + n$ seconds, where n is an integer parameter. Display an alarm if a safety violation is found.

- Interpret and provide an initial response to all operator commands within 2 seconds. For commands that require communications to and from aircraft, the initial response should occur after the appropriate message is sent to the communications subsystem.

- Receive and interpret input to the communications subsystem. This could be data sent from aircraft in the space or from neighboring sites.

- Maintain the airspace database. This requires functions to add, remove, and change the data of aircraft records.

- Store the airspace state in a history file every 60 seconds. There should be enough information in this log to generate an approximation to the history of the airspace over time.

- Handle lost or unidentified objects, for example, by first broadcasting messages such as "Where are you?" or "Please identify yourself."; and then alerting the operator who can switch to the radio and attempt voice contact.

---

[2]Note that these data are only a model of the airspace, as known to the ATC computer system. They approximate the state of the actual space. How close this approximation is to reality depends on many factors, including the accuracy of the radar, communications reliability and transmission times, aircraft modelling assumptions, computer and IO overhead, and clock precision.

- Detect and handle failures including missed deadlines and failure of an aircraft to respond to an operator command.

▶ A.5 PROJECT REQUIREMENTS

The exercises comprising the project are listed below. All or part of these may be done.

1. Fill in the missing details of the environment, inputs and outputs, and software functions and data.

2. Express the basic minimum separation requirement as an RTL formula (Section 5.3). Assume that the radar hits are events, that $@(AC, i)$ gives the time of the ith hit on aircraft AC (if such a hit occurs or exists), and that the value function $v(AC, i)$ returns the location and velocity of aircraft AC at the time of its ith radar hit.

3. Describe the functional behavior of the software with data flow diagrams (DFDs) (Section 3.2).

4. Specify the behavior of the ATC system and its environment, using either state-charts (Section 4.2) or communicating real-time state machines (CRSMs) (Section 4.1). The environment comprises any object that sends or receives data from the computer system. Your description should contain several concurrent machines, as well as several levels of hierarchy.

5. Implement the ATC system and a simulator for the environment. Part of the simulator should permit entry of environmental data from the workstation terminal during execution. The active part of the system should consist of a set of periodic processes, where periodic polling is used to handle sporadic events (Section 6.3). Assume that all processes or threads share a single processor. Instead of accessing the computer system's clock for ATC software times and the environmental simulator's time, implement a virtual clock that can be set, started, stopped, and stepped from the terminal. Use a real-time programming language, such as Ada, if available.

6. Test your system under various operating conditions—low, medium, high, and over loads. The system load is determined primarily by the number of aircraft in the space, the degree of congestion in the space, and the amount of IO traffic.

7. Measure the execution times of each process, best and worst cases if possible (Section 7.2). Test for scheduling feasibility using rate monotonic fixed priority assignment (Chapter 6).

BIBLIOGRAPHY

[Ada95] *Annotated Ada Reference Manual*, Version 6.0, Intermetrics, Inc., 1995.

[Ada&Beyond97] *Ada and Beyond, Software Policies for the Department of Defense*, National Academy Press, Washington, D.C., 1997.

[Alger&Lala86] L. S. Alger and J. H. Lala, "A real-time operating system for a nuclear power plant computer," *Proc. IEEE Real-Time Systems Symp.*, Dec. 1986, pp. 244–248.

[Anderson90] T. Anderson, "The performance of spin lock alternatives for shared memory multiprocessors," *IEEE Trans. on Parallel and Distributed Systems*, vol. 1, no. 1 (Jan. 1990), pp. 6–16.

[Ashby94] N. Ashby, "Relativity in the future of engineering," *IEEE Trans. on Instrumentation and Measurement*, vol. 43, no. 4 (Aug. 1994), pp. 505–514.

[Avizienis89] A. Avizienis, "Software fault tolerance," *Proc. IFIP 89*, pp. 491–498.

[Avizienis,Kopetz&Laprie87] A. Avizienis, H. Kopetz, and J. Laprie (eds.), *The Evolution of Fault-Tolerant Computing*, Springer, 1987.

[Baker&Shaw89] T. P. Baker and A. Shaw, "The cyclic executive model and Ada," *Real-Time Systems Journal*, vol. 1, no. 1 (June 1989), pp. 7–25.

[Baril99] A. Baril, "Using Windows NT in real-time systems," in [RTAS99], pp. 132–141.

[Bernstein&Harter81] A. Bernstein and P. Harter, Jr., "Proving real-time properties of programs with temporal logic," *Proc. 8th Annual Symp. on Operating Systems Principles*, 1981, pp. 1–11.

[Berry&Gonthier92] G. Berry and G. Gonthier, "The Esterel synchronous programming language: Design, semantics, implementation," *Science of Computer Programming*, vol. 19, 1992, pp. 87–152.

[Bic&Shaw88] L. Bic and A. Shaw, *The Logical Design of Operating Systems*, 2nd edition, Prentice-Hall, Englewood Cliffs, NJ, 1988.

[Booch_et_al99] G. Booch, J. Rumbaugh, and I. Jacobson, *The Unified Modelling Language User Guide*, Addison-Wesley, Reading, MA, 1999.

[BrinchHansen73] P. Brinch Hansen, *Operating System Principles*, Prentice-Hall, Englewood Cliffs, NJ, 1973.

[Brooks87] F. Brooks, Jr., "No silver bullet: Essence and accidents of software engineering," *IEEE Computer*, vol. 20, no. 4 (April 1987), pp. 10–19.

[CACM99] "UML in action," Special Issue, *Comm. ACM*, vol. 42, no. 10 (Oct. 1999).

[Callison95] H. Callison, "A time-sensitive object model for real-time systems," *ACM Trans. on Software Engineering and Methodology*, vol. 4, no. 3 (July 1995), pp. 287–317.

[Callison&Shaw91] H. R. Callison and A. Shaw, "Building a real-time kernel: First steps in validating a pure process/adt model," *Software-Practice and Experience*, vol. 21, no. 4 (April 1991), pp. 337–354.

[Cardelli&Pike85] L. Cardelli and R. Pike, "Squeak: A language for communicating with mice," *Proc. SIGGRAPH '85*, San Francisco, July 1985, pp. 199–203.

[Chandy&Misra88] K. Chandy and J. Misra, *Parallel Program Design: A Foundation*, Addison-Wesley, 1988.

[Cheriton79] D. Cheriton, "Thoth, a portable real-time operating system," *Comm. ACM*, vol. 22, no. 2 (Feb. 1979), pp. 105–114.

[Cheriton88] D. Cheriton, "The V distributed system," *Comm. ACM*, vol. 31, no. 3 (March 1988), pp. 314–333.

[Chi&Shaw86] U. Chi and A. Shaw, "Using flow expressions to specify timing constraints in concurrent systems," TR 86-05-03, Dept. of Computer Science and Engineering, Univ. of Washington, Seattle, May 1986.

[Clapp_et_al86] R. Clapp, L. Duchesnau, R. Volz, T. Mudge, and T. Schultze, "Toward real-time performance benchmarks for Ada," *Comm. ACM*, vol. 29, no. 8 (Aug. 1986), pp. 760–778.

[Cordy&Holt81] J. Cordy and R. Holt, "Specification of Concurrent Euclid," TR CSRG-133, Computer Systems Research Group, University of Toronto, August 1981.

[Craig93] T. Craig, "Queuing spin lock algorithms to support timing predictability," *Proc. IEEE Real-Time System Symp.*, IEEE Computer Society Press, Dec. 1993, pp. 148–157.

[Cristian89] F. Cristian, "Probabilistic clock synchronization," *Distributed Computing*, vol. 3 (1989), pp. 146–158.

[Cristian93] F. Cristian, "Understanding fault-tolerant distributed systems," *Comm. ACM*, vol. 34, no. 2 (Feb. 1991), pp. 56–78.

[Dana97] P. Dana, "Global positioning system (GPS) time dissemination for real-time applications," *Real-Time Systems Journal*, vol. 12, no. 9, 1997, pp. 9–40.

[Dertouzos&Mok89] M. Dertouzos and A. Mok, "Multiprocessor scheduling of hard real-time tasks," *IEEE Trans. on Software Engineering*, vol. 15, no. 12 (Dec. 1989), pp. 1497–1507.

[Dijkstra75] E. Dijkstra, "Guarded commands, nondeterminacy, and formal derivation of programs," *Comm. ACM*, vol. 18, no. 8 (Aug. 1975), pp. 453–457.

[Fidge91] C. Fidge, "Logical time in distributed computing systems," *IEEE Computer*, vol. 24, no. 8 (August 9, 1991), pp. 28–33.

[Fortino&Nigro00] G. Fortino and L. Nigro, "A toolset in Java2 for modelling, prototyping and implementing communicating real-time state machines," *Microprocessors and Microsystems*, 2000.

[Fortino_et_al00] G. Fortino, A. Furfaro, L. Nigro, and F. Pupo, "Hierarchical communicating real-time state machines," Laboratorio di Ingegneria del Software, Dipartimento di Elettronica Informatica e Sistemistica, Universita della Calabria, I-87036 Rende (CS)—Italy, 2000.

[Furht_et_al91] B. Furht, D. Grostick, D. Glutch, G. Rabbat, J. Parker, and M. McRoberts, *Real-Time Unix Systems: Design and Application Guide*, Kluwer Academic Publishers, Boston, 1991.

[Gallmeister95] B. Gallmeister, *POSIX.4: Programming for the Real World*, O'Reilly & Associates, Sebastopol, CA, 1995.

[Gerber&Lee92] R. Gerber and I. Lee, "A layered approach to automating the verification of real-time systems," *IEEE Trans. on Software Engineering*, vol. 18, no. 9 (Sept. 1992), pp. 768–784.

[Gheith&Schwan93] A. Gheith and K. Schwan, "CHAOS[arc]: Kernel support for multiweight objects, invocations, and atomicity in real-time multiprocessor applications," *ACM Trans. on Computer Systems*, vol. 11, no. 1 (Feb. 1993), pp. 33–72.

[Ghezzi_et_al91] G. Ghezzi, D. Mandrioli, S. Morasea, and M. Pezze, "A unified high-level Petri net formalism for time-critical systems," *IEEE Trans. on Software Engineering*, vol. 17, no. 2 (Feb. 1991), pp. 160–172.

[Ghezzi_et_al91b] G. Ghezzi, M. Jazayeri, and D. Mandrioli, *Fundamentals of Software Engineering*, Prentice-Hall, Englewood Cliffs, NJ, 1991.

[Goguen_et_al88] J. Goguen, J. Meseguer, K. Futatsugi, P. Lincoln, and J. Jouannaud, "Introducing OBJ," TR SRI-CSL-88-8, Computer Science Lab, SRI International, Menlo Park, CA, August 1988.

[Guttag&Horning93] J. Guttag and J. Horning, *Larch: Languages and Tools for Formal Specification*, Springer-Verlag, 1993.

[Haase81] V. Haase, "Real-time behavior of programs," *IEEE Trans. on Software Engineering*, vol. SE-7, Sept. 1981, pp. 454–501.

[Halang&Stoyenko90] W. Halang and A. Stoyenko, "Comparative evaluation of higher-level real-time programming languages," *Real-Time Systems Journal*, vol. 2, no. 4 (Nov. 1990), pp. 365–382.

[Harel87] D. Harel, "Statecharts: A visual formalism for complex systems," *Science of Computer Programming*, vol. 8, 1987, pp. 231–274.

[Harel_et_al90] D. Harel, H. Lachover, A. Naamad, A. Pnueli, M. Politi, R. Sherman, A. Shtull-Trauring, and M. Trakhtenbrot, "STATEMATE: A working environment for the development of complex reactive systems," *IEEE Trans. on Software Engineering*, vol. 16, no. 4 (April 1990), pp. 403–414.

[Heitmeyer&Lynch94] C. Heitmeyer and N. Lynch, "The generalized railway crossing: A case study in formal verification of real-time systems," *Proc. IEEE Real-Time Systems Symp.*, IEEE Computer Society Press, Dec. 1994, pp. 120–131.

[Heninger80] K. Heninger, "Specifying software requirements for complex systems," *IEEE Trans. on Software Engineering*, vol. SE-6, no. 1 (Jan. 1980), pp. 1–13.

[Hoare69] C. Hoare, "An axiomatic basis for computer programming," *Comm. ACM*, vol. 12, no. 10 (Oct. 1969), pp. 576–580, 583.

[Hoare78] C. Hoare, "Communicating sequential processes," *Comm. ACM*, vol. 21, no. 8 (Aug. 1978), pp. 666–677.

[Hoare84] C. Hoare, *Communicating Sequential Processes*, Prentice-Hall, Englewood Cliffs, NJ, 1984.

[Holt&Cordy85] R. Holt and J. Cordy, "The Turing Plus Report," Computer Systems Research Institute, University of Toronto, February 1985.

[Hopcroft&Ullman79] J. Hopcroft and J. Ullman, *Introduction to Automata Theory, Languages, and Computation*, Addison-Wesley, Reading, MA, 1979.

[Humphrey_et_al99] M. Humphrey, E. Hilton, and P. Allaire, "Experiences using RT-Linux to implement a controller for a high speed magnetic bearing system," in [RTAS99], pp. 121–130.

[Hurley83] R. Hurley, *Decision Tables in Software Engineering*, Van Nostrand Reinhold, New York, 1983.

[Inmos84] *The Occam Programming Manual*, Prentice-Hall, Englewood Cliffs, NJ, 1984.

[Inmos88] *Occam 2 Reference Manual*, C. Hoare (ed.), Prentice-Hall, Englewood Cliffs, NJ, 1988.

[Jahanian&Mok86] F. Jahanian and A. Mok, "Safety analysis of timing properties in real-time systems," *IEEE Trans. on Software Engineering*, vol. SE-12, no. 9 (Sept. 1986), pp. 890–904.

[Jahanian&Mok94] F. Jahanian and A. Mok, "Modechart: A specification language for real-time systems," *IEEE Trans. on Software Engineering*, vol. 20, no. 12 (Dec. 1994), pp. 933–947.

[Jahanian_et_al94] F. Jahanian, R. Rajkumar, and S. Raju, "Runtime monitoring of timing constraints in distributed real-time systems," *Real-Time Systems Journal*, vol. 7, no. 3, 1994, pp. 247–273.

[Jeffay,Stone&Poirier92] K. Jeffay, D. Stone, and D. Poirier, "YARTOS: Kernel support for efficient, predictable real-time systems," in W. Halang and K. Ramamritham (eds.), *Real-Time Programming*, Pergamon Press, New York, 1992.

[Jeffay_et_al91] K. Jeffay, D. Stanat, and C. Martel, "On non-preemptive scheduling of periodic and sporadic tasks," *Proc. IEEE Real-Time Systems Symp.*, IEEE Computer Society Press, Dec. 1991, pp. 129–139.

[Jeffay_et_al92] K. Jeffay, D. L. Stone, and F. D. Smith, "Kernel support for live digital audio and video," *Computer Communications*, vol. 15, no. 6 (July 1992), pp. 388–395.

[Jones86] C. Jones, *Systematic Software Development Using VDM*, Prentice-Hall, Englewood Cliffs, NJ, 1986.

[Jones&Regehr99] M. Jones and J. Regehr, "The problems you're having may not be the problems you think you're having: Results from a latency study of Windows NT," in [RTAS99], pp. 287–292.

[Jones&Rosu97], M. Jones, D. Rosu, and M-C. Rosu, "CPU reservations and time constraints: Efficient, predictable scheduling of independent activities," *Proc. 16th ACM Symp. on OS Principles*, OS Review, vol. 31, no. 5 (Dec. 1997), pp. 198–211.

[Kligerman&Stoyenko86] E. Kligerman and S. Stoyenko, "Real-time Euclid: A language for reliable real-time systems," *IEEE Trans. on Software Engineering*, vol. SE-12, no. 9 (Sept. 1986), pp. 941–949.

[Kopetz97] H. Kopetz, *Real-Time Systems: Design Principles for Distributed Embedded Applications*, Kluwer Academic Publishers, Boston, 1997.

[Kopetz_et_al89] H. Kopetz, A. Demm, C. Koza, and M. Mulozzani, "Distributed fault tolerant real-time systems: The Mars approach," *IEEE Micro*, 1989, pp. 25–40.

[Krishna&Shin97] C. Krishna and K. Shin, *Real-Time Systems*, McGraw-Hill, New York, 1997.

[Lamport78] L. Lamport, "Time, clocks and the ordering of events in a distributed system," *Comm. ACM*, vol. 27, no. 7 (July 1978), pp. 558–565.

[Lamport&Mellior-Smith85] L. Lamport and P. M. Mellior-Smith, "Synchronizing clocks in the presence of faults," *J. ACM*, vol. 32, no. 1 (Jan. 1985), pp. 57–78.

[Lampson&Redell80] B. Lampson and D. Redell, "Experience with processes and monitors in Mesa," *Comm. ACM*, vol. 23, no. 2 (Feb. 1980), pp. 105–117.

[Laplante_et_al95] P. Laplante, E. Rose, and M. Gracia-Watson, "An historical survey of early real-time computing developments in the U.S.," *Real-Time Systems Journal*, vol. 8, 1995, pp. 199–213.

[Lea97] D. Lea, *Concurrent Programming in Java, Design Principles and Patterns*, Addison-Wesley, Reading, MA, 1997.

[Leung&Merrill80] J. Leung and M. Merrill, "A note on preemptive scheduling of periodic real-time tasks," *Information Processing Letters*, vol. 11, no. 3 (1980), pp. 115–118.

[Leung&Whitehead82] J. Leung and J. Whitehead, "On the complexity of fixed priority scheduling of periodic, real-time tasks," *Performance Evaluation*, vol. 2, no. 4 (1982), pp. 237–250.

[Leveson86] N. Leveson, "Software safety: What, why, and how," *ACM Computing Surveys*, vol. 18, no. 2 (June 1986), pp. 125–186.

[Leveson95] N. Leveson, *SAFEWARE: System Safety and Computers*, Addison-Wesley, Reading, MA, 1995.

[Leveson&Stolzy87] N. Leveson and J. Stolzy, "Safety analysis using Petri nets," *IEEE Trans. on Software Engineering*, SE-13, no. 3 (March 1987), pp. 386–397.

[Leveson&Turner93] N. Leveson and J. Turner, "An investigation of the Therac-25 accidents," *IEEE Computer*, vol. 26, no. 7 (July 1993), pp. 18–41.

[Leveson_et_al94] N. G. Leveson, M. Heimdahl, H. Hildreth, and J. Reese, "Requirements specifications for process control systems," *IEEE Trans. on Software Engineering*, vol. 20, no. 9 (Sept. 1994), pp. 684–707.

[Levi&Agrawala90] S. Levi and A. Agrawala, *Real-Time System Design*, McGraw-Hill, New York, 1990.

[Li&Malik95] Y-T. Li and S. Malik, "Performance analysis of embedded software using implicit path enumeration," *Proc. 32nd Design Automation Conf.*, June 1995, pp. 456–461.

[Li_et_al95] Y-T. Li, S. Malik, and A. Wolfe, "Efficient microarchitecture modeling and path analysis for real-time systems," *Proc. IEEE Real-Time Systems Symp.*, IEEE Society Press, Dec. 1995, pp. 298–307.

[Lim_et_al95] S. Lim, V. Bae, G. Jang, B. Rhee, S. Min, C. Park, H. Shin, K. Park, S. Moon, and C. Kim, "An accurate worst case timing analysis for RISC processors," *IEEE Trans. on Software Engineering*, vol. 21, no. 7 (July 1995) pp. 593–604.

[Liu&Layland73] C. Liu and J. Layland, "Scheduling algorithms for multiprogramming in a hard-real-time environment," *J. ACM*, vol. 20, no. 1 (Jan. 1973), pp. 46–61.

[Liu_et_al94] J. Liu, W. Shih, K. Lin, R. Bettati, and J. Chung, "Imprecise computations," *Proc. IEEE*, vol. 82, no. 1, pp. 83–94.

[Locke92] C. Locke, "Software architectures for hard real-time applications," *Real-Time Systems Journal*, vol. 4 (1992), pp. 37–53.

[Lynch&Tuttle89] N. Lynch and M. Tuttle, "An introduction to input-output automata," *CWI-Quarterly*, vol. 2, 1989; Tech Memo MIT/LCS/TM-373, Laboratory for Computer Science, MIT, Boston, MA, Nov. 1988.

[Lynx93] *LynxOS Application Writer's Guide*, Lynx Real-Time Systems, Inc., Los Gatos, CA, 1993.

[Lynx00] http://www.lynxworks.com.

[Manna&Pnueli93] Z. Manna and A. Pnueli, *The Temporal Logic of Reactive and Concurrent Systems*, Springer-Verlag, New York, 1992.

[Markatos92] E. Markatos, "Multiprocessor synchronization primitives with priorities," in Y. H. Lee and C. Krishna, *Readings in Real-Time Systems*, IEEE Computer Society Press, Piscataway, NJ, 1992, pp. 111–120.

[Martin65] J. Martin, *Programming Real-Time Computer Systems*, Prentice-Hall, Englewood Cliffs, NJ, 1965.

[Marzullo84] K. Marzullo, "Maintaining the time in a distributed system," OSD-T8401, Xerox Office Systems, Palo Alto, March 1984 (also Stanford Univ. Ph.D. dissertation).

[Metzner&Barnes77] J. Metzner and B. Barnes, *Decision Table Languages and Systems*, Academic Press, New York, 1977.

[Mok83] A. Mok, "Fundamental design problems of distributed systems for hard real-time environments," MIT/LCS/TR-297, Laboratory for Computer Science, MIT, Boston, MA, 1983 (Ph.D. thesis).

[Mok87] A. Mok, "Annotating Ada for real-time program synthesis," *Proc. IEEE COMPASS '87*, June 1987.

[Mok_et_al89] A. Mok, P. Amerasinghe, M. Chen, and K. Tantisirivat, "Evaluating tight execution bounds of programs with annotations," *Proc. 6th IEEE Workshop on Real-Time operating Systems and Software*, May 1989, pp.74–80.

[Molesky,Shen&Zlokapa90] L. Molesky, C. Shen, and G. Zlokapa, "Predictable synchronization mechanisms for real-time systems," *J. Real-Time Systems*, vol. 2, no. 3 (Sept. 1990), pp. 163–180.

[Mostert94] S. Mostert, "Constructing a heterogeneous real-time system," *Proc. 11th IEEE Workshop on Real-Time Operating Systems and Software*, IEEE

Computer Society Press, Piscataway, NJ, May 1994, pp. 34–38.

[Obenland_et_al99] K. Obenland, T. Frazier, J. Kim, and J. Kowalik, "Comparing the real-time performance of Windows NT to an NT real-time extension," in [RTAS99], pp. 142–151.

[Oh&Baker98] D. Oh and T. Baker, "Utilization bounds for N-processor rate monotonic scheduling with static processor assignment," *Real-Time Systems Journal*, vol. 15, no. 2 (Sept. 1998), pp. 183–192.

[Ostroff&Wonham87] J. Ostroff and W. Wonham, "Modelling and verifying real-time embedded computer systems," *Proc. IEEE Real-Time Systems Symp.*, Dec. 1987, pp. 124–132.

[Park92] C. Y. Park, "Predicting deterministic execution times of real-time programs," TR 92-08-02, Dept. of Computer Science and Eng., Univ. of Washington, Aug. 1992 (Ph.D. dissertation).

[Park93] C. Y. Park, "Predicting program execution times by analyzing static and dynamic program paths," *J. Real-Time Systems*, vol. 5, no. 1 (March 1993), pp. 31–61.

[Park&Shaw90] C. Y. Park and A. Shaw, "Experiments with a program timing tool based on source level timing schema," *Proc. IEEE Real-Time Systems Symp.*, Dec. 1990, pp. 72–81; a modified version appears in *IEEE Computer*, May 1991, pp. 48–57.

[Patterson&Hennessey98] D. Patterson and J. Hennessey, *Computer Organization & Design*, 2nd ed. Morgan Kaufman, San Francisco, 1998.

[PD96] *Journal of Parallel and Distributed Computing*, Academic Press, vol. 36, no. 1 (July 1996).

[POSIX93] *Portable Operating Systems Interface (POSIX)*, POSIX P1003.4, IEEE, 1993.

[POSIX98] *POSIX Real-Time Applications Support (AEP)*, IEEE std 1003.13-1998, IEEE, Piscataway, NJ, March 1998.

[Puschner93] P. Puschner, "Zeitanalyse von echtzeitprogrammen," Technical University of Vienna, Vienna, Austria, 1993 (Ph.D. dissertation).

[Puschner&Koza89] P. Puschner and C. Koza, "Calculating the execution times of real-time programs," *Real-Time Systems Journal*, vol. 1, no. 2 (Sept. 1989), pp. 159–186.

[Puschner&Schedl97] P. Puschner and A. Schedl, "Computing maximum task execution times—a graph-based approach," *Real-Time Systems Journal*, vol. 13, no. 1 (July 1997), pp. 67–91.

[Raju&Shaw94] S. C. V. Raju and A. Shaw, "A prototyping environment for specifying, executing, and checking communicating real-time state machines," *Software-Practice and Experience*, vol. 24, no. 2 (Feb. 1994), pp. 175–195.

[Randall75] B. Randall, "System structure for software fault tolerance," *IEEE Trans. on Software Engineering*, vol. SE-1, no. 2 (June 1975), pp. 220–232.

[Reed&Roscoe86] G. Reed and A. Roscoe, "A timed model for communicating sequential processes," *Proc. ICALP '86*, Springer-Verlag, New York, LCAS 226, 1986, pp. 314–323.

[Riddle72] W. Riddle, "Modelling and analysis of supervisory systems," Computer Science Dept., Stanford Univ., Stanford, CA, March 1972 (Ph.D. dissertation).

[RTAS99] *Proc. 5th Real-Time Technology and Applications Symp.*, Vancouver, Canada, IEEE Computer Society, Piscataway, NJ, June 1999.

[RTJEG00] Real-Time for Java Experts Group, http://www.rtj.org.

[RTMX00] http://www.rtmx.com.

[Saksena_et_al95] M. Saksena, J. da Silva, and A. Agrawala, "Design and implementation of Marutti-II," Chap. 4, in [Son 95], pp. 73–102.

[Scallon&Nast87] G. Scallon and D. Nast, " A sample problem in real-time control," Real-Time Systems Newsletter, vol. 3, no. 3 (Fall 1987), pp. 6–12.

[Schwan,Gheith&Zhou90] K. Schwan, A. Gheith, and H. Zhou, "From CHAOS^{base} to CHAOS^{arc}: A family of real-time kernels," *Proc. IEEE Real-Time Systems Symp.*, IEEE Computer Society Press, Piscataway, NJ, Dec. 1990, pp. 82–91.

[Selic99] B. Selic, "Turning clockwise: Using UML in the real-time domain," in [CACM99], pp. 46–54.

[Selic_et_al94] B. Selic, G. Gullekson, and P. Ward, *Real-Time Object-Oriented Modelling*, John Wiley & Sons, New York, 1994.

[SG90] L. Sha and J. Goodenough, "Real-time scheduling theory and Ada," *IEEE Computer*, April 1990, pp. 53–62.

[Sha,Lehoczky&Rajkumar87] L. Sha, J. Lehoczky, and R. Rajkumar, "Task scheduling in distributed real-time systems," *Proc. IEEE Industrial Electronics Conf.*, 1987.

[Sha,Rajkumar&Lehoczky90] L. Sha, R. Rajkumar, and J. Lehoczky, "Priority inheritance protocols: An approach to real-time synchronization," *IEEE Trans. on Computers*, vol. 39, no. 9 (Sept. 1990), pp. 1175–1185.

[Sha,Rajkumar&Sathaye94] L. Sha, R. Rajkumar, and S. Sathaye, "Generalized rate monotonic scheduling theory: A framework for developing real-time systems," *Proceedings of the IEEE*, Jan. 1994, pp. 68–82.

[Shaw78] A. Shaw, "Software descriptions with flow expressions," *IEEE Trans. on Software Engineering*, vol. SE-4, no. 3 (May 1978), pp. 242–254.

[Shaw80] A. Shaw, "Software specification languages based on regular expressions," R. Fairley and W. Riddle (eds.), *Software Development Tools*, Springer-Verlag, New York, 1980, pp. 148–175.

[Shaw89a] A. Shaw, "Reasoning about time in higher-level language software," *IEEE Trans. on Software Engineering*, vol. 15, no. 7 (July 1989), pp. 875–889; an updated version appears in S. Son (ed.), *Advances in Real-Time Systems*, Prentice-Hall, Englewood Cliffs, NJ, 1995, pp. 379–409.

[Shaw89b] A. Shaw, "Real-time systems = processes + abstract data types," *Proc. Euromicro Workshop on Real-Time*, IEEE Computer Society, June 1989, pp. 188–197.

[Shaw91] A. Shaw, "Deterministic timing schema for parallel programs," *Proc. 5th Int. Parallel Processing Symp.*, IEEE Computer Society, Piscataway, NJ, April 1991, pp. 56–63.

[Shaw92] A. Shaw, "Communicating real-time state machines," *IEEE Trans. on Software Engineering*, vol. 18, no. 9 (Sept. 1992), pp. 805–816.

[Shaw93] A. Shaw, "A more formal definition of communicating real-time state machines," TR 93-08-01, Dept. of Computer Science & Engineering, University of Washington, Seattle, August 1993.

[Shaw94] A. Shaw, "On scalable state-based specifications for real-time systems," TR 94-02-03, Dept. of Computer Science and Engineering, Univ. of Washington, Seattle, Feb. 1994.

[Shaw98] A. Shaw, "Time-stamped event histories: A real-time programming object," *Control Engineering Practice*, vol. 6, no. 3 (March 1998), pp. 417–420.

[Shaw00] A. Shaw, "A case for object-oriented real-time systems," *Real-Time Systems Journal*, vol. 18, no. 1 (Jan. 2000), pp. 71–74.

[Son95] S. Son (ed), *Advances In Real-Time Systems*, Prentice-Hall, Englewood Cliffs, NJ, 1995.

[Spivey89] J. Spivey, *The Z Notation: A Reference Manual*, Prentice-Hall, Englewood Cliffs, NJ, 1989.

[Stankovic&Ramamritham91] J. Stankovic and K. Ramamritham, "The Spring kernel: A new paradigm for hard real-time operating systems," *IEEE Software*, vol. 8, no. 3 (May 1991), pp. 62–72.

[Stankovic_et_al98] J. Stankovic, M. Spuri, K. Ramamritham, and G. Buttazzo, *Deadline Scheduling for Real-Time Systems: EDF and Related Algorithms*, Kluwer Academic Publishers, Boston, MA, 1998.

[Stoyenko87] A. Stoyenko, "A real-time language with a scheduability analyzer," TR CSRI-206, Computer Systems Research Institute, Univ. of Toronto, Dec. 1987, Ph.D. thesis.

[Tokuda&Mercer89] H. Tokuda and C. Mercer, "ARTS: A distributed real-time kernel," ACM Operating Systems Review, vol. 23, no. 3 (July 1989).

[Tokuda,Nakajima&Rao90] H. Tokuda, T. Nakajima, and P. Rao, "Real-time Mach: Towards a predictable real-time system," *Proc. Usenix Mach Workshop*, Oct. 1990.

[WindRiver00] http://www.windriver.com/products/html/vxworks54.html.

[Wirth77] N. Wirth, "Toward a discipline of real-time programming," *Comm. ACM*, vol. 20, no. 8 (Aug. 1977), pp. 577–583.

[Wirth86] N. Wirth, "A fast and compact compiler for Modula-2," TR 64, Institut fur Informatik, ETH, Zurich, July 1986.

[Uckun&Gasperoni98] S. Uckun and F. Gasperoni, "Making Java real-time," *IEEE Spectrum*, Dec. 1998, pp. 22–23.

[Xu&Parnas93] J. Xu and D. Parnas, "On satisfying timing constraints in hard real-time systems," *IEEE Trans. on Software Engineering*, vol. 19, no. 1 (Jan. 1993), pp. 70–84.

Index